The Branches and the Vine

Jabez

A MEMOIR

Copyright

Some names have been changed to protect the rights of certain individuals.

Front cover art: T.G.
Back cover art: R.G.
Cover design: M.G.

ISBN: 9798830029124
10 9 8 7 6 5 4 3 2 1

For my forever love

I hope one day we meet and you really get to know me

CONTENTS

Preface

My life was never simple, and before I could properly pronounce the words 'spiritual life', I had a spiritual life. I began dreaming early, and over time, my agglomeration of dreams grew to include people outside my circle and events outside my bubble. I have faced some skepticism from those around me who think my experiences strange, simply because they have never experienced the things I have, and not only that, have shut themselves off to the possibility.

It has been said to me that God does not speak to people in dreams as He did in days past although the Bible states, in Acts 2:17, that God will pour out His Spirit upon all flesh and that people will prophesy, see visions, and dream dreams. It is hard for some to perceive that which they cannot see or have not lived through themselves, so God allows others to have experiences that bear witness to His truth.

I have had some of those experiences. In the spiritual realm, I have talked to God, seen Jesus, received messages and protection from angels, faced off with demons, been threatened by the devil, walked in The Valley of the Shadow of Death, been put through tests, and seen things that are to come.

Some have offered helpful suggestions—out of genuine concern I'm sure—for why I experience the things I do, like medications or a medical condition—specifically a brain tumor. This is so because they find it hard to accept that the things they read about in the Bible are still possible today.

However, The Bible describes the Word of God as living, enduring, alive and active; as such, it is relevant and will continue to be relevant. As Ecclesiastes 1:9 says, "What has been will be again, what has been done will be done again; there is nothing new under the sun" (NIV).

Although this book contains some end-time dreams, it is by no means a study in the Book of Revelation. It is simply an account of my personal experiences, which I hope will be helpful in bringing insight and hope because "as iron sharpens iron, so one person sharpens another" (Proverbs 27:17, NIV). I also discover new and interesting things about myself, which I hope the readers of *Before Journey's End* appreciate.

If you are a Believer, I pray that this book encourages you to walk the faith instead of simply talking the faith. If you are not a Believer, I pray this book encourages you to be more open to the possibility that there truly is a God, and He is good.

Blessings

Glossary of Words and Terms

ah--is/are/to

awright----------------------------------alright

bly--chance/break

bredda----------------------------------brother

bringle----------------------------------angry

bwoy------------------------------------boy

cyaan------------------------------------can't

crawses----------------------------------problems

dat--that

deh/yah----------------------------------there/here

dem--------------------------------------them/their/they

dis--this

di--the

draw mi tongue----------------------provoke me to quarrel

duh--do

dutty--------------------------------------dirty

eeh--eh

eeh-hee----------------------------------really

enuh--------------------------------------you know

fi--for/to

guh/guh ah----------------------------go/go to

gyal--------------------------------------girl

gwaan------------------------------------go on

haffi--------------------------------------have to

innah------------------------------------in

know seh-------------------------------know that

macca------------------------------------prickle/burr/thorn

madda----------------------------------mother

mek/mekking---------------------------make/making

mi---my/I/me

nevah----------------------------------never

no sah-----------------------------------no

nobaddy------------------------------nobody

nuff--------------------------------------plenty

nuh--------------------------------------doesn't/don't

nuh mussi suh------------------------it must be so

nutting---------------------------------nothing

seh---------------------------------------say

set-on----------------------------------one who eggs a situation on

shi--she

si--see

sugah----------------------------------sugar

suh--------------------------------------so

tan ah dem yaad---------------------stay home

tek--------------------------------------take

to not spit on someone-----------ignore him/her

waah-----------------------------------want

wah------------------------------------what

weh-------------------------------------where

weh yuh deh-------------------------Where are you?

wid--------------------------------------with

yuh/unnuh--------------------------you(sing)/you(pl)

Putty in the Potter's hand

Ashes, Dust, Clay

No pottery like the other

Each made His perfect way

Wheat

My hands froze over my laptop keyboard, and I cocked my ears like a dog listening for a high-pitched-soft sound in a far-off place—except this sound had come from inside Logan's closet, a mere six-feet away. Moments ago, the night had been eerily quiet—just the way I liked it and just the way I hated it. It was hard to be creative in the day, and since I had no access to a remote cabin flanked by woodlands and a bumbling brook, the night had to do; however, the night was not without its *crawses*.

I dared not breathe or blink.

Maybe I had imagined it.

My closet was an overcrowded mess. It was not unusual that things dislodged because they were not packed in properly or made weird noises due to the contraction of molecules in objects as the temperature dropped in the night . . . or something like that (I didn't pay much attention in Physics class). Anyway, it was what I told myself whenever something went *bump* in the night.

Only, the sound had not come from my closet.

My mind began to run wildly through a list of possibilities, none of which were comforting.

"Pfft." I rolled my eyes. "This is so stupid." Logan had taken most of his stuff when he moved out, and what was left was so sparsely laid out, his closet looked like an island supermarket after a hurricane. There was no way a sound had come from there.

My heart clenched painfully at the thought of Logan. I missed him like I would miss air were it to suddenly be taken from me. Even though Logan had moved downstairs before he had filed divorce papers, he was still in the house. At least when he was there, he wasn't with someone else. All that had changed, a few nights ago, after a huge argument. I had gone to bed hopping mad and had taken forever to fall asleep. No sooner had I drifted off than I was awakened by Logan calling me from outside my bedroom door. Annoyed, I had groaned and covered my head with my pillow, ignoring him. Not dissuaded, he had called me again—more insistently that time—and I had yelled at him, asking what he wanted. Instead of answering, he had called my name again, which had me ready to blow a fuse. I had sucked my teeth and sat up, yelling that the door was open. It had not been until that moment that the sounds coming from downstairs had registered. The alarm had not gone off, so I was sure the house had not been broken into. If Logan was downstairs hauling and tossing things about, who was outside my door? With my heart thumping in my ears and every nerve in my skin prickling, I had tiptoed to the door and flung it open to find exactly what I suspected I would find. As I stood there gawking at the empty doorway, I should have been in total awe of my Samuel experience. However, whatever heebie-jeebies I had been feeling, in that moment, were totally overridden by something far more powerful. I would have woken up in the morning to find Logan gone without so much as a word. No feeling could trump how I felt at the thought of that.

I sighed and pictured Logan's face. I missed opening my eyes and seeing that face. I'd lie there whenever I woke before he did—which was extremely rare—and drink in every detail, including the smallest freckle, as though it were the last time I'd ever see his face. He would sometimes catch me and ask if I was watching him sleep. To my 'yes', his response was always, "That's really creepy. You're weird." I'd simply grin and keep mum about the mornings I would pretend to be asleep—peeking through my lashes—as I watched him watch me sleep, except he did something I dared not do—and that was only because he knew I slept like the dead. He would gently touch my face, his fingers—no heavier than feathers—tracing every detail of my features—etching each to memory as though it were the last time he would ever see my face.

I missed the mornings.

The plastic bag rustled again, bringing my focus back to the closet.

My heart leapt hard, slamming against my chest and causing my breath to hitch in my throat. I listened intently, and after a few eerily still moments had passed, I began pounding away at the keyboard again.

I almost wanted to laugh as the bag rustled again the moment I started typing. "Are you kidding me? God, is this for real?" I had no time for shenanigans. My bedroom was supposed to be my retreat, and too often it was anything but.

I flung the comforter off and stomped over to the closet, hesitating for a split second to allow for curiosity to overrule fear. I flung the door open, and after a cursory scan, tentatively walked over to the overstuffed garbage bag on the floor. Logan had left some of his clothes behind. I kicked the bag—which was far more satisfying than it should have been—and stepped back. There was no movement. I should have been relieved, yet I wasn't. Those noises had not been in my head. A handful of sparsely spaced hangers dangled from a rod, an almost empty laundry basket sat by its lonesome in a corner, and a few of the kids' comic books laid single pile on one of the shelves. There was nowhere for a critter to hide, except in the folds of the garbage bag. The thought of having a critter jump out at me was almost as scary as finding no explanation at all for the noise. I kicked the bag a few more times before moving it. When nothing crawled out after I had tossed it about a bit, I gave up and headed back to the bed.

Thwack

A book fell and slapped the closet floor hard when I was almost half-way there. I jumped, my blood immediately curdling. I wanted to run, but my feet felt tethered to the floor. I wanted to turn around, but I was too chicken. I simply stood mannequin stiff, not daring to breathe.

Waiting.

For what? I had no clue. The only thing audible to me was my heartbeat thumping in my ears, which in itself was disconcerting. I held my breath so long my head began to feel light. I was going to keel over, and there was no better place than my bed to do that.

I took another step forward.

Thwack

Another book fell to the closet floor.

Fear wrapped tendons around my heart.

That was no critter.

I was sure of it.

It had been what—a few weeks since I had had any kind of supernatural attempt at terrorization and oppression?

Although the time had been short, it had seemed like forever, and I was becoming rather accustomed to the peace and quiet.

I should have known better.

I wanted to bolt from the room, but I knew I could show no fear regardless of how my insides were churning. I dashed to the bed and jumped in, my eyes immediately becoming glued to the closet.

The laundry basket slid across the floor and, after a few suspenseful moments, fell over.

A chill doused me from head to toe—causing all the hairs on my body to stand up—as my heart ping-ponged all over my chest. My head felt as though it had detached from my body and was floating somewhere high above me. I should go look, but I could not. So, I listened instead. After about two minutes had gone by and there were no more sounds, I sidled up to the closet. I took a deep breath—pausing only long enough to wonder why I was bothering to look when I already knew what I would find—and opened the door.

Everything was in its place. The laundry basket was still in its corner, the books were still stacked on the shelf, and the garbage bag was just as I had left it. My heart was really hammering now as I closed the door and began backing away from the closet. With my eyes glued to the door, I kept going and did not stop until I felt the back of my knees hit the edge of the bed. I let my knees go limp and plopped down on the bed so hard, I bounced a couple times.

When the laundry basket slid across the floor once again, I almost lost it. I started hyperventilating, and jolts of heat started coursing through my body. I was struggling hard to control my breathing and slow my heart, before it gave out, when a book fell.

I immediately held my right hand up. "God, I can't," I whispered. "This is too much. I need your help."

Another book fell.

I squeezed my eyes tight until I was seeing spots of white swimming in the blackness. "God, please."

The garbage bag rustled.

"I don't know what to do. I don't know what to say to make this go away. You said if I need help, I should ask for it, and you would do what I ask. I'm asking."

I held my breath and squeezed my eyes even tighter until they began to hurt. When a few minutes had passed and I heard nothing, I knew it was over—for now.

I hated the nights.

* * *

I slouched on a stool at the peninsula, bearing the entire weight of my upper body down on my elbows, as I sipped on a large mug of coffee. I had not slept a wink the night before although the only noises I had

17

been subjected to for the rest of the night, after the noises in the closet had stopped, was the occasional call and answer of some neighborhood dogs.

My back stiffened as I heard the gate slide.

Logan.

I was tired and cranky and so not in the mood to deal with Logan. So why did my heart skip a little? After the way he had left the other night, his face should have been the last face I wanted to see, yet it wasn't. After the way he had left the other night, I should leave him to stand outside banging on the door all day. However, I was too exhausted to channel my inner pettiness. I sighed and reluctantly slid off the stool to fly both latches, and intent on a certain nonchalance, hurried back to my perch to continue slurping my coffee with my back to him.

"Hey," he called out casually.

"Hey yourself," I called over my shoulder, equally as casual although my insides were slush.

"Here," he said, coming up alongside me and holding out an envelope.

I took it, and without checking its contents, placed it on the counter. What I wanted to do was talk because I did not like having unresolved issues between us, but my pride would not let me.

Logan putz-putzed around downstairs a bit before going into his bedroom to get his backpack. He stopped in the kitchen to shove a receipt book at me.

"Sign this," he said aloofly.

I had so many questions, including where he was staying, but I signed the book and held my tongue. At this point, it did not matter where he was staying. Logan had made sure his business was not my business anymore. He took the book, and without another word, went through the front door. It dawned on me that I had not heard him drive into the yard, so I got up and slowly peeled the curtain back, inch by painstaking inch. The last thing I wanted was to attract attention because abject humiliation was not something I could currently handle. I had sworn I would never be *that* woman—the woman who spied on her man, pug-nosed against a smudgy window or croc-eyed over some overgrown bush. Scoffing, I made to step off.

And then I saw her.

Logan said something to her as she alighted from the car, and she threw him a smile hot enough to melt the sun. My nails dug into my palm as my fist closed like a vice on the slinky material in my hand.

Oh my God. The woman in my dream I thought. Something raw and ugly clawed at my chest, but I had time to neither name nor nurse it.

Move, I chided myself. *Suppose one of them looks and sees you? Now that would be a real doozy.* My heart won out over my head, and I did not move a muscle. Instead, I stood transfixed, becoming what I swore I would never become.

I watched their interaction as they walked to the trunk for Logan to toss in his backpack. They were comfortable with each other. She seemed to hang on his every word, and I got that.

There was something about Logan, and women were often drawn to that something. He possessed Adam Levine's musical acuity and Barack Obama's charm. For me, Barack and Adam were the perfect package, and together they were Logan. He often feigned indifference to all the adoration, but I knew deep down he relished it. I would often stand aside while women dusted his ego with sugary compliments like *Mr. GQ* and slipped him phone numbers on napkins. I would often roll my eyes and ignore all of it, except the time Chaka Khan had moseyed over to his table and called him *cutie* during a performance at a jazz club. I had not been there, but he could not stop talking about it. He was so over the moon and—I have to admit—so was I. After all, the legendary Chaka Khan had noticed not just any man; she had noticed *my* man.

I stood there for a long time after the car drove off. The shock was not seeing Logan with another woman—that was a different emotion entirely. I simply could not believe I was just looking at the woman I had seen in one of my dreams two months before Logan served me divorce papers. In the dream, Logan had come over to me, waving divorce papers in my face and demanding I sign them. When I refused, the woman had gotten in my face and screamed at me to sign the papers because she was not hiding anymore.

For a brief moment, before the car had driven off, I had wanted to rush outside and scream at Logan about how much of a liar he was because I had asked him countless times—before this—if he was leaving me for someone else, and his answer was always no. Of course, I did not tell him that the reason I had asked so many times was that God had already shown me the truth, but I wanted to hear him say it.

Over the space of our marriage, I hardly told Logan any of my dreams because he always dismissed them. Even after a truck coming in the opposite direction in which he was travelling had jack-knifed on a hill, and he had to take to the banking to avoid being hit—just as I had seen in a dream and told him about that very morning—he had remained dismissive. He had even gone so far as to call me a witch in a fit of rage once. About two weeks after his brother Caleb had been shot, I told Logan about a dream I had had—three months prior to his death—in which I saw how Caleb was killed. He had brushed over it, like he had not heard me, and had steered the conversation in another direction. It wasn't until a year later that I found out Logan was actually terrified by my dreams—and because he was mad—he had thrown in that his parents thought me a witch and were afraid of me too.

I probably would have remained at the window half the day had I not suddenly thought of what I must look like standing there. I pictured myself as the ominous figure in a horror movie, that nobody sees watching through a window, and chuckled. I hastily dropped the curtain, as though it had caught on fire, and stepped back.

* * *

Sometime in the wee hours of the morning, when everything was eerily still, I panicked. I had less than a second to open my eyes before the seizure hit. I had had a few of those now, so I knew roughly how much time I had to play with. Once the big wave hit, I would be rendered immobile. I had never succeeded in opening my eyes in time before, but this time would be different . . . if only I could open my eyes. Seizure always only crept up on me while I slept—a bandit hiding in the shadows, waiting for sleep to happen by. It would wait patiently until I had had my fill of sleep, and when the time neared for me to stir, it would deftly pounce, viciously tackle, and then strategically shackle me. By the time I realized my stalker was upon me, it would always be too late, guaranteeing its inexorable triumph in assaulting not only my body, but my peace. I could never relax and let Seizure simply have its way with me. I fought tooth and nail to be free of its grasp. I always tried to call out to someone, kick my feet, flail my arms, open my eyes, scream. However, Seizure always proved too strong.

As my ears clogged and my brain buzzed, my body began to vibrate at what felt like a quadrillion judders per second. I did the only thing I could because, somehow, my mind was the one thing that worked totally fine—every single time.

Oh, God! Help me, please! I screamed from a cavernous place inside my head—a place so far off my voice seemed to echo back at me. Even in that moment, I took fleeting comfort in knowing God was with me. I didn't know, however, whether He would shorten my ordeal because He had never done so before. Still, I called on Him.

As my heart slowed, a new wave of panic hit. This time was different. It was slowing way too fast and for far too long. I struggled even more. *Open your eyes,* I chided myself.

My heart sounded so loud in my ears. *Buboom . . . Bu Boom . . . Bu . . . Boom . . . Bu . . .*

I looked down at myself on the bed and gasped. I don't know how I even knew it was me because all that lay there was pure skeleton—no muscles, ligaments, tendons, skin. I watched in horror as my skeleton vibrated, my bones rattling and clattering as Seizure continued its assault.

Whoa! What the—? I thought, mesmerized . . . momentarily forgetting that I was desperate to rouse myself. My heart, my lungs, my brain—they were all lit up like the Fourth of July, giving off a bright-shocking-neon-red glow. I had never seen that dazzling a red before. I watched, momentarily frozen.

And then I wasn't.

"*Nooooo!*" I screamed over and over again because—if I were looking down at my body—I must be dead. However, no matter how hard I screamed, Seizure refused to let go.

That left fighting the only way I could. "*God, save me! I am begging you, please. I don't want to die!*" I begged over and over—not necessarily with the exact words or in the same order—but my pleadings seemed to ricochet off invisible walls, returning to me hollow.

Why aren't you hearing me? I screamed. I was growing increasingly weary, but I refused to wave the proverbial white flag.

All of a sudden, Seizure grudgingly let go of my body, and I was slammed back inside the shell that housed my soul. All was blackness around me, and I still could not hear my heart. Worse, I was not breathing. I struggled frantically to suck air into my lungs. My insides felt hollow—empty—like parts were missing or things were not where they should be.

Please, please, please God. I want to live, I begged from deep inside the void, *I'm not done doing everything you want me to do.*

I felt a jolt to my heart so jarring, it would have been less painful had a freight truck slammed into my chest. As I gulped air into my lungs, my chest caught fire. I wanted to hold my breath indefinitely, but when I tried to not breathe, the pain worsened. Like a fish floundering out of water, I took rapid, shallow breaths.

When I eventually opened my eyes, I was lying on my left side. For a moment, I did not know where I was. My eyes travelled up the empty cream walls in search of some recognizable detail, coming to rest on the intricate patterns of the tray ceiling, and I sighed my relief. However, my neck felt as though it might snap from being in that position, so very slowly and very deliberately, I began lowering my head to its original position.

My tears burned like acid as they trailed across the bridge of my nose into my left eye, down my cheek, and onto my pillow. I did not realize it right away, but my tears were due not only to the pain wracking my body, but the relief of being alive. I tried to call out, but my voice was hoarse and brittle, my throat too parched and gravelly.

Maybe if I lubricate my throat, I thought, swallowing hard a few times before calling out again, but my cry was nothing but a scratchy croak.

My phone.

My kids always made sure I had it beside me should the need arise for me to call for help in the middle of the night. I reached for it, but my hands refused to move as though they had—along with the rest of my muscles—somehow atrophied. I could only lie there and feel . . . feel all the hurt that Seizure had wrought on me.

The tears flowed faster as the veins in my hands puffed to almost bursting. My blood felt as though it had congealed somehow, forming teeth that chomped paths along my body.

I tried to cry out once again, but my throat had closed up.

God, please, I begged from some place deep in my spirit. *I can't take anymore.*

Mercifully, darkness engulfed me.

Clay

For it is God who works in you
To will and to act according to His good purpose.

Philippians 2:13 (NIV)

Oh great, I thought as I walked by Logan's pouch on the center table. Now, he had a reason to come over, which I really did not want. I definitely was not going to be the one to call him. He would have to figure out on his own where he had left it.

Hmph, I thought bitterly, *might take him a while.*

I was still weak from the seizure and was in no mood to deal with Logan. I had spent all day in bed the day before, but still, I did not feel quite myself. I sat down to a bowl of oatmeal that tasted—at best—like soggy cardboard and took way too much energy to finish, so after about a half an hour of pushing it around in the bowl, I got up from the counter and left it there.

As I passed the living room, I got a prompting to pick up Logan's pouch, which I balked at because I was never in the habit of searching through anything of Logan's—not his wallet, not his pockets, not his glove compartment, not his phone—except the one time I was playing a game and a racy message popped up, quite fortuitously, at the top of the screen.

Pick it up, God said again, as I came to stand in front of the table.

As I reached for the pouch, I said, "Just so you know, I *really* don't want to . . . but then you already know that." I clutched it, waiting for instructions because I was not taking a single step on my own. My stomach was turning over—mostly for fear of what curiosity purportedly did to the cat. "God, I hope I don't regret this."

Open it, He instructed.

I slid the zipper and stood there waiting.

Pull out a piece of paper.

"Which one?" I asked, gawking at the numerous pieces of folded paper in the overstuffed pouch.

Pull out a piece of paper.

"Okaaay." I shrugged, reaching in and pulling out a piece of paper from the middle of the wad. I felt like a contestant on a game show. I held it and waited.

Open it.

I unfolded the paper tentatively. My eyes grew huge, and my mouth gaped open as I looked at the balances of four bank accounts I knew nothing about.

Another one.

I did not ask any questions this time or wait to be told twice. I eagerly yanked another piece of paper out and unfolded it. "Oh, my God," I whispered, "more accounts."

Another one, God instructed again and then a few more times after that.

Several bank statements, a couple dividend statements and several insurance policy premium receipts later, I put the pouch down although it was extremely hard. I wanted to know all, but I knew better. I took a few steps back until the back of my knees hit the couch, and then I let myself fall.

Shaking the papers in the air, I asked, "God, what is all of this?"

The bread, He said, referring to a dream He had given me some time ago.

In the dream, I had needed to feed my family, but had grown increasingly frustrated to find only the end portion of a loaf of bread. After a lengthy search, I had finally found the larger portion hidden in the back of a cupboard. When I had confronted Logan with it, he had forbidden me from using the bigger piece as he had reserved it for other people. Furious, I had gone to God, who had instructed me to cut up the bread end. The remarkable thing was that after my family had eaten their fill, I had been able to gather up a platterful of leftovers.

I squealed, "Yes! The bread! I can't believe this!" . . . except I could because God was cool like that. As I sat processing everything, I should have been angry. Money had been a huge source of stress in our marriage and the cause of many an argument, most of which had left me feeling like an albatross around Logan's neck. However, any anger I should have felt was completely eclipsed by far more potent emotions—awe, wonder, gratitude, joy. I was stoked to have another dream come true, especially one that had nothing to do with anything ominous. In a way, I also felt vindicated because, hard as I tried, I was never able to remain unaffected by Logan's cynicism.

God had promised me that I would never be hungry nor beg for bread and that nothing I needed to know would ever remain hidden from me. This definitely beat anything anybody could have come to me with because God had shown it to me himself. In that moment, I thought of Numbers 13:19 (NIV): "God is not human that He should lie, not a human being that He should change His mind. Does He speak and then not act? Does He promise and not fulfil?" To me, this summed up the essence of God, and it felt good to have that truth manifested in my circumstance. It did not matter to me that I was not going to be able to confront Logan with my discovery.

This was not about Logan.

This was about me.

* * *

27

I was happy to hear the lock clanging against the gate the next morning. Annalise.

Somehow, whenever Annalise came to work, I felt better in my spirit. She was a force unto herself. She maintained a warrior-like posture in both her spiritual and personal life, which some found abrasive despite the colorful way in which Jamaicans communicate.

I call the art of this communication *Jamaicanese*. It is not just what a Jamaican says, it's how he or she says it. It is Patois (Jamaican Creole) stylized—to boot—with exaggerated inflections, gestures, and facial expressions, totally made-up terms, and quotes of old-time expressions. There is nothing quite like it. When a Jamaican *styles* you, you are well and truly classed—and not in a good way.

If putting people in their places were an artform, Annalise would own a degree. What most people didn't know, though, was that under the copious layers of tough, she was a softie at heart. I, for one, liked that she did not mince words.

"Hey, Annalise," I said, flinging the door open.

"Morning, teacher."

'Teacher' was a name she called me because that was my occupation. Jamaicans have a thing with pet names, so most people have been gifted at least one. I had started collecting pet names as soon as I turned five months old, and was up to six, not including the ones Logan had given me.

"What's up? Everybody good?" I asked, taking a seat at the kitchen counter, which was where I always sat to chat with Annalise while she unpacked the produce she had bought at the market.

"Yes, teacher. Yuh awright?"

"Not really, but I'm not letting it bother me." I did not have to debate in my head whether I was going to tell her about my week because I was seeing that she had a huge problem herself. I furrowed my brow. "Annalise, do you have water stored in containers outside your house?" Most homes in the country areas had tanks for storing water because service from the water company was either non-existent or poor.

She did not hitch with the unpacking. "Yes, because di tank empty. Why?"

"As soon as you get home, push them over. I had a vision, just now, of someone putting something inside the drums. You would never know because, whatever it was, has already dissolved."

She immediately stopped, her mouth gaping open. "Teacher, the Spirit showed me the same thing, so I have been using the water for other things, but not drinking and cooking."

"What?" I screeched, goosebumps spreading all over my arms. "This is crazy! Really?"

"Yes, teacher. Whatever dem put in di drums was round like a tablet but bigger."

"That's it. That's exactly what I saw—some things looking like white tablets . . ." I made a circle, the size of a golf ball, with my thumb and index fingers. ". . . this big."

"Yes, around that size."

I shook my head. "My God. People are so wicked."

"Yes, you can't trust them. That's why anything di Spirit tell mi, mi listen."

"Me too. Annalise, can you believe the two of us saw di same thing?" My voice was breathy in my excitement. That was the cool thing about Annalise and me. Over the years, we had confirmed so many things for one another. The biggest thing she had yet confirmed for me was the presence of angels God had told me to call, but whom I could not see.

"*Bwoy*, teacher, mi nuh know how much longer mi can stay there."

Annalise had had nothing but problems with some of the residence since she moved into that neighborhood because outsiders were not welcome. Now, she was having problems with her landlord, who was entering her apartment when she was not home and helping himself to her food, using her washing machine, watching television, ironing his clothes, and even entertaining guests.

"You're always telling me that God makes the impossible possible, so He will make a way for you to move. One thing we know for sure, and that is that God has our backs. That means we don't need to worry about anybody and what they are trying to do to us." It was at this point I changed my mind and brought up the woman at the window.

"Teacher, yuh know that when I was coming a while ago, I saw Japheth? He was talking about you and how yuh nice . . . and how yuh husband nuh have no sense for leaving yuh for somebody wid no character. When him start talking about di other woman's family, I realized she is someone mi know. She's Apostolic like me, and her father is a pastor."

My mouth fell open. "Seriously?"

Japheth was the neighborhood drunk, who walked about in the wee hours of the morning maligning residents. I never paid attention at all to the things he said—that was until I had heard him ranting about Logan one night. Japheth had been at our gate, flailing about like a *moko jumbie* and shouting at the top of his lungs. I had known he never liked Logan because Logan was standoffish with him, so I had ignored him at first until I had heard the words 'hypocrite' and 'ah guh ah church and have girlfriend wid him wife'. I had been all ears after that because Jamaicans have a saying, 'if it nuh guh suh, it near guh suh', which means that even if something is not the truth, it is close enough to the truth to be believable. Logan had denied it when I had confronted him, of course, and then had served me with divorce papers only six months after that. After that incident with Japheth, I had become a firm believer in the saying, 'there is truth in wine'—well in Japheth's case, overproof Jamaican white rum.

I listened, kind of in a haze, as Annalise told me what she knew about the woman and her family. However, none of that mattered. What mattered was that after all the garbage I had put up with in my marriage, I had stayed. I had not stayed because I had seen any evidence that things would get better, but I had prayed, kept the faith, and did as God had asked of me. I had left Logan once and had packed my bags twice after that. However, my packing had been in vain because, in each instance, an angel had come to me in my dreams. And to think . . . I had not lost my husband to a woman out in the world. I had lost him to a woman who claimed to be in the church. That infuriated me more than I could explain.

"You know what?" I jumped in the second Annalise paused to take a quick breath, "It's amazing that some people want to beat others over the head with the Bible. They are judgmental and act like they are the only ones capable of righteous living, but when they want to indulge their flesh, they chuck their holiness aside. How is that? How do people do that? The problem is dem tek God fi joke. I can't afford to do that. I can't deliberately do something, consequences be damned, because I decide that what I want supersedes God's will. One thing I don't do and that's *ramp* with God because my consequences are as swift as they are sure."

"So true, teacher. I don't play with God either because him *ramp* rough."

* * *

When my cell phone rang, I frowned and jumped to answer. "Hey, Annalise. What's up?" She rarely called me at that hour on a weekday. Besides, I had seen her a couple days ago.

"Hey, teacher."

"Yuh good?" I asked, my tone tense and anticipatory.

"Yes. Everything awright. I'm at church."

I slapped my forehead. "Oh yeah. I forgot you told me this week is crusade."

"Service nuh start yet."

"Seriously? You're not going home tonight."

Annalise laughed. "How yuh know suh, teacher?" She lowered her voice. "Anyway, you'd never guess who come ah church."

I immediately knew. Not sure what it was. Maybe it was her

tone. "You've got to be kidding me. Is Logan with her?" I don't know why I had asked—on account it would devastate my heart if the answer happened to be 'yes'.

"No, mi nuh see him. Looks like she's here by herself."

I disguised my relief by asking gruffly, "What is she doing there? The way that church condemns adultery and divorce, she shouldn't be let in the door. Why is it okay for her to waltz up in there, quite comfortable, like she's not with somebody's husband? It's so hypocritical. Does she get a *bly* because she's a pastor's daughter?"

"Same thing I'm wondering, teacher. It's like di rules don't apply."

"Did she see you?"

"No, she actually walk by and sit down innah di bench in front of me. I came out same time to call yuh. Teacher"—her voice dropped even lower—"I have to go. Service starting. I'll call yuh later."

"Bye—" I did not get to say anything more because she had rung off.

I began pacing back and forth between the refrigerator and the stove, the food I had been about to heat up—before Annalise called—forgotten.

"Oh, my God! Seriously? I don't even want to leave my house because all of my business is in the street, thanks to Constance. She will not leave my name out of her mouth even though I'm not in her way . . . and this woman—the other woman—is walking around like nothing?" I knew I looked a sight, but if I did not let off steam, my head was likely to blow clear off my body. "Apparently, Constance hasn't heard about her . . . then again, maybe she has and is quite fine with her because *anybody* would be a better alternative to me."

Over the years, Logan's mother had done little to hide her disdain for me because I had refused to be manipulated by her. Constance used money to control her sons, and because I cared little about her money and would rather die than ask her for anything or allow my kids to ask her for anything, she loathed me. During our marriage, she had done her best to sabotage my relationship with Logan by encouraging him to keep in touch with as many of his female friends as possible. She would sometimes ask him when last he had heard from this woman or when last he had spoken to that woman. She had even gone as far as to tell me that I should not stop Logan from talking to his girlfriends because he had many, and they were all around before me. This had infuriated me beyond words because I had known Logan since I was eight years old, and dictating who he could speak to, was never something I had ever done. I always knew that Logan leaving me trumped all of her heart's desires, which she made evident by showering him with expensive gifts immediately after he moved out.

Anger seeped from my pores in the form of heat. I felt like I was burning up. "I have a mind to drive over to the church and sit right up front where that homewrecking hypocrite can see me."

And you would surely die, God said.

My phone clattered across the tile. "What?"

And you would surely die, God said once more.

As an image of my car—wrapped around a lamppost—flashed before my eyes, the blood drained from my face.

* * *

"Come on, Annalise!" I said through gritted teeth, tossing the phone onto the bed. I had picked it up at least a hundred times already in the last two hours. However, each time, I had gained control of the impulse to dial because having her phone ring during service would get Annalise chastised. Right about when I thought I might expire from anxiety, the phone rang.

I snatched it up. "Annalise. Oh, my goodness. I have been *dying* for you to call," I said, bumbling my words. "I have something to tell you."

"Teacher, *I* am the one who has somet'ing to tell *you*."

As much as I was burning with what I had to tell Annalise, my curiosity won out. "Really? What happened?"

33

"You're not going to believe this, teacher, but during the service, I decided I was going to take a picture of di woman to show yuh. Just as I was about to snap di picture, mi phone went dead." Annalise was talking fast, her voice filled with something more than excitement. I couldn't pinpoint whether it was fright or wonder.

"Really?" My heart did its fluttery thing—and it had the tiniest bit to do with wonder. This had to be a coincidence. "How? The battery was low?" Even as I asked, I already knew.

"No. It was fully charged. Mi don't know what happened to it because no matter how mi try turn it on, it would not power up."

My heart was drumming extremely loud now—so loud I could scarcely hear myself think. I wanted to say, *It's more like who happened to it,* but instead I said, "Hmm. That's strange."

"Yuh nuh hear strange yet."

A chill ran up my back. I almost did not want to ask . . . almost. "What do you mean?"

"When the phone shut off, mi borrow Ciara's tablet, but it was locked. She was sleeping, suh mi ask Raheim for the password. Teacher, could he remember it? Dis is a tablet that dem live on every day." I could not believe what I was hearing. Every time I had asked Annalise for her kids, she would tell me they were watching something on the tablet. "Anyway, mi decide to wake Ciara, but she would nevah budge . . . no matter how much mi shake her, she wouldn't wake up."

I shuddered hard. "Oh, my God. This is so crazy."

"I know. It's like no picture nevah fi tek." Annalise sounded like she was just as shaken up as I was.

"No, you *definitely* weren't supposed to take any pictures. God could *not* have made that *any* clearer." My mind immediately began racing far ahead of my mouth.

It was surreal how the night had played out, and how none of what happened had to do with me and how badly I had been wronged. It was about me doing what was right in God's sight. He had reminded me, several times in the past, to live in peace with everybody as much as it was possible with me (Romans 12:18, NIV), and this trainwreck—that had been averted—would have undoubtedly come to rest with me. I don't know what would have happened had Annalise taken that picture; however, I knew whatever the outcome, it would not have been good. God had promised me a long time ago that He would never let me do anything that would lead to my destruction, and this was Him keeping that promise.

"This is too much! This is crazy!" I knew I was screeching but could not contain what I was feeling. I took a deep breath and kept telling myself over again to calm down. "Oh, my God. Wait until you hear what happened to *me*—" I began, way too fast and far too animated.

Putty

So that you may be able to discern what is best
And may be pure and blameless for the day of Christ.

Philippians 1:10 (NIV)

The doctor had seen only two patients in the four hours Michael and I had been waiting. We were definitely going to be there all day because Michael was ninth in the patient log. The waiting room of the surgery was small, and I was claustrophobic. It did not help that the room had way too many seats, or that I could feel the hot breath—of the person behind me—fanning my neck back. Every space that didn't have a chair had a six-drawer filing cabinet, and every time I looked up, I could swear the cabinets flanking me had moved in a little closer.

The room had no air conditioning, and although the doors and windows were open, the breeze was hot and the air humid and suffocating. The bottle of water I had bought an hour ago was sitting on my lap, full three-quarters of the way, because there was no way I was going to use the same restroom as *everybody and dem madda*. The plastic chairs were extremely uncomfortable, and I was constantly shifting to ease the persistent butt-cramp and back pain I was experiencing. I was trying hard not to think about what had happened

37

with Annalise and me the night before because, while I understood about keeping the peace and all . . . what about Logan and the other woman? If I was to be punished for my actions, where was Logan's punishment? Where was hers? I knew God showed mercy to whom He chose to show mercy . . . but still.

I had given in to the distraction of people-watching. However, nobody had come out of the pharmacy across the way for at least half an hour, and the trail of ants I had been watching carry food single-file across the tile, since then, had begun to bore me. I glanced over at Michael whose mouth was set in a firm line as he concentrated hard on the hand-held game he was playing. I was happy he did not seem uncomfortable because that would have made matters worse. A figure darkened the doorway of the entrance, and I glanced up, relieved to see an older woman with whom I was vaguely acquainted. I had chitchatted with her a few times in her daughter's salon while I was having my nails done. Any conversation would be a welcome distraction now.

My eyes stayed glued to her as she walked in, but another woman—sitting a few seats from me—caught her attention. She chatted with the woman for a short while before swivelling her head to find a seat. Her eyes eventually came to rest on the chair next to me— the only empty seat. My heart leapt a little as she walked towards me, but sank quickly, as the eyes that met mine were devoid of recognition. I wanted to call to her as she sat down, but I hesitated—averting my eyes and fiddling with my cell phone instead.

I hated being embarrassed. I had called to people in public before—people that I thought should recognize me—only to be left egg-faced and tongue-tied. She was sitting for at least five minutes before I worked up the nerve to turn in my seat.

"Hi," I said softly, waving a bit hesitantly.

She turned her head slightly. "Hi." Her smile was warm, but her eyes squinted, and her brows furrowed as she tried to place me.

My stomach turned over a little. "It's Jabez, Collette's sister-in-law. I come to your daughter's salon sometimes."

"Oh, yes! I didn't see it was you." Her eyes lit up, and her smile spread even wider. "How yuh doing?"

"I'm fine." I grinned and relaxed into my seat. "How are *you* doing?"

That one question opened up the door to a host of topics, and in no time, I was totally immersed. After a while, she got a call, so I resorted to games on my phone. I spotted a movement out of the corner of my eye and looked up to see Logan standing in front of Michael.

"Wha' ah gwaan yout'?" Logan asked Michael, handing him his insurance card. "Yuh good?"

"Yeah. I'm fine." Michael remarked indifferently; his don't-care demeanor short a shrug.

"Okay. Later," Logan said and turned to leave without so much as a glance in my direction.

My cheeks flamed as tears pricked the back of my eyes. I was shocked that Logan would make it so obvious to everyone looking that he held me in such low regard I did not even deserve to be spat on. Maybe no one noticed.

Fat chance, I thought. Because I knew better. I stole a glance at the only person who would have so much as a remote interest in what was going on, and my heart sank when I caught her intently watching Logan take his leave—a look of disgust on her face.

Oh, my God. This is so embarrassing, I thought. The heat already burning my cheeks spread to my earlobes, and I wanted nothing more than to be caught up like Elijah.

Michael, on the other hand, had already returned to his game, which did not surprise me. He had gotten so used to not having much of a relationship with his father lately that it didn't seem to bother him that all Logan had to say to him—the first time he saw him since he moved out—was, 'what's going on, youth.' Well, if Michael was not mad, I would be mad for him. I never thought I would see the day our family would end up in a place where Logan and I would be acting like virtual strangers, and all he would have for his kids were stupid questions. What did he think was going on?

"How comes yuh husband jus' ignore yuh suh?" The older woman leaned over and asked, interrupting my thoughts. And it was a good thing she did.

I tried as best as I could to mask my shame, which was hard to do because my face typically read like an epistle. "We're in the middle of a divorce," I said with all the lightness I could muster, except my throat was constricting rather painfully.

"Eeh hee?" She had dressed back and looked at me as one would look over a pair of glasses.

"Yes." My tone was blah. "Really." And before I could stop myself, and lest she thought it was *my* fault, I added, "He left me for another woman."

She shook her head, her mouth turning down at the corners. "These men. They don't think twice about going after what they want, and they don't care who they hurt. Look how yuh family nice, and he is willing to just walk away . . . for what? Why people cyaan satisfy with what dem have? God bless them, and dem throw it back in His face."

"I know. I don't know why people always run instead of fight to keep what they have."

"Because they think they can do better."

The story of the greedy dog and the bone flashed in my mind, and I muttered, "So true."

"But wait . . . aren't you sick?" she asked, her face laden with concern.

I nodded. "Yes."

"Are you doing any better?"

I shook my head, unable to respond, because I felt the tell-tale pricking at the back of my eyes again. Tears. Such an annoyance!

The older woman scowled. "Wicked! Don't let no man stress yuh, yuh hear. Stress only mek your kinda sickness worse. If you dead, yuh husband ah enjoy life same way and nuh business." She had ramped up the volume quite a bit.

Oh, Lord, I thought, looking around nervously as she kept at it. I was relieved that even if people had their ears perked up, they at least had the decency to feign disinterest.

My eyes flew to the older woman's face because she had suddenly fallen quiet mid-sentence and was looking dead ahead of her. I looked towards the spot she was staring at and saw nothing. She wasn't blinking, and the faraway look she had in her eyes set me a tad on edge.

Oh, my God. Maybe I should call the nurse, I thought, looking towards the nurses' station.

Just as suddenly as she had stopped speaking, she started up again. "He's going to come back," she said without affect.

I knitted my brows. "What?"

"Your husband . . . he's going to come back, and you're going to turn around and feel sorry for him." She was looking at me now, but her eyes—they were blank as though someone had flipped a switch, turning off the lights.

Thousands of tiny, featherlike fingers tickled my back.

It can't be.

"What? Why?" I asked, my heart pounding hard because I knew where she was going with this. Yet I didn't . . . not really.

"Because you're going to have to take care of him." Her voice was a little firmer—surer.

Oh, my God! It is.

"But when that happens, you are not to rejoice in it," she warned firmly. Her eyes met mine, and I shivered. She was not seeing me.

"Okay," I whispered.

Her eyes shifted, and she stared off past me. My chest ached with the pressure building up in it, and I felt cold—like the temperature in the room had plunged thirty degrees. I wanted to ask for details, but I already knew. I wanted to ask for details, but I was afraid. And so, I sat there dumbly, staring at her—anticipatory.

"And it won't be long," she said, quite matter-of-factly.

Oh, my God. Oh, my God!

Bug-eyed, I worked my lips, but no sound emerged. My throat spasmed and ached so badly I wanted to weep. It took me a few long moments before I was able to push sound past my lips.

"Okay," I said so softly that I was sure she had not heard me, because I had barely heard myself.

The older woman reached over and patted my hand. Shocked, I looked up. She was looking at me, her eyes twinkling. "God has a way of working things out. Just make sure you do your part when the time comes."

I could only nod.

The already small room was closing in on me, and I struggled to take in air. I was pulling hard, but it was like there was a film blocking my windpipe. I shot up out of my seat and mumbled, "Excuse me, please," before bolting.

As soon as the air hit my face, I began gulping. I moved away from the door because I did not want anybody inside to see me, especially Michael. I paced and breathed, talking myself through it as though my lungs had to be reminded how to function. *Breathe . . . breathe . . . breathe*, I told myself over and over until my breathing slowed and I was able to think.

Oh, my God! This is about what Abby and I got. This is about my dreams. I realized I was pacing and stopped. The hospital emergency room, several doctors' offices, and a pharmacy were across the way, and anyone seeing me would think I had lost my mind. *Well, at least I'd be in the right place.* I stifled a chuckle. If I started laughing, I knew I would not stop because panic was welling in me.

I could not believe that *this* woman—a woman I barely knew—had just confirmed what God had given my sister Abigail and me some time ago. I was on my way to her house when I had gotten a vision of Logan, on his back, unable to move as a result of a car accident. At that precise moment, Abigail had gotten her own vision of Logan, confined to a bed, and I was feeding him. I had also had several dreams, including one with Logan in a casket.

Why are you surprised that God used this woman? Didn't He use a man who wasn't so right in the head to confirm one of your dreams? I chided myself. *You already know that He can use anybody. And who better to use than people you don't know? What better confirmation is there than that? Get a grip! If you think about it, this is actually pretty crazy-cool.*

I always got caught off guard by the people God used to confirm the things He showed me. My first response was always panic, and it should not be. 2 Timothy 1:7 dropped into my spirit—God hath not given us the spirit of fear; but of power, and of love, and of a sound mind—and a twinge of shame washed over me. *God, I'm sorry. I should be used to this by now. Thank You for confirming this for me— just like I asked You to do with everything. It's just that sometimes the way You do things* blows *my mind.*

I had been outside long enough, so I decided to head back inside. As I neared the door, I thought, *That was freaky, though. No lie. I wonder if she remembers anything. I need to ask her if she knows what happened to Logan.*

My heart sank when I saw the older woman in deep conversation with someone else. I was stuck with only what she had told me. *Maybe it's for the best,* I tried to comfort myself. *Maybe digging would not be pleasing to God because it's not like you don't already know.* I sighed and made my way to my seat.

"Hey," I said to Michael.

He looked up and frowned. "Hey, Mom. Are you okay?"

"I'm fine." I grinned big, but my stomach was roiling up a storm.

***

I was having trouble falling asleep that night because—as if what had happened with the older woman was not enough—I had gone to use Michael's insurance card at the pharmacy, and it would not go through. The pharmacist said he had gotten a 'subscriber not on file' message.

When he tried my card, he had gotten the same message. Logan had cancelled our insurance. Who does that? It was a good thing the doctor only took cash because I would have been twice embarrassed.

I was having trouble falling asleep because my anger was giving way to something far worse. The hate I was feeling had steadily crept in like a weed, wrapping itself around my heart and strangling any love I might have had left for Logan. I covered my face with my pillow and screamed when what I really wanted to do was cry. However, I would rather die than give Logan that power—never mind that he was not there to see the tears. I had already spent hours ruminating on all Logan had done, throughout the marriage, that made me unhappy. The entire night ended up being about more than just that day. It ended up being about twenty-plus years.

I needed to get my head right because if my head was not right, my heart would not be right either. *Come on, Jabez! Since you left the doctor's office, you haven't once thought about what God did today through the older woman. You've wasted the* entire *day focusing on what Logan did to you instead. You've spent all your energy hating on Logan instead of loving on God. God cannot be pleased with that,* I chided myself.

Just then, Romans 12:2 dropped into my spirit: Do not be conformed to this world, but be transformed by the renewing of your mind, that you may prove what is that good and acceptable and perfect will of God (NKJV).

"God, please be patient with me—" I began as I closed my eyes. I continued talking to Him until my own words lulled me to sleep.

Almost as soon as I dozed off, the air in the room shifted. Panicked, I tried to open my eyes, but I could not. My body seemed to be humming, and my head felt as though I was under water. I could feel the menace intensifying and knew I would soon be out of time. I began thrashing about, and though I was growing increasingly tired, I knew I had not really moved. A hand closed around my throat and started squeezing. I struggled for air, but I could not breathe. I tried to reach for my neck to grab at the hand, but my hands refused to work.

God, help me please! I begged, but the hand only tightened.

I struggled to move, but I was pinned.

God, please. You promised to always help me. Where are you?

My throat was immediately released. The lids of my eyes peeled open with some difficulty—as though they were being held in place by sticky putty. I was breathing so hard and fast my chest was heaving, and my brow was covered in sweat.

I rolled over and grabbed the TV remote. There was no way I was going back to sleep after that.

Inner Sanctum

What's more, I consider everything a loss,
Compared to the surpassing greatness of knowing Christ Jesus my Lord,
For whose sake I have lost everything.

Philippians 3:8 (NIV)

It felt as though I had only just fallen asleep when the phone rang.

"Hey *babsey*," I said in my brightest *Cheery Mary* voice.

"Hey, Mom." Christine had dragged her words.

"What's wrong?" I asked, immediately going into stress mode. Christine and Nathan were staying in Florida with my parents while attending school. Despite the fact that they were not on their own, I was still concerned for them.

"Nothing. Nate and I are good, but I'm worried about you." Her voice was laced with anxiety. I did not like hearing it.

"I'm fine." I said in a singsong.

"Are you sure?" She sounded hesitant, like she was trying to discern whether she should believe me.

"Hmm . . . yup."

"Are you sure there isn't something you're *not* telling me?" she asked, her tone accusatory.

I shook my head and rolled my eyes.

Oh, Lord, I thought. *This child.*

Christine was not one to give up easily, and so if I didn't tell her something, she would call me ten times for the day. I knew deep down that she had called because there was something *she* wanted to tell me, and I wanted to hear—just not today.

I sighed. "Okay . . . some things have been going on, but I *honestly* don't want to talk about them right now."

"Really? What happened?"

I could not help chuckling. "Seriously, *chica*? I just said I *don't* want to talk about it."

"You're sure?" She sounded disappointed.

"Yes, I'm sure. It'll keep."

We chitchatted a while longer, mostly about school, before I dragged myself out of bed to unenthusiastically face the day.

***

That night, I fell asleep almost as soon as my head hit the pillow.

I dreamed that Michael and I were walking through a town I did not recognize. It was eerily quiet, and for as long as we had been walking, we had yet to see a single soul. Most of the buildings were either severely damaged or completely destroyed. I held on to Michael's hand and hastened my steps because the stillness was giving off an ominous vibe. It was not until we got to a building I recognized as once being a hospital, that I realized I did know the town. I paused to survey the damage.

Most of the building was gone, and the part that was left standing was missing its roof and more than half of all its top floors. Parts of the walls, that had not fallen to the street below, seemed to have crumbled in on themselves. Spikes of steel stuck straight up from the ground impaling the belly of cars once parked in the garage above. Fixtures, furniture, and equipment—that had once been inventory—were now crumpled bits of scrap metal strewn like confetti all around. Electrical wires that were either dangling precariously or hanging low—like draping on a cake—gave off occasional crackling sparks and popping noises. The place looked like a tornado had danced like a gig through it, and I wondered if it was possible anyone had survived. I shuddered and held on tighter to Michael's hand as we put some distance between us and the town.

Not long after, we happened upon a group of people being led by a police officer, and I was happy to tag along—because what better guide could one ask for? However, the longer we walked, the more uneasy I grew. Something about the police officer did not sit right with me. However, I could not put my finger on what that was. It did not take long for me to find out, though, because when he thought no one was looking, he shoved a little girl into a stream. Before anyone else could come to her aid, he rushed in to fish her out, cooing and whispering soothing words as he passed her off to someone on the bank. Applause and compliments rang out. He smiled and pretended it was no big deal—like he was simply doing what anyone else would have done. When his eyes swept in my direction, I quickly averted my eyes. Although there was a low-lying feeling in my gut, I continued on with the group, darting occasional daggers at the officer's back. He would sometimes turn and look at me, and I would flash him a strained smile. I got the niggling feeling, however, that he knew I suspected he was not altogether what he appeared to be.

He led us to a church that looked centuries old with its mildewed-moss-covered-brick walls and intricate-stained-glass windows—their colors muddied by years of caked-on grime. Instead of being a thing of beauty, they offended the eyes. The roof, with its peeling shingles—some curled like paper held to flame—looked unable to withstand the slightest puff of wind. The wooden boxed eaves had turned an ugly shade of black rot from obvious water damage. Giant trees of gnarled branches and sun-scorched leaves, prickly overgrown weeds with purple flowering, and brittle shrubs that were more vine than bush, had transformed the yard into a small forest. Yet, there was nothing that spoke life there.

As we moved closer to the back door, a nauseating sense of foreboding settled itself in my spirit. I did not want to go inside. I threw a furtive glance at the policeman, who took no notice of me. I glanced around at the others, but nobody exhibited any signs of concern. As soon as the policeman got the door opened, he marshalled us inside, becoming increasingly agitated because we were not moving fast enough. He promptly locked and chained the door behind the last person in the queue.

I frowned at him.

"For your safety." His smile did not reach his piercing, obsidian eyes. "People,"—he turned his attention to the others, dismissing me, but not before I caught the glint of menace in his eyes—"it is not safe out there. Now, I'm going to have to ask you all to take a seat . . . Please.*" He looked at me as he sardonically tacked on the gesture of politeness. He swept his hand towards several rows of chairs and watched with a gleam of satisfaction as people clambered for a seat. It was like watching a game of Musical Chairs. Michael and I took the two remaining seats in the front, which nobody occupied, but only because we had been standing in the way of them.*

"I will come back and get you when it's time," the policeman said, before sauntering towards a door that was dead ahead of where we had entered.

Time for what? *I wondered but dared not ask.*

He paused abruptly, with his hand still on the doorknob, and slowly turned his head to glower at me—as though he had heard my thoughts. "Oh, and one more thing that you should consider a warning. Do not dare *leave your seats."*

I shifted uncomfortably in my chair but held his gaze. He opened his mouth as if to say something else, and I tensed. However, he pursed his lips and took his leave.

"Get up," God commanded me, shortly after the door had closed behind him.

Obediently, I rose from my seat, my eyes wandering around the

room to meet many disapproving glares. They all had the same look—
the   there-always-has-to-be-one-of-you-who-gets-everyone-killed-
trying-to-be-a-hero look.

Ignoring them, I crept up to the door, my heart in my throat. What
if the policeman turns back? *I fretted to myself. If I had any sense at all,*
the intense spasming in my stomach at the thought, should have
deterred me.

Upon my approach, God spoke again. "Open the door."

Instead of turning the knob like the officer had done, I pushed one
of the panels in the top half of the door, which was saloon style. The
bottom part of the door was solid and housed the knob that opened the
entire door. I tentatively eased the panel outwards, and as soon as the
opening was big enough, I stuck my head around. My free hand
immediately flew to my mouth to stifle a scream.

At the front of the hall, below the pulpit, people were being
restrained around an altar. Indescribable horror froze their faces on
their screams—or maybe I had simply blocked out the sound. Their
struggling was in vain as they were grossly outmatched in brawn and
number. A woman was dragged forward and stretched out on the altar,
one person holding each limb, as she writhed and pleaded. A sinewy
tower of a man, whose face was obscured by a hood, stepped forward.
He effortlessly raised a huge dark-grey-medieval looking-battle axe—
that was already dripping with blood—high above his head and
brought it down with extreme force, cleanly severing the woman's head.
When he rolled her body off, it landed with a sickening thud right next
to the altar, but her head rolled a significant distance further. A man
rushed forward to drag her body out of the way, leaving bloody drag
marks behind him. I pressed my hand hard against my lips, not only to
keep at bay the sound that was bubbling up in my throat, but to swallow
the bile that was now flooding my mouth. As the man stepped back to
allow someone else to be dragged by him and laid on the slippery slab,
I slowly eased the door closed and stepped back, clumsily making my
way back to my seat.

"God, what am I going to do?" I asked, my mouth still bitter with gall. "They are killing people." The corners of my eyes burned with tears I could not afford to shed. "I don't want to die here. I don't want my son to die here."

"Look up," He said.

I slowly raised my eyes to the ceiling and saw the faintest outline of a square. I carefully carried my chair over, nervously darting my eyes around the room, but no one was paying me any mind. I cringed and tentatively climbed up onto the chair. I was afraid of heights, and even a chair was too tall for me. Because I kept worrying about falling, and because my fingers barely touched the panel even when I was tiptoeing, I made slower work—than I would have liked—sliding it out of the way. I brought my fingers up to my lips before waving Michael over. I dragged him up in front of me. With my hands trembling violently from the weight, I hoisted him so that he could pull himself up and over the ledge.

When he was safely situated, I glanced around. "God, what about all these people?"

"Pull yourself up," He said.

Once I was in the crawl space, I gently slid the panel back into place—my heart heavy. These people were going to die, and there was nothing I could do about it. I could not save anybody, least of all myself. Michael and I were going to be saved only because God had willed it.

Michael and I crawled through the dark, narrow opening, careful not to make too much noise. All the while, I had to be whispering to myself to keep calm. I was relieved when we got to a grate that led to the outside. Michael sat back on his hunches with his palms resting slightly behind him and kicked with all his might. It took several kicks for the grate to eventually loosen and fall with a clang unto the paved walkway below.

I held on to Michael's arm listening for sounds of alarm being raised. Although I did not hear any, I was still cautious. "Stick your head out a little and make sure no one is coming before you jump."

He nodded, did as I had instructed, and—after two enthusiastic thumbs-up—jumped to the ground. When my turn came, I stayed in place, frozen—too afraid to jump. Michael began flapping his arms urgently, encouraging me to hurry. I dangled on the ledge for a few moments before I closed my eyes and let myself drop. I glanced around quickly before grabbing Michael's hand, heralding us towards a disintegrating wrought-iron gate. As I stood outside the gate, trying to decide in which direction we should run, I was faced with a conundrum. I dared not look back—not wanting to see what was behind me . . . but I hesitated stepping off—not wanting to see what lay ahead either.

"Wake up," I screamed from some far-off place inside my head.

When I opened my eyes, my breathing was uneven. I willed myself to steady it while I looked around my room—grateful to be where I was. I was also relieved to see the faint light peeking through the glass at the top of my balcony door.

"God, what was that?" I whispered.

I got no response.

***

The entire day was garbage. I barely dragged myself through the day and could hardly summon enough energy to do mundane tasks. The dream plagued me. I kept remembering every detail, including the smells that wafted towards me from inside the church hall—the smell of stale blood mixed with fresh blood, the smell of vomit, the stench of uncontrolled bodily functions.

I talked to God throughout the day, and He addressed everything—except the questions I had about the dream. Although I recognized it as an end-of-days dreams, I wanted to know so much more, like when, what caused the destruction, how Michael and I ended up where we did, why Nathan and Christine were not with us, who the policeman was . . .

It took me forever to go to sleep that night.

When I eventually did, *my heart pummeled my chest wall as I charged at the glass door. I was not sure of anything, except that they were coming. I had no clue who 'they' were, but I knew they could not find us. Even though I was unaware what we would find inside, I pushed hard against the door and—bracing it with my back—waved about ten others inside. I recognized my kids but no one else, an inconsequential detail as we were all in the same capsizing boat. I had no clue where we were, which soon would not matter if we could not find a hiding place.*

"Quick! We don't have any time!" I urged, not sure how I knew that, except for my gut.

As I let the door go, a raw metallic scent tickled my nose, and I knew what it was before I saw the bodies. I had an aversion to blood, and the mere sight of it—even from the tiniest of scratches—turned my stomach. I blanched and froze for a moment, trying to stem the nausea welling in my belly.

You don't have time for this, *I chided myself and moved towards the middle of the room. I had minutes—if not seconds—to excogitate a survival plan, or the state of my stomach would be the least of our worries.*

Furniture, equipment and personal items were tossed about. I ignored the gasps of horror and the 'oh-my-gods' coming from the people who had fallen in line behind me. It was not as though I wasn't equally awed by the mayhem, but my gut knew things my mind did not. Time was almost up. The splintered glass of a picture frame crunched under my feet as I jerked into action. My eyes, wide and wild, ping-ponged all over the room.

I rushed forward. "We don't have time to look for hiding places." I got to the lifeless body of a woman and rolled her unto her side. I gagged and swallowed hard. So much blood. I wanted to move away from her—come up with another plan—but we were almost out of time. I shook my head vigorously to clear it and called over my shoulder. "Hide under a body."

Blocking out the stunned protests, I waved my daughter over. She obeyed immediately. "Quick! Lie down!" As soon as her chest hit the ground, I rolled the body of the woman partially on top of her. I had no time to process how revolting it was; instead, I cautioned, "No matter what you hear, do not move. When the door opens, try to hold your breath as long as you can. Pretend you're swimming underwater. Remember that game we used to play to see who could hold their breath the longest?" I did not wait for her to answer. "Do it just like that."

"Okay, mom," she said, her voice barely a tremor, and my heart clenched. As much as I wanted to, I could not hang back to console her. My boys needed me. I glanced around, relieved to see that all the adults were moving to follow my instruction. I spotted my youngest and charged forward.

When I got to my baby, he was standing frozen over a body. He didn't respond to my voice, so I bent down slightly—until my face was level with his—and roughly grabbed both his arms. "It's okay, son-son." His eyes rose slowly to meet mine, and the tears began to flow furiously. "Listen, if you don't do as I say, we're all going to die. You have to stop crying. If you cry, they'll find you. Do you understand me?" I shook him gently. "Stop crying." He calmed down and nodded. "Come on." I grabbed his hand and yanked.

I knew I was being rough with Michael, but our hunters were almost upon us. I could hear someone shouting, "Over here!" I glanced back at the door, beside myself with panic.

I looked around for my eldest and saw his sneakers. He was under a torso lying crossway his lower back and legs. Someone must have helped him, which was good because I would not have been able to get to him on time. I urgently nudged Michael to the ground and yanked the arm of the man—over whose body he was standing—across his upper back, wedging Michael in tight under his armpit. I did not dare put any weight on Michael's back because he was so winjy he might get crushed. "Please, please, please, baby. Do not move. Do not breathe."

Before he could answer, I took off running to find a body of my own. I rolled a man's body on to its left side, lay on my left side as well, and pushed back as hard as I could. Ignoring the squishy wetness, I yanked his arm hard, rolling us both onto our stomachs. His body did not completely cover mine, but I did not have time to adjust because just then, the hinges of the heavy door creaked and groaned. I stiffened and held my breath. The heavy footfall of boot-clad feet thundered on to the tiled floor.

"Search everywhere," a deep, grating voice commanded.

It was hard to tell how many of them there were, but it sounded like a small army. I held my breath as footsteps approached and stopped next to me. The body on top of me was rolled off, and my heart made a racket. It thumped so hard I could feel my chest slapping against the tile. I knew *I was going to die. My blouse was soaking wet and clung to my back. Bile rose up in my throat, but I dared not swallow. My lungs burned, as the oxygen I had inhaled and trapped there, began eating holes in them. I listened as things were kicked and tossed about. I was running out of air, and if the hunters stayed a minute longer, we would all be found out.*

Not a moment too soon, a voice said, "Nobody here. Move out."

As the heavy door banged shut, we let out a collective sigh, but I was far from relieved. "Wait," I whispered loudly, "stay where you are for a few minutes—just in case they circle back." Nobody protested.

After a long while, I got up and peeled my bloodstained shirt off my skin. Several members of the group lost the contents of their stomachs, and the smell of vomitus—rising to mingle with the already foul stench in the air—had me retching hard.

Suddenly, a wave of panic surged inside me. I had to get out of there. "Get ahold of yourself. Your kids are counting on you," I whispered. That fact should have mattered, but it didn't. Whatever control I had had earlier had now crumbled. Eyes wild, I charged forward, searching for a back door. There was none. "Oh my God! We're going to die!" A scream welled up in my throat, but I swallowed it. The room seemed even smaller. I could not breathe. I sucked air hard into my lungs, but it was not enough. I was suffocating. I began braying, trying to force the air in, but I was still dying.

"God, I don't want to die here." I could not believe I had survived being slaughtered, only to drop dead from fear. My braying grew increasingly louder.

"Open your eyes!" I heard my own voice call out to me from someplace within the dark recesses of my mind.

And I did just that.

* * *

I checked the pantry, trying to figure out what I could eat that would not further upset my stomach. I glanced over at the kettle, annoyed. It was taking way too long to whistle. My whole body felt like garbage—weak and unsteady, and I looked worse than anything the cat could have dragged in. Sitting with my legs splayed, I slumped forward and rested my head on folded arms. It felt good to lie down on the cold counter.

I had been having end-of-days dreams for a while but had not had any recently—until now—and honestly, I had welcomed the break. The weight of those dreams rested heavily on me, and sometimes that weight was overwhelming. God still had not talked to me about the first dream . . . so, did it even make sense to ask Him about the second?

It had been over an hour since I woke up, and I had spent the entire time essentially moping around. I had ended up deciding to save myself any further frustration and simply wait. Problem was—patience was not one of my virtues.

I started gently banging my head on my arms, and kept that up for maybe ten seconds, before I sat up and said, "Jehovah, I really can't take this anymore. The waiting is driving me crazy. I need to know. Why do you keep giving me these horrid dreams? I already believe in the things that are to come. I don't *need* convincing or constant reminders. I'm aware . . . I'm *always* aware. So why?"

It is so that you can bear witness to the truth, God said.

I should have been relieved. My heart should have felt light, but it felt heavy—the weight sitting squarely on my chest. Shuddering, I began running through the scenes of death and destruction and wished I could ask that He show someone else. But just as soon as the thoughts came, I quickly pushed them aside. I knew considerable responsibility came with being chosen, and I had claimed to have accepted that, so flakiness was not an option.

I sighed heavily. "Okay. I understand."

One day, God said, *your children will call you bles-sed.*

"What?" I was all teeth, my smile so wide my cheeks hurt. "Really?"

I let it sink in for a moment. This was one of the rear times I did not follow up with a bag o' questions after God had told me something. I did not need to ask why, or under what circumstance, or when. It did not matter to me. The reason God had chosen now to tell me this was of greater import.

"That's pretty crazy-cool," I whispered in total awe of His heart. "Thank you for your kindness."

The Advocate

Now I want you to know, brothers, that what has happened to me
Has really served to advance the gospel.

Philippians 1:12 (NIV)

That night, I felt someone blowing air into my lungs. Horrified, I tried to catch my breath but could not. My chest ached as my lungs stretched—and then stretched some more—to accommodate the unwelcome air. I struggled to move and open my eyes, and when I could not, I tried holding my breath, but my lungs kept taking in air.

Oh, God! I thought, blowing with all my might to counter the pressure. However, the offender gave no quarter, increasing the force of the air being pushed into my lungs. *Oh, God! This must be what it feels like to drown.* I thrashed about in earnest at the thought of the number one worst way to die on my worst-ways-to-die list.

My lungs burned as they reached capacity, and though it should not have been possible, air continued to steadily fill my lungs. I fought to roll over and break contact, but I still could not move.

I was going to die.

God, help me please, I screamed in my head. *I don't want to die.* Air continued to steadily fill my lungs. *God, please! I'm dying! You promised to help me, so help me. Please!*

Instantaneously, the pressure was released, and air *whooshed* from my lungs. The deflation caused immediate relief from the fullness but not from the pain. I struggled awake and took tentative breaths—afraid to breathe too deeply. Tears ran down my face as little by little, I inhaled a bit more deeply.

I stayed awake for hours, wondering what that was about. I wanted to be left in peace, and that was what I prayed for. I dared not close my eyes again until I saw a glimpse of the morning.

* * *

Christine called not too long after I had fallen asleep.

"Hmmm?" I groaned loudly, not hiding my frustration.

"Mom—" She hesitated. "Are you okay?"

"I just fell asleep," I grumbled. "What?"

"Sheesh! I guess I'll call back later."

"Mm-hmm."

"Okay, then."

The disappointment in her voice jolted me. I sighed. "It's okay, *babsey*. What is it?"

"I'm just calling to see if you're okay."

I frowned and sat up. "Really? That's the second time you're doing that this week. Wha' happen?"

"It's . . ." She hesitated. "I-it's just that I had a strange dream the other night, and I did not know if it meant anything, but when I called, you said you were okay. But . . . it *really* has been bothering me."

"What is it about?" My heart revved up and switched gears.

"I dreamt that we were in a void, and I could sense two evil entities approaching. I immediately began praying, and as soon as I did, they left."

My blood ran cold. "What?"

"Yes."

"So how did you know they left if you did not see them any at all?"

"Because I felt the energy leave."

"That explains a lot. Some weird things have been happening lately."

Christine gasped. "Really? Why didn't you tell me?"

"I just didn't want to worry you."

"Why do you do that? You shouldn't hide things from us." She sounded highly annoyed.

I felt sort of bad. "I know. Wait . . . you've never done that before. You've never prayed. You've always used your right hand."

"I know. I don't know how I knew to pray instead, but I did . . . and it worked. So, tell me what happened to you."

I took a deep breath. I really did not want to talk about this. However, if Christine was dreaming about it, it was important. "It began with a sound in your dad's clo—"

"By the way, Mom," she interrupted, "Nate's been hearing everything. You're on speaker."

"Hey, Mom," Nate said.

"Hey, *son-son*. Yuh good?"

"Yes," he said, his voice solemn. "Before you start telling us about what has been happening, I want to say something. I know you're kind of surprised Christine prayed—but remember that Jesus spoke about this? Do you remember when the disciples could not cast a demon out of a boy who could not speak and was having seizures?"

I sighed. "Nate, I just woke up. I don't even remember my name."

"Okay. So, the father went to Jesus instead. After Jesus cast the demon out, the disciples asked Him how come they were unable to do it, and He told them that that kind of spirit could only be driven out by prayer and fasting."

"Hmm. Yes, I do remember that story," I said. "I'm shocked that Chrissy knew to do that in her dream, though."

"Mom," Christine butt in impatiently, "tell us what happened."

***

That night, *I dreamed that I entered my bedroom. It was exactly as it was in the physical realm. Michael was lying on my bed, just as he had been before I fell asleep. He had come to lie down because he was not feeling well. Because I could not move him, I had decided to leave him there.*

As I began walking towards my bed, I froze. I could not see it, whatever it was, but I knew its eyes were trained on me because of the way my skin prickled. I glanced over at Michael and was relieved to see that he seemed fine. My immediate instinct was to protect him, but instead of that instinct giving way to unbridled fierceness, it gave way to unadulterated fear.

Disgusted with myself, I willed my feet to move. However, they had upped and declared themselves emancipated. I was so tired of having these face-offs. Why me? It was beginning to feel like I did not share the planet with seven billion other people.

I wanted to petulantly stomp my feet and throw a fit. Instead, I choked out, "I rebuke you in the name of Jesus Christ of Nazareth."

The being did not move.

Good air was getting sucked out of the room and was being replaced by air that was dense and heavy. My room—which very easily swallowed up the oversized furniture in it—suddenly felt tiny. My nerves felt worn already although the standoff had only now begun.

Assuming a more authoritative stance—head up, shoulders back—I raised my voice. "Leave, in the name of Jesus Christ of Nazareth."

Still the entity refused to budge.

My stomach churned and pitted. I honestly wanted to tuck tail and run, but Michael was lying right there. I screamed at the top of my lungs, "I command you to leave in the Name of Jesus Christ of Nazareth."

Menace swirl in the air as the entity stood its ground.

Frustrated, I opened my eyes.

Ignoring the erratic thumping of my heart and the heaviness sitting in my chest, I said, "Pfft! Seriously? God, what was that?" Not really expecting an answer because I was not really asking, I flung the covers off and headed to the bathroom. I should have been relieved that I was out of the dream, but I was annoyed—and highly so. This was not supposed to happen. Getting rid of a spirit should not be *this* hard.

"God, why does this keep happening to me? This should be so easy, yet sometimes what I say works and sometimes it doesn't. How is it that I commanded this spirit, and it did not flee?"

You're fighting the wrong spirit using the wrong words, He explained.

"What? What's that supposed to mean?"

Silence.

"What am I fighting?"

Silence.

"What are the right words to say?"

Silence.

"Seriously? You're done talking?"

Silence.

"Great. So, how am I supposed to know what to do?

Crickets.

"Really, God? You're just going to leave me hanging?"

Silence.

I wanted to scream, but I was afraid that if I started, I would not be able to stop. Dejected, I sighed and climbed back into bed. I could not believe God was not answering me. I understood that He did whatever He wanted . . . but why bother saying anything in the first place if He knew I would not understand? Why leave me more confused? I tossed and turned, chasing sleep for hours before finally catching it.

I found myself standing in the exact spot I had been in before I woke. The hairs on the back of my neck stood at attention. The sinister spirit was still there. My heart sank. Was it too much to ask for a little peace in my life? I really did not want to fight anymore, but I had no choice. I glanced over at Michael, who was still sleeping. At least he was still alright.

Spreading my legs wide and planting my feet firm, I began rebuking the spirt in as loud and authoritative a voice as I could muster. Still, the spirit persisted, and so did I—for what seemed like forever. At the moment I began to feel like there was no hope, I remembered what God had said to me when I was awake.

"Show yourself," I commanded, feeling quite pleased to have remembered that titbit.

Immediately, the spirit revealed itself, but I was unprepared for what I saw. I made an ugly choking sound and took a huge step backwards—but only because one step was all my feet allowed.

One demon, a female, was lounged on a recliner—that had not been there before—on the far side of my nightstand, parallel to my bed. She began cackling incessantly, the sound so loud and grating, I wanted to rip my ears off. Not wanting her to see me squirm, however, I feigned indifference and averted my eyes.

As my eyes landed on the other demon, every hair on my body stood up as if supercharged by wild levels of static electricity. The Male was no joke. He emanated sheer power and even greater evil. The high-ranking demon (not sure how I knew that) smirked, and my entire body chilled.

I watched, dazed, as he slowly walked over to my side of the bed. I held my breath as he rested a knee on the mattress and, with a hand on either side of his knee, leaned forward with exaggerated slowness.

Michael!

I had not spoken aloud, but The Male seemed to have heard me. He looked over at me—the intensity of the threat in his glare—pinning me where I stood. I grimaced as he turned and slowly inhaled, pulling air from Michael's lungs. It instantly dawned on me that he was the one blowing air into my lungs the night before.

I wanted to scream at him, but my throat had clogged and was spasming painfully. My skin felt like tiny ants were crawling all over it—just beneath the surface, and my head felt as if it had grown to twice its normal size-becoming way too heavy for my body. I itched to charge forward, but my feet simply would not cooperate.

The demon kept pulling hard without once pausing to breathe. It was as though his lungs had limitless capacity. If he kept at it, Michael would not last much longer.

It sunk in.

Michael was going to die.

Finding my voice, I screamed, "Noooo! Stop!" Michael had not awakened, and I could not tell if he was in distress. He had not flinched or squirmed or struggled. His tiny eighty-pound body was merely lying there completely still. "Leave him alone!"

The Male ignored me, intent on his task.

"I'm the one you're here for—not my son—so come get me," I hollered, hoping to at least distract him until I could figure out what to do. However, he was not to be deterred. "You have no authority to touch him because you are here for me; therefore, you cannot harm him. Let. Him. Go." I had dragged the last word out so long that my lungs painfully ran out of air.

The Male immediately stopped inhaling. And, as if someone had hit a rewind button, he seamlessly straightened his torso, lifted his palms and knee, and moved off and away from the bed—all in one fluid movement.

He snarled, his attention now solely on me. However, he made no move to approach. It was only then that I noticed The Female was still cackling. I had been so focused on Michael that I had managed to tune her out completely. Although her cackling was insufferable, I knew it would be a waste of time to spare her a moment's notice because, of the two, she was the less malignant.

I stared The Male dead in the eyes and said firmly, "Leave! I'm commanding you in the name of Jesus Christ of Nazareth." I had been unsuccessfully in hiding the quiver in my voice but had managed a fierce expression.

The corners of his mouth turned up almost imperceptibly, causing my stomach to plunge to indescribable depths. He had actually smiled.

Although I wasn't sure one could call it a smile. It was more like a menacing smirk. Anyway, whatever it was, it was all I could do to not drop dead. My heart was not even beating anymore. It was doing a weird quivery thing, and my skin had gone cold and clammy.

Oh, my God. Oh, my God. What am I going to do? *I wondered.* This is so much bigger than me. I am nothing but a joke to these two. They are *never* going to leave . . . wait—but I got him to back off of Michael.

I thought about what I had said in Michael's situation and commanded, "Leave. You have no authority here."

Immediately, they both vanished.

As easy as that? Oh, my God! Finally! *I thought, exhaling on a tremendous sigh. All of a sudden, I felt too weak to stand, so I walked over to the wall and sagged against it. My relief was short-lived, however, because my body began buzzing—a low, humming vibration.*

No-no-no-no-no, I whispered, running frantically into the bathroom. It was empty. I ran back into the bedroom, but Michael was alone. I tore the curtain away from the window and looked outside.

My heart sank.

The Male—standing tall, his stance wide—was glaring at me. My skin crawled, and I was sure they could hear my heart all the way out there. I took a deep breath in, and then let it out very slowly, all the while maintaining eye contact with The Male.

"Okay," I whispered before whipping my head to the left to look at The Female, who in keeping with her role as the set-on, *was lying back on a mound of grass, cackling and pointing at me. The sound of her voice wore on my nerves, but it had no other effect.*

I returned my attention to the real threat. We stood glaring at each other—me waiting on him to make a move—him waiting for God alone knew what. At some point in our standoff, I convinced myself it was safe to assume Michael and I would be alright because enough time had passed, and he had done nothing. As far as I was concerned, he could stand there as big and as bad as he wanted because I was inside, and he wasn't. Smug, I cut my eyes, dropped the curtain, and moved away from the window.

I had scarcely made it halfway across the floor when the humming in my body intensified, and all the hairs on my neck back stood up. My blood ran ice cold. I swivelled around, and my mouth gaped open.

The Female was lounged on the recliner, grinning widely, and The Male was parked, firm-footed, beside my bed.

No-no-no-no-no, *I thought, shaking my head vigorously.* What the hell! They can't just waltz back in here!

Scowling at The Male, I yelled, "Didn't I tell you you have no authority here? Leave!"

The Female began cackling even louder than before, the timber of her voice and the intensity of her caterwauling gravely offending my senses. Every sound slinked across my skin, leaving no surface untouched. I wanted to yank all the hairs from their follicles and rip the flesh from my body. Grimacing, I covered my ears and screamed until my voice was ugly and throat raw. Mentally tapped out, I was ready to give up, but something deep inside me was not having it.

She doesn't matter. She's just a distraction, *I chided myself.* Don't lose focus. Don't lose focus. Don't lose focus.

Steeling myself, I removed my hands from my ears. I balked at the blood on them but kept focus. "Leave. Now!" I shouted at The Male.

He laughed, his voice a deep-rolling-raucous boom.

Gasping, I backed away, stopping just inside the bathroom doorway. I turned my eyes heavenward. "G-God, w-why isn't this w-working?" I sputtered.

Your faith is not strong enough, *He said.*

"What? H-how can that be?" I cried out. "How much more faith do I need?"

I stood frozen, waiting for an answer, and when none was forthcoming, a strong wave of anger engulfed me.

"Well, faith, o' no faith, I'm done. I can't do this. Send some angels to take care of this," I screamed before promptly opening my eyes.

"Oh, my God! Oh my God! Jehovah, I'm sorry I talked to you like that. I-I didn't even say 'please'. I-I d-didn't m-mean to do that." I tripped over my words, terrified I had offended God because as scary as those demons had been, they were nothing compared to Him. The weight of everything suddenly bore down on me, and tears started to trinkle down the sides of my face and into my ears. "I'm really sorry."

I did not hear the words 'I forgive you', yet I knew I was forgiven—and still, that did not make me feel any better because I knew I was not going to be able to forgive myself.

I looked over my balcony door and saw faint beams of light punctuating the darkness, and although I knew the darkness would soon be overrun, I dared not close my eyes.

I reached for the remote. There was nothing on but infomercials, but I was not about to complain. Anything was better than the silence. Before long, sleep crept up on me, and—try as I might—I could not resist its lull.

* * *

I was awakened by a clanging at the gate.

Annalise.

I almost could not believe it was Saturday again. The week had blown by so quickly. I groaned and looked at my cell phone. It was only seven thirty. I felt like I had been run over by a dump truck, and I wanted nothing more than to sleep for days. I rolled out of bed, let Annalise in, and crawled back into bed right away because I was not up for conversation.

"Yes, Annalise," I called out—not five minutes later—in answer to the knock on my door.

She came in and stood at the foot of my bed, concern plastered on her face. "Teacher, you've been on my mind for the past few days. Everything okay?"

I shook my head. "No. Actually, the past week and a half have been horrible. I've been coming under constant attack—with last night being the worst."

"Lawd Jesus! Teacher, mi *know* seh something was going on wid you, enuh."

I waited for her to explain herself, and when she didn't, I said, "Well, it's been really crazy. Night before last night—"

Annalise frowned and held up a hand, cutting me off. "Wait deh, teacher."

She looked distracted—as though something had arrested her attention. Before I could ask what was wrong, she scowled and took off towards Logan's closet.

I frowned. "What happen?" Although it knew nothing as yet, my heart took off galloping.

Annalise did not answer me. Instead, she slowly opened the closet door—stopping short at the entrance. "They're in here." Her voice was calm and soft.

My heart did a somersault, backflip, nosedive—seemingly all at once. My head did not feel right. It was a good thing I was already in bed. "Oh, my God! What?"

I did not have to ask who *they* were. My mind was blown. I could not believe I had said nothing about the noises in Logan's closet, and yet there she was. My thoughts were all over the place as I watched her intently. There was no sign of fear on her face as she closed the door with deliberate care and made her way back to the foot of the bed.

Although I wanted to hear what Annalise had to say, I raced ahead of her to speak, unable to contain myself. "Oh, my God! This is so crazy! I can't believe you did that! I really can't!" I was talking so fast I could scarcely catch my breath. "You walked right over to Logan's closet? Just like that? I've been hearing noises coming from in there."

Annalise's eyes widened. "Oh, Lawd . . . well . . . now yuh know why." She paused, getting that far away gaze once again. "Hold on, teacher."

She walked back to the closet and opened it.

This is madness, I thought. *What is she doing?*

Standing just outside the door, she asked firmly, "What unuh come here for?" The look on her face was intense—vexed almost—as she listened briefly before heading back to the foot of the bed. I braced myself.

"Teacher, dem seh dem come fi information."

My blood curdled—not so much because of what was said, but more so because anything had been said at all. *A casual conversation with demons? Seriously? This is some next level @&%#,* I thought.

I had ever only heard one other person speak to demons thus, and that had been the pastor from whom Logan and I had sought help in dealing with Christine's woes of demon oppression.

As I let what was said sink in, I frowned and asked incredulously, "What information?" I racked my brain. "There's no information here for them to get. Ask them what information."

As I watched Annalise walk over to the closet, I rubbed my throbbing temples and thought, *Oh, my God! I can't believe I sent her back over there . . . and she's actually going . . . but then again—this is Annalise. Shi nuh 'fraid ah nutting.*

To say Annalise was not afraid of anything was an understatement. I had heard stories from her about her encounters with demons, and she had never cowered nor quaked. She had always dealt with them as though she were dealing with regular people. However, none of those encounters—so far as I knew—had involved face-to-face conversation.

"What unuh *really* come here for?" Annalise asked brusquely. I shivered, not sure I wanted to hear the response. She listened for only a moment before heading back to her spot. "Teacher, dem seh dem come fi get results."

I gulped. "What? What results?"

She shrugged. "They didn't say." Her expression grew somber. "Teacher, mi tell yuh already seh ah *long* time yuh suppose fi dead."

Even though I had heard it before, the effect was the same. My stomach clenched. "I don't understand that. Why am I supposed to die?

Who would want that? I-I-I don't even know what to say." Shrugging, I held both hands out, palm up, and shook my head. "I-I can't even."

Annalise abruptly charged towards the closet. Yanking the door open, she said in a harsh, authoritative voice, "The blood of Jesus is against unuh. Return to unuh sender!"

I held my breath, waiting. For what? I was not sure.

"Feel dat, teacher?" Annalise's asked after a few moments, her face beaming.

Instead of answering, I held my back ramrod straight—my anticipation heightening.

And then I felt it.

My face split into a huge grin.

"Yes," I whispered and fell back against my pillow, basking in the sudden airiness of the room.

* * *

About an hour later, the phone rang, and my heart did a little leap.

Christine.

This could mean only one thing. I thought of every conceivable reason not to answer, none of them good. After the night I had had, I needed a respite, but my kids and I were in this together whether I liked it or not. If they were not complaining about what they were going through, I did not get to call timeout.

I sighed. "Hey, *girlie*!" I said, a bit too cheery.

"Hey, mom." Christine had dragged her words.

Oh, Lord, I thought, but said, "You have something to tell me, don't you?"

"Yes." She sounded like I felt. "I had a weird dream. You weren't in it, but I knew it had something to do with you. Yuh okay?"

My stomach knotted. "Yes, I'm fine. Something *did* happen that I'll tell you about later, but first—tell me your dream."

"Well . . . I was in a huge room filled with people. I missed my belt and went to go look for it on the chair where I thought I'd left it. I spotted it, but as I was walking towards it, a woman went and sat right on it. I approached her and told her she was sitting on my belt. She ignored me. So, I repeated myself. She reached for the belt and smirked as she handed it to me. I quickly took it, suddenly feeling an urgent need to get out of there. Something about her creeped me out . . . like she was pure mischief or something. But, as I was leaving, I spotted a man—behind a display table—talking to Nathan. I had to get Nathan out of there because the instant I laid eyes on the man, I *knew* he was pure evil. I got to Nathan just in time to hear the man saying, 'Demons are great and all-powerful. They know everything and can be anywhere at any time.' I could *not* believe this man was glorifying demons with such bold-faced lies. Mom, I was getting *so* mad. As—"

"*Waiwaiwaiwai*-wait," I interrupted, the knot in my stomach tightening. *It couldn't be.* "When did you have this dream?"

"Why? What does it matter?" Christine asked impatiently. "Can I *finish*?"

"In a minute," I promised. "Just tell me."

"Umm . . . last night." She had said that as though it were a question—like she had suddenly grown afraid of what that might mean, and she was wishing she did not have to say it.

The gasp sounded before I could contain it. My head felt like it was growing and had already reached twice its size.

"What?" Christine sounded frightened.

I tried to tamp the excitement—no—*horror* I was feeling, by speaking in measured tones. "Look, I'll explain when you're done. I want to hear the rest of *your* dream first."

"Okaaay." Christine sounded hesitant, but she continued anyway. "Let's see . . . where was I . . . Okay, so when the man was talking to Nathan, I focused on his eyes. They suddenly began to flash. I could not believe it. His pupils began expanding to eclipse the white in his eyes. Then a white dot appeared where the pupils had been and began to expand. As the white overtook the black, a black dot appeared in the center. That black dot then expanded outward until it totally covered the white in his eyes . . . kinda like a spirally effect. The process kept repeating itself—over and over—but it was fast. I jumped back in shock and said, 'Demon, show yourself!'"

"What!" I screeched, immediately picturing myself in my dream commanding the entity to show itself, except I had not known what I was dealing with. Christine had stopped talking. "Sorry. Continue."

"His name immediately came to me, so I called him by his name."

A chill crawled up my spine. "What? What name?"

"I can't remember it now . . . and I'm not sure how I knew it either. I *do* know it wasn't a name that I've ever heard before. Anyway, as soon as I said the demon's name, he disappeared and then took shape—as a taurus—at the top of a staircase. The taurus was huge—tall and bulky. It stood there looking at me with its arms folded."

I gasped. "Wait, what arms? Isn't a taurus like a bull . . . like in astrology? So how come it had arms?"

"Well, I'm not really sure if 'taurus' is the right word because it had a bull's head, but not a bull's body. The head was attached to a human torso, and it stood tall like a man—a giant man."

"Oh, my God," I said, mortified. "So, what happened next?"

"At first, I was pretty amazed because I had never seen anything like it, but then I quickly remembered what it was. I took off running really fast towards the stairs. When I was almost at the top, I jumped up really high and—as I did that—I swung my right hand back, forming a fist. Then, I swung it forward with all my might and hit him with an uppercut to his chin. As his head went back, everything began playing in slow motion. And that's when I woke up. I was so scared, Mom, because I knew this wasn't about Nathan and me. It was about you. So, what happened?"

"I don't even know what to say . . . except this is all so surreal." I took a deep breath. "Okay, so . . . last night—"

Seed

Whatever happens, conduct yourselves in a manner
Worthy of the gospel of Christ.

Philippians 1:27 (NIV)

I sat in the office of the chemical factory, waiting for someone to bring my cleaning supplies to me. Annalise had used up everything over the weekend, and although I would rather wait until she could go get the stuff herself, it was only Tuesday. I sighed.

I hated that it was Christmas again. The radio stations had been driving me crazy with Christmas songs since the beginning of November. Annoying as I had found that, I had occasionally caught myself singing along to some of the Reggae Christmas songs I used to listen to when I was growing up. Despite how I felt about Christmas, there was something nostalgic about it. The music took me back to my mom's excellent cooking and even better baking. Her rum cake was among the best I had ever eaten and that was why nobody else could have made my wedding cake. I also loved her sorrel—a drink made from the sorrel plant (family to the hibiscus). The flowers are steeped and then flavored with spices (ginger, dried orange peel, cinnamon stick, cloves), sugar, and rum to taste—the more rum the better.

It was exciting, too, to have Christine and Nathan home. With the demon fiasco weeks behind me, my only worry was how the kids would handle their first Christmas without Logan. Even though my middle name could very easily have been Ebenezer, I had vowed to make this Christmas a good one. I had to fill underneath the Christmas tree, which had remained permanently posted below the staircase since the kids and I had assembled and decorated it roughly nine years ago. People often expressed shock—or maybe it was confusion—at seeing the tree still up in the middle of the year. They could always judge me, but I knew what they did not know—and that was—if I took it down, it would never go up again. I had ordered some stuff on Amazon and was praying they would be delivered on time. The kids were not fussy about gifts because they had learned to be grateful for the smallest things but—given the circumstances—gifts would certainly bring cheer.

Our Christmas Eve routine had included baking cookies and watching Hallmark movies until Logan came home from Grand Market—a traditional Christmas affair where stores remain open (all night Christmas Eve till the wee hours of the morning Christmas Day) to accommodate last-minute shoppers and revellers. Logan would get maybe three hours sleep before he had to get up to play for Christmas morning service. When he got back, we would have breakfast and open presents. We were going to have to create new memories. The kids had already suggested that, instead of cookies, we bake cinnamon buns, and I had told them it was a fantastic idea—never mind my being allergic to cinnamon.

I smiled at the man who handed me my cleaning chemicals and said my goodbyes to a group of workers sitting underneath an open shed. I was struggling a little with the bottles, but I did my best not to let on. I had two two-gallon bottles in one hand and my keys and another gallon bottle in the other. My keys—wedged between my fingers and the bottle—were squeezing the living daylights out of me.

"Want some help with that, Mama G?" a voice called out. The voice was jovial, and I could tell its owner was laughing at me.

I turned around to see a man who looked to be at least seven or eight years older than I was. His face was hard as though life had not been kind, but his eyes—they told their own story. The word, 'mama' was used to address one's elders.

What a way yuh bright and bumptious, I wanted to say—but instead—chuckled and said, "Sure." I handed him two of the bottles, but he leaned in and took the other.

After he had put them in my trunk, I smiled and said, "Thank you, Sugah." His eyes widened slightly at my mention of his name.

I knew his name only because—when he had offered me help—some of the guys were touting, "*Gwaan,* Sugah," while some were chiding, "Lawd, Sugah. How yuh suh *nuff?*" I could have explained this to him, but I chose to let him wonder. Served him right!

"Awright, Mama G. Take care of yuhself." He grinned widely—so wide his smile seemed to take up his entire face.

"You take care too, Sugah," I said, and thought, *I like you.*

And I didn't like a lot of people.

* * *

A couple days later, *I dreamed that I was standing in conversation—well, more like in argument—with Logan's mother. Constance was being really animated and made no bones about her feelings towards me. I was equally as vocal, and—before long—we were rounds-deep in a screaming match. Eustace stood on the side-lines with his head going from side-to-side like an umpire at a tennis match.*

After a long while, I decided I had had enough and made to leave but stopped myself—not wanting to be rude. I said goodbye, trying my best to keep the scowl from my face and the huffiness from my tone. I succeeded at neither. Constance harrumphed and threw me a contemptuous glare while Eustace smiled pleasantly and said, "Goodbye, baby. Take care." I cringed and stalked off.

"I am so tired of these people, especially the one Constance," I

mumbled to myself when I was far enough from them.

God said something, then, that stopped me in my tracks right before jolting me from my dream. "Eustace is the one to watch."

The dream bothered me, but I was not surprised by it. Watching my back with Eustace was not going to be hard as I already avoided him and Constance anyway. I had not been to their house since the last time I had gone to Sunday dinner, which was ages ago. I had not wanted to go, and had gone only to please Logan.

The entire time, I had felt like an inmate, on death row, eating her last meal. I had mostly pushed the food around on my plate, picking at it occasionally only because Constance had kept eyeing me. The dinner had been nothing but awkward silence punctuated by splotches of strained conversation. I had wanted to leave right after dinner, but in Jamaica, it is in poor taste to eat and then immediately take your leave. There are even expressions used to describe the act, like: *nyam and scram* (eat and scram) or *eat an' lef'* (eat and leave).

After dinner, in the middle of our having tea and dessert, Eustace had asked Nathan what he wanted to study. I had cringed inside because I could foresee where this was heading, yet I had remained quiet. Eustace had scoffed when Nathan had said he was interested in the sciences and had told him that business was the only sensible way to go.

"*Nothing* beats being one's own boss," Eustace had remarked emphatically. "With the sciences, you will be nothing but a glorified slave."

I had gnashed my teeth and continued to bite my tongue, not wanting to seem interfering—that had been until Eustace had brought up someone else's child. According to him, the young lady had started college with the intention of going to medical school and had to change her major because she had been unable to manage the demands of the program.

"What does that have to do with Nathan?" I had asked icily. I had grown so sick of these people thinking they knew better what was best for my kids. "They are not one and the same. I make it a point not to push my kids towards any career or compare them to other people's kids. I talk to them about their interests and encourage them to research and explore opportunities. I have absolutely no plans to live vicariously through my kids. Their lives are theirs to do with what they will."

Eustace had gone on to point out my folly in thinking that the kids should be given slack reins. He had droned on, basically implying that I was failing at my parental obligation to strongarm Nathan into doing what he wanted him to do as there was an expectation that Nathan would come back to Jamaica to work in the family business as Logan had done. What had irked me, even more than what Eustace had said, was his highly superior tone.

He had called for us all to join hands in prayer just as we were leaving—malapropos, but not surprising. Whenever we had any disagreements, he had to be seen as taking the moral high road—no matter the situation—and he almost always used prayer.

Before Eustace had begun praying, he had asked Nathan if he knew what to do with an obstacle. To Nathan's 'no', his response had been, "What you do with an obstacle is, you go around it, and if you can't go around it, you roll over it." And, without the slightest hint of the malice he had just made clear he harbored in his heart towards me, Eustace had belted out a lusty and unctuous benediction.

* * *

I was at the garbage bin outside the gate, struggling to toss a heavy bag in before Japheth got to me. I had not heard him coming, or I would have waited inside the house until he passed the gate. He was staggering, but he was unusually quiet. Instead of his usual rantings, he was deep in conversation with someone he alone could see. He was pointing at stuff, explaining, and then asking if the person understood. I was praying hard he would not see me.

"Oi deh!"

Great! I thought, but said, "Hey, Japheth," as lightly as I could to hide my irritation.

"How di people leave in front o' yuh gate suh?" he asked, shakily pointing to any other spot near the pothole—except on the pothole itself—that the water company had left when they removed the fire hydrant months before. He sounded indignant like the offense was fresh, and like he had not seen the eyesore every day he staggered by it.

"Yeah, I don't think they're fixing that."

He stumbled back and pointed at the gate. "Suh, wah di *man* ah duh 'bout dat?"

I stifled a giggle. Japheth disliked Logan so much he never called him by name. "To tell you the truth, I don't know what he's doing about the gate."

"It ah rotten down." His tone had bite to it. "Di man ah gwaan like mi cyaan duh di job."

I rolled my eyes. *Seriously?* "Logan knows you can do the job because you painted the gate in the first place. I really don't know what the hold-up is. You have to check with him." I was relieved to see Sugah coming towards us. I waved and smiled at him.

"Hey, Mama G," he called out. He frowned at Japheth. "Why yuh nuh *gwaan* home?"

Japheth did not take well to being dismissed, and the cuss words started flying. Fortunately, he did not tarry but immediately started moving away.

Sugah shook his head. "No matter what time of day yuh si dat man, he's drunk."

I chuckled.

Japheth had swung his hands up and to the left of his body and was swaying—one step forward and then two steps back, then two steps forward and one step back—like he was doing a choreographed dance routine. I was *actually* fascinated.

"Mama G," Sugah said, regaining my attention, "yuh nuh si seh yuh lawn waan cut?"

The nerve! I rolled my eyes on the inside, but my face and ears grew extremely hot from my embarrassment. "Yes, I know. But I don't have anybody to cut it."

The crab grass—not the best grass—was shabby and full of weeds and looked like I had planted a purple garden in the midst of it. Dried leaves that had stripped from the palm trees lay scattered on top of that. The bougainvillea and ficus benjamina shrubs that lined the walls were overgrown and misshapen. The black olive trees had grown way too tall and wide—one of them so out of control—the branches would every so often rap on Nathan's window.

"I'll send somebody."

I raised my eyebrows. "*Really?*"

"*Yes*, man."

"Make sure you don't send Blacka." I could not stand the man Logan had hired to cut the yard, and as soon as he had moved out, I had stopped Blacka from coming. Besides the fact that he gave me the creeps, he could sell you the shirt off your own back.

Sugah frowned. "*Shame* on you, Mama G, man. I wouldn't do a thing like dat."

I chuckled. "Okay, that's good."

"Sunday work fi yuh?"

I stepped inside the gate. "Yes, Sunday's fine. Thanks a lot."

"No problem, Mama G," he said, his grin wide.

He locked the gate and waited until I had reached the front door before he stepped off. The only other person who would have done exactly that was Caleb, Logan's older brother. In that moment, a wave of sadness crashed down on me, hitting me like a mack truck. Caleb had been shot and killed almost three years now, and every time I thought about him, the pain was as fresh as it was that tragic day.

* * *

"Mom, look at this!" Nathan said, holding up his cell phone to show me a flyer with a picture of a woman, along with an extremely inflammatory description of her as a homewrecker—among other things too salacious to mention—typed up underneath. The flyer had been stapled to a wooden lamppost. There was a message accompanying the forwarded message that read, 'Yuh father's woman.' Nathan's eyes were wild with disbelief and anguish. "Can you believe this?"

My heart began to ache intensely for him. "Who sent that?"

"I don't recognize the number."

"I'm going to call Auntie Collette. Maybe she knows something about this."

I disappeared into my bedroom to call Collette because I always tried to shield the kids from what I could. She explained that the flyer was not new, but that someone had recently begun recirculating it. She told me a couple other things, including that Logan wasn't *just* seeing this woman. Their relationship had been ongoing—for a few years—at least as far back as when Caleb had gotten shot.

I felt I had been sucker-punched. *The whole community knew? Apparently, it's true that the wife's always the last to know. This is* so *humiliating,* I thought, imaging people laughing at me behind their hands. *So much for a very merry Christmas.*

After I rang off from Collette, I waited about ten minutes to collect myself before going out to Nathan. As soon as I came out of my room, the questions started firing at me—from all directions—because Nathan had obviously done some talking of his own. I answered what I could, which was not much because most of the answers lay with Logan.

"Dad called, but I didn't answer." Nathan's tone contained quite a bit of grit that was unmatched by his eyes. "I wanted to hear what you had to say before I called him back. We've been calling him for days, and he hasn't answered. Who does that to his kids? So now he wants to call? Well, he's only calling because I forwarded the picture of the flyer to Grandma and told her not to expect us for Boxing Day dinner."

I gasped. "You did what? Why would you do that?"

"Because we all decided we're not going." He shot me an I-dare-you-say-any-different look.

I groaned. "Y'all know this is going to come back on me—right? Somehow this is all going to be *my* fault." Christine was standing arms akimbo, and they were all glaring at me as though I were a nefarious dictator, and this were a coup d'état. "Fine." I threw my hands up. "Duh unnuh thing." After all, they had a right to their feelings, and I was not about to force them to do anything they felt uncomfortable doing. They needed space and time to process and deal with things.

"Mom, we don't want to be around any of them. We just want answers," Christine said, frustration heavy in her tone.

"But y'all know how this is going to go. It makes no sense to call your dad back. You're going to hang up angry and no closer to having any answers.

"We don't care." Nathan's voice was as hard as the expression on his face. "We have to try."

"Fine," I conceded, but Nathan was already dialling. He looked up at me and held a finger up to his lips before he put the phone on speaker.

"Hey, Dad," he said as soon as Logan answered.

"Nathan," Logan bellowed, "why would you do a thing like that, eeh? Why did you send that to your grandmother?"

Nathan did not cower. "Who is that woman?"

"None of yuh business. I'm a grown man, and I can do whatever I want. I'm not with your mother, so I don't have to answer to you. As a matter of fact—I don't have to answer to *any* of you."

"Not even Mom?" Nathan was blowing hard, and I could tell he was fighting to keep his rage in check.

"*Especially* not yuh madda. I don't owe her anything."

"Really? So, what about your vows?"

"Look, Nathan, I've tried for over twenty years. And I'm done. I can't live with your mother."

"*You've* tried? Really? So, mom hasn't tried? This is her fault? Mom has had to live with you too. You do things to upset her, and then when she gets mad, she's the problem. You're always complaining to us about her, even when we tell you we don't want to hear it—like you're perfect. The sad thing is that whatever you complain about are things that can be fixed, but you have to *want* to fix them. Mom has had bigger things to forgive you for, and she always does even though you *never* apologize. Dad, I know we are kids, but we are not stupid. What you're doing is basically trading up."

"Look, Nathan, I'm a grown man. *Mind yuh business*! I don't know why you think this concerns you."

"Of course, it concerns me. It concerns all of us because we are a family, whether you like it or not. So, what? You're divorcing us too? Is that it? You're starting a new family? Well, the grass is not always greener on the other side—so, good luck!"

Logan sucked his teeth. "Yuh madda put you up to dis?"

"No!" Nathan shouted. "This has nothing to do with mom. Don't make this about her. Who is this woman? How long have you been dating her?"

"I'm not dating her!" Logan was practically screaming now. "She's just a friend. But I tell yuh what—since you're accusing me of dating her, I'm going to date her—starting today."

The phone went dead.

"Dad!" Nathan called out. He spun around to look at me. "Mom, can you believe him?"

"Yes, I can," I said sympathetically. This was classic Logan; however, this was no time for 'I told you so's'. "Listen, I'm sorry you guys have to go through this. I never wanted any of this drama to reach you. You don't deserve this. Your dad suggesting that you are in any way responsible for *his* actions? Utter rubbish!" I looked over at Christine and Michael, who were busily texting away.

Christine gasped. "Dad just blocked me!"

"Me too!" Michael said, incredulous.

"Seriously?" I hissed.

I grabbed my phone to give Logan a piece of my mind.

I didn't even get to give him two-cents worth.

He had blocked me too.

* * *

My heart sank when I heard Sugah calling at the gate. I was in the middle of flipping pancakes and had not even made my coffee. He had said he was coming early, but this was *way* too early. I was no *Cheery Mary* on any given morning. It usually took time—a very *long* time—for me to thaw out on account of my stiff joints and sour disposition.

"Hey," I said as I opened the lock on the gate.

Sugah grinned. "Si mi bring him come, Mama G."

I could not help it. I chuckled. "You had to *bring* him?"

"Yuh know how di young *bwoy* dem stay."

I looked over at the young man. "Hey, Enzo."

"Hi, miss," he said, shyly averting his eyes.

"Well, I was in the middle of making breakfast. Do you guys want some?"

Enzo did not answer, but Sugah said, "Sure, Mama G."

Shucks, I thought before quickly adding, "But, it's not Jamaican breakfast. It's pancakes and eggs and bacon." I should have thought about that before I offered. Now, it would be awkward if they did not want the food because I was not going to be making anything else.

Logan had hated when I made pancakes for breakfast. As far as he had been concerned, it was not real food, and he did not stand alone in this belief. For him, a good Sunday morning breakfast consisted of ackee and saltfish, roast breadfruit (fried over), callaloo, and fried plantain. He would cook that outside almost every Sunday on a double-burner-coal stove he had had made. He would trek in and out of the house for utensils and seasoning and pans and bowls, and the breakfast would take forever. Every time I would offer to cook some of it on the gas stove, he would turn me down. I never complained, though, because the food was always so good I could eat it into tomorrow.

"I won't feel bad if you guys say no—seeing as it's not ackee and saltfish and stuff," I added to let them off the hook.

"How yuh mean, Mama G, man! Of course, wi want it," Sugah piped up.

"Okay, great." Sugah had answered for both of them. I looked over at Enzo. "How about you?"

He nodded. "Thanks."

We sat on stools at the peninsula and chatted and laughed as we ate. Soon, I did not mind the time at all. Sugah did most of the talking while Enzo interjected every once in a while.

About thirty minutes into the conversation, Sugah gave out, "Mama G, mi nevah know seh ah suh yuh stay."

My brows creased. "What do you mean?"

"Yuh so easy-going and down-to-earth."

I beamed. "Yeah, a lot of people misjudge me because I'm quiet and stick mostly to myself. *You*"—I paused a little and pointed—"on the other hand—you're *exactly* as I thought you'd be."

He dressed back a little and raised his eyebrows slightly. "How yuh mean?"

"Yuh full o' joke, and you're super sweet. I see why you got that name."

"Eeh hee?" Sugah grinned wide.

"Yup. Definitely."

Glancing at his cell phone, he pushed back from the counter. "Anyway, Mama G, it's getting late. We'll be outside."

"We? You're staying?"

"How yuh mean, Mama G. Mi haffi mek sure di *bwoy* duh di job right."

"Yuh don't have stuff to do? You could always come back and check the work once he's done."

"I'm not leaving until him finish," Sugah said firmly.

"Okay." I held up both hands in surrender and laughed.

* * *

The next morning, I heard someone calling, "Nurse!" I almost did not look out, but it sounded like it was coming from right outside my gate. I looked out to see Enzo with a five-gallon water bottle propped up on his shoulder.

Quickly donning my robe, I opened the door and hollered up to the gate. "Hey, Enzo. I didn't order any water."

"Sugah sen' mi wid it," he explained.

I frowned. "Really? Let me grab the key." I did not realize Sugah had noticed the empty dispenser as his eyes had not been all over the place at breakfast.

Enzo took the water straight into the kitchen, pulled the tab open and loaded the water onto the dispenser.

"How much do I owe?" I asked.

"Nothing. Sugah says no charge."

I widened my eyes slightly. "Really?"

"Yes."

"Oh, okay," I said, a bit hesitant, because it was hard for me to accept help from people or to trust that they were helping me out of the goodness of their hearts. "Wow. Well, thank you. And tell Sugah I said thanks."

Why would he send me water out of the blue? I wondered. *He doesn't know me.*

You needed it, God said.

I smiled. *That's pretty cool. Thank you.*

I waited for a reply, but God was done talking. I wondered—as I climbed the stairs to crawl back into bed—if one day, I would hear Him say, "You're welcome."

* * *

The day after Boxing Day, when Logan, Constance, and Eustace arrived for the meeting Nathan had called, I was washing dishes. I barely called out a greeting over my shoulder, leaving the kids to seat their guests. I was not happy to see any of them, especially Logan because of what he had done Christmas Day. Nathan had called him to come for his gifts, and he had not answered his phone. He had called way into the evening to say he was in St. Ann's Bay—where his woman lived—and would not be able to come by. His gifts were still under the tree—and only because I knew Jesus.

As I listened, I grew increasingly angry because Constance kept gaslighting the kids, refusing to hold Logan accountable for his part in the conflict, and insisting that the kids owed *him* an apology. She even tried justifying why Logan felt he had to block them. Apparently, he felt disrespected by their texts.

Although Constance was dominating the conversation, Nathan was determined to be heard. "I'm not saying that Chrissy and Michael handled things right, but Dad's the adult here. What parent blocks his kids? It's like we don't have a right to our feelings. Why can't you guys see how this is affecting us?" Nathan's voice was so heavy-laden it was like a booted foot to my chest. "What would Uncle Caleb say if he were here? He'd be so ashamed. Is this how family treats family? No—and Uncle Caleb seems to be the only one who knew that." His voice had broken, and without seeing him, I knew he was tearing up.

The mama bear in me was rearing to come out at this point. However, I remained where I was because I knew that once I set foot in the room, all hell would break loose. I could not hear what Logan or Eustace were saying, and only knew one of them was speaking because of the mumbling.

When Constance said that the other woman and her family were close-long-time-family friends, I almost blew a gasket. I had known Logan since I was eight years old and was married to him for over twenty years, and I had *never* heard mention made of that girl or her family. Constance explained that the poster the kids were upset about had been put up by a jealous politician's wife, who thought that he and the other woman were having an affair. The wife had been wrong, of course. The politician and the other woman were good friends, yes, but nothing untoward had happened between them.

Right, I thought bitterly. *Because you were in di bed.*

She went on to say that Logan had been wrongly accused, just as the politician had been. And this was the thing. Logan could do no wrong and Constance would defend her son even if it meant doing it with boldfaced lies and manufactured alibis. I should be used to this by now, but it always managed to hit me square in the gut—every time. When she turned the conversation back on the kids, I decided enough was enough. I had to pace myself so as not to blow into the living room like a typhoon. I took a seat on the far side of the couch on which Eustace was sitting. Logan was on a couch by himself, brushing imaginary lint off the arm of the chair, and all three kids were sharing a sofa with their grandmother.

"Kids, go upstairs," I said, trying to keep my tone even and my voice soft. Hopefully, nobody noticed the tremor.

Constance looked over at me, worry all over her face. "We were just about to catch up," she said, doe-like in her tone and demeanor. She turned to the kids. "Nate . . . so how is school?"

Seriously? Always using Nate, I thought, bitterly. *I wonder what she thinks she's playing at.* "Kids, please go upstairs." My voice had become granite, but the volume had remained low. Christine got an uh-oh look on her face and shot up off the couch. The boys followed suit.

As soon as the kids were out of earshot, I pounced on Constance. "I don't appreciate you coming in here and making the kids feel like they did anything wrong. You act as if their feelings aren't valid. This has been hard on them, but do you guys care about that? The *only* person you care about is Logan. When are you going to lay the blame where it truly belongs?"

Constance slowly smoothed out the folds in her skirt. "Well, Miss Jabez," she dragged my name the way I hated, "all I know is that every story has three sides."

"Sure," I scoffed, holding up a finger. "Logan's side." I held up another finger. "Logan's side." I held up a third finger. "And Logan's side."

"Why yuh making trouble?" Logan asked, his tone scalding, his eyes shooting darts at me.

"Me?" I laughed sardonically. "*I'm* the one making trouble?"

"Yes, *you*," Eustace said, his tone caustic.

I glowered at him. "Wow, this is actually very funny. Now *this*"—I used my index finger to draw several air circles—"*this* is family."

Logan shot up out of his seat and breezed past everybody, slamming the front door behind him.

"*Hellooo*, Logan!" I scoffed. "Now, *that's* the Logan the kids and I have to deal with—the one who refuses to sit through an entire conversation—because he doesn't give a crap."

"So?" Eustace bellowed, drawing out the word and looking at me like something the dog left on the pavement that he had just stepped in.

I jumped out of my seat, not caring about decorum now. "*So? . . . So?* Who do you *think* you're talking to? Have I *ever* disrespected you? All when yuh deserve it . . . Talking about '*so*'. Have you *ever* spoken to me, and I look at you and seh, '*so*'? Really? Mi ah *big* woman. And *nobaddy* nah *chat* to mi suh."

My ire was not about this single moment in time. It was about the culmination of years of blatant slights. Marching over to staircase, I held on to the banister and shouted up the stairs, "Kids, come say goodbye to your grandparents." I flung the front door wide open.

When the kids came and hugged their grandparents, I detected a slight tremor in Constance's voice when she said goodbye. She could bawl for all I cared. As a matter of fact, I hoped she would. After all, I had done a lot of that lately, and nobody gave a crap. Constance and Eustace were barely out the door before I slammed and locked it.

* * *

"Aaarrrgh!" I screamed through my teeth. "Gaaaaaad! This is the reason I asked you to keep people away from me!" I was pacing like a wroth bull rearing to be let out of a holding pen to rampage and rail. God had told me once that I had a *Peter Spirit* when I had asked why I was so 'passionate'. For all the good that knowledge had done.

It does not work that way, God admonished.

I halted in my tracks. "Well, I wish it would. These people are the worst. They only came here to give Logan the right and to *draw mi tongue*. I don't know *why* dem nevah *tan* ah dem yaad." I began pacing once more. "I was fine until they showed up, and I'll be fine as long as they stay *far* away from me. I need you to keep people away from me."

The children of Israel were wilful and irreverent and ungrateful, but that was no excuse for Moses to lose his temper and disobey me. As it was with Moses, so it is with you. You too have a responsibility to act, but only in accordance with my will. I have told you about your temper and your tongue, and you keep making promises. Your tongue is your greatest weapon. With it, you have the power to heal, and you have the power to harm.

God's words doused the flames of my self-righteousness like a heavy shower of rain on a campfire. My belly trembled, and my heart squeezed under the weight of its agony. God had warned me many times about my anger. Now, He was bringing up Moses? Moses did not see the Promised Land. The seriousness of that hit me.

What if tonight is the night God decides He's had enough of me? I fretted. I stopped pacing and held up both my hands as if to say, 'whoa, hold up'. "So, what are you saying, Jehovah? Am I to be like Moses?"

Crickets.

Fear squeezed my heart tighter. "Jehovah, answer me, *please*. Am I going to die before I finish what I'm supposed to do?"

More crickets.

My heart froze.

The Art of Warfare

When you walk through the fire, you will not be burned;
The flames will not set you ablaze.

Isaiah 43:2 (NIV)

The new year found me alive—but far from well. Every time I made progress where Logan and his family were concerned, he would do something atrocious, and Constance would say something viperous. It seemed the more I struggled, the more they did. And the more they did, the more I struggled. It became a vicious cycle of begging God forgiveness and then invariably finding myself back at square one.

About two months after the start of the year, *I dreamed that my cell phone rang, and I grabbed it up off my bed.*

"Hello," I said, but immediately became aware that I had unwittingly become an interloper in a conversation already in progress. However, instead of hanging up, I cocked my ears.

"Can you believe Jabez? She sued Logan for child support, and if he misses one payment, she threatens him with court or jail. On top of that, he can't get to develop a decent relationship with his kids because he can't even see them."

Lowell? What the heck! *I thought, gasping upon recognizing Logan's best friend's voice. However, I quickly picked my mouth up off the floor and tried to control my breathing so as not to reveal myself.*

"Jabez doesn't pay any bills. Logan is the one paying for everything, including the utilities, health insurance, school fees, medical bills . . . mortgage. Honey, the worst thing about it is he can't even go into his own house." Lowell's voice was peppered with contempt.

He was talking to his wife? I was over my shock and was now hopping mad. Lowell had already established himself as a backstabber, but I only knew what people had said he told them. To actually hear, for myself, the garbage spewing from his lips—like it was gospel at that—was beyond words.

He paused to listen and then said, "No. Every time he goes over there, a big argument ensues . . . instigated by Jabez, of course. The last time he went over there, she ran him out like a dog—out of his own house—the house that he alone built and is paying for—and she wouldn't even let him see Michael. Can you believe that, honey?"

My blood boiled even hotter. Where is Lowell getting this rubbish? I have never—and would never—run Logan out of the house. And what does he mean by 'Logan's house'? *I fumed to myself.* This house has been our home for the past twelve years. Logan's house? Seriously?

He paused for a while and then said, "Well, anyway, that's what happens when yuh have wifey and matey."

I gasped.

"Jabez!" Lowell growled angrily.

Oh, my God! *I thought, covering my mouth.* How did he know it was me?

"Jabez!" he growled once again.

I threw the phone as though it were a lump of hot coal and began backing away from the bed. I did not stop moving until I had backed out of the dream.

"God, what was that?" I asked, more out of habit than need, as it was obvious I had been given a ringside seat to an assassination. Nothing cryptic about that.

I jumped out of bed and immediately started pacing. This was the thing I hated about moving back to Jamaica. For over twenty years, I had grown accustomed to living in the United States, where people minded their own business. In Jamaica, people lived for the thrill of minding other people's business. I often wondered if they had nothing better to do than sit and *watch mi like TV*—like my life was the best soap opera they had ever seen, and they could not wait for the next salacious episode. Deacon Lowell Lovelace, whom Logan had dubbed 'brother', was no different. The thing, though, was that I had trusted Lowell because I knew him since I was about ten years old. Unfortunately, that trust had been woefully misplaced. I had come to find out that some of the things the church had heard about me had come from him. Logan had planted seeds of half-truths and innuendos, and Lowell had been the fertilizer—and from this dream, it was apparent it was still happening.

What was now clear, as well, was something I had been wondering about for a while. Prior to Logan's filing the divorce papers, every time I had broached the subject of a possible affair, Lowell had waved it off as gossip and innuendo. He would say that people just wanted to bring Logan down because of who he was. However, Lowell's use of the word 'matey' in the dream—a word Jamaicans use for a man's side-chick or mistress—meant he had known about Logan's affair all along.

Normally, I would have wondered—if a conversation I had overheard in a dream could possibly be an actual conversation—had it not been for something that had happened only a week prior to this dream with Lowell. I had dreamed that I was sitting in the back of a car with Abigail and her husband George. They had been unaware of my presence. George had been voicing his opinion about my part in the failure of my marriage. Somehow, he had not gotten the impression that I was trying hard enough to save my marriage. He had insisted that if I had tried harder, my marriage would have been saved. The entire time he had been speaking, Abigail had said nothing. I had willed her—with my mind—to clear up his misconceptions, but she had just sat there. Once George had slowed enough, I had jumped from the car at the foot of a mountain. At first, I had been so preoccupied that I had not noticed how dirty the hill was—a far cry from the one Abigail and I had climbed together in a previous dream. Bottles, plastic shopping bags, cans, old tires, and pieces of paper were scattered all about. Not caring, I had trudged up the hill alone, quite let down and forlorn.

When Abigail had come over a few days later, I had asked her if she and George had had a conversation about me because I had dreamed that they had. Shocked, she had admitted it. And as I had begun relaying the details of the dream, she had looked as though she had wanted the ground to swallow her up. To hear her confirm the details of the conversation had been jolting although I had recognized, eventually, that George had been coming from a place of concern. When I had asked Abigail what she had said in my defence, she had hung her head and admitted she had said nothing. That had stung far more than George's comments, and it had taken some work to get over that.

I could never imagine a conversation in which Lowell would be talking anything but flak about me. However, to be making stuff up? Who did that? I did surprise myself, though, because of all the things he had said, most offensive was that Logan could not come inside the house. Logan trapsed in and out whenever he had a mind, without the courtesy of calling first, and I had never made a fuss about that.

I was going to have to pray *long* and hard about Lowell because, if I did not, my anger towards him would fester into deep-seated hatred. And hatred was a pox to the soul. The thing was that people like Lowell were in my life for one reason only, and that was as a test of my faith and spiritual mettle. If I remained mindful of that, I could jolly well remain unaffected.

* * *

Later that week, Logan came by to drop Michael to private lessons. I met him in the garage.

"Hey. Michael's not quite ready," I said casually.

Logan glanced at his watch.

It's not that I did not respect Logan's time. However, Michael had two autoimmune illnesses as well as scoliosis, so getting out of the house—any morning—was a feat. Sometimes he would end up having to stay home after dragging himself about for hours trying to get ready. This always irritated Logan because he hated to wait, and it was worse if his waiting was in vain. It was his belief that Michael was not going to be able to survive in the real world because nobody was going to care if he was sick. He thought that my coddling encouraged Michael to give up too easily and that if Michael set his mind to it, he could grind through the pain—never mind his swollen joints and inability, at times, to hold up his own weight. Sometimes walking was made possible only with the aid of crutches—providing Michael's fingers were not swollen. If that was the case, he would drag his butt on the ground to get to where he wanted to go, or he would get piggyback rides from one of his siblings or me. Once, his joints were so swollen, the orthopedic surgeon had put one of his feet in a cast so his bones would not break. Michael was always a trooper and did not complain. Most times, I was unable to gauge whether he was in pain or how bad his pain was unless I caught him crying.

"When is Michael's orthodontist appointment?" I figured that if I started up a conversation, it would distract Logan from obsessing about the time.

Logan looked at me sideways. "Mi nuh know." When I did nothing but stare at him, he jerked his head in a slight up-and-down motion—his lips curling in disdain. "You know?"

I gnashed my teeth. It was going to be one of those days. I should have simply walked away. But no. Not me. I had to be heard. "Seriously? If I knew, why would I ask you? You are the one who is responsible for Michael's orthodontic care, and it has been three months since his last visit."

"You can call and make the appointment too. It's not dependent on me."

This got my back up. Logan had one appointment to make for Michael once a month . . . and he could not do that? "Look, I'm not making the appointment because I don't know when you're available to take him. You keep cancelling and rescheduling, and his visit is long overdue."

Logan did not respond. Instead, he walked around the car, seemingly disconcerted. "What's wrong with the car?"

"It's not starting."

"Give me the keys, so I can take a look at it." He looked around the garage contemplatively. "I had a box with some stuff on top of the grill. Have you seen it?"

I did not bat an eyelash as I said, "Mi nuh know." I jerked my head up and down, looking at him sideways as he had done me. "You know?"

As I walked off, he made a sound in his throat, and without turning my head, I knew that he was shaking his. I was glad my back was to him, so he couldn't see the smile playing on my lips. I had an innate mischievous streak that either lightened tensions or fuelled intense aggravation. Thankfully, in this case, it was the former.

I thought Logan would wait in the garage for me to return with the car key, but when I got to the front door, I realized he was hot on my heels. I definitely did not want him to come inside to stress Michael because he was already in pain, and stress made the pain worse. However, I said nothing because I did not want Logan to leave and go complain to anybody that I had barred him entry.

"Where's Michael?" he asked as he closed the front door.

I was already halfway up the stairs. "He's in the bathroom," I called over my shoulder.

Logan began to take the stairs two at a time.

Stopping abruptly, I turned to face him. "Logan, Michael will be right down. Please wait downstairs."

He ignored me and kept coming. I stood where I was and placed one hand on the wall and held on to the rail with the other. "Logan, I told you Michael will be right down. You need to wait downstairs, please."

He scowled and said angrily, "Yuh cyaan tell *me* that."

"Logan, I said wait downstairs. I don't want you up here. Michael will be down in ten minutes." I had raised my voice, and my whole body had begun shaking.

"Where is he?" Logan demanded to know, pushing past me. He went to look in Michael's bathroom, and when he didn't see him, he yelled for him. Michael didn't answer.

"He's probably in my bathroom, but you can't come in here. I do not want you in my bedroom." I was already standing in my doorway with both hands on the jamb. I resented that Logan consistently saw fit to disregard my wishes. My bedroom was no longer a place he could simply waltz into as he saw fit. He had lost that right. It irked me that even now—after he had assumed the role of someone else's man—he still thought it appropriate to assert his dominance. I did not bother trying to count to ten because all the counting in the world could not calm me. There was always a point of no return for me, and I was there. Apparently, Logan was at that same point.

"What do you mean you don't want me in your room? This is *my* room. Ah *me* ah pay fi *this*!" he barked.

"I don't give a @&%# what you're paying for. You don't live here!"

"*Lawd Jesus!*" Logan said, incredulously, charging at me. He pushed the full weight of his body against my upper arm. Pain shot through my shoulder. I had dislocated that shoulder many times before, and it did not take much for the joint to pop out of place. Ignoring my cry of pain, Logan marched into the room. "Michael!" He checked the bathroom before looking in both closets. It was not so much what he was doing, but the way he looked at me. It occurred to me, then, that maybe he really was not looking for Michael. Maybe he thought I had someone there.

I pointed to the door. "Logan, get out of my room. You're invading my personal space." He did not budge. "Get out! Get out of my spaaaace!" I was screaming like a banshee and was so blinded by rage I could barely see straight. "I can't come to where *you're* living whenever I feel like and push into *your* bedroom when yuh up under yuh woman."

"No! You don't get to do that," Logan bristled—'that' meaning dare to make mention of the other woman. He took his cell phone out of his pocket, fiddled with it for a few seconds and then held it up to my face. I grabbed the car keys from the T.V. stand before reaching up to try and bat his phone away because it was practically touching my nose, but Logan persisted.

It did occur to me that he had backed out of the room as soon as he began recording me and had immediately stopped talking. As I moved to make my way downstairs, he positioned himself in front of me, walking backwards as he kept the camera close to my face. His moving ahead of me made it look as though he was trying to get away from me, but I kept following him. I was so mad, though, I did not even care.

I batted at the camera. "Get the phone out of my face, Logan." When he touched my nose with it, I grabbed at it. However, his grip was too firm. This was what was typical. Logan would light a fuse and sit back and watch the fireworks.

And I did not disappoint.

My whole body began shaking. "Get out of my space!" I batted at the camera again. "Logan, you need to take the camera out of my face. I know it's your intention to make me look bad, but *you're* the one who's going to end up looking bad. You've moved out . . . so how are you going to explain, first, pushing your way upstairs and then pushing your way into my room? All of this—I might add—you did *after* I asked you, repeatedly, to wait downstairs. I'm *tired* of you bullying me and then acting as though yuh cyaan mash ants when you're in front of other people. You think yuh can come in here and simply *push-push* me around?"

Logan remained silent.

"Your mother asked me once why God was going to allow you to be chained, and *this*—*this* is it right here." I was breathing so heavily I could hardly get the words out. However, underneath all the rage, I felt smug and deeply satisfied that Logan would one day get his comeuppance. And he would deserve *Every. Single. Blow.* dealt to him by the chain-wielding supernatural beings I had seen, flaying the skin from his flesh, in one dream. The car keys jingled in my hand. I had forgotten them there. "Here are the keys, Logan." Instead of taking them, he kept backing up.

When we got to the bottom of the stairs, he made a mad dash for the guest bedroom and locked himself inside. That was odd and totally uncalled for, but I immediately recognized the game for what it was. That added extra coal to the fire. I began ranting about Logan and his behavior, my vocabulary heavily seasoned with choice words I would be ashamed of later, as I made my way into the kitchen to see to Michael's snack. My hand was in the sink when—a few short minutes later—I heard the bedroom door open. I spun around in time to see Logan make a mad dash for the front door like fire was at his tail.

Why, God? Why must I be subjected to this man and his bloody foolishness? I wondered, shaking my head. Before I checked on Michael, I rushed to bolt the door in case Logan decided to turn back. Michael and I met at the top of the staircase.

"Where were you?" I asked, trying to keep my voice from tremoring.

"In my room."

"Didn't you hear your dad calling you?"

Michael flashed me a sheepish grin.

"Why didn't you answer?"

He shrugged.

"Were you in the closet?"

The corners of his mouth turned up slightly. "Mm-hmm."

I rolled my eyes. "Seriously?"

His grin widened.

I moved in to hold him tight. "I'm really sorry you had to hear that."

"It's okay, Mom." He leaned back a little to look me square in the eyes. "You do realize Dad just set you up, right?" His face was serious, his voice heavy with concern.

I sighed, "Yeah. He certainly did. I should not have lost my temper."

"No, I don't think you understand, Mom. You really got set up. You gave Dad exactly what he wanted. He got you angry, and now he has you on video. Nobody is going to see what he did to upset you; they're just going to see you going off."

I frowned. "What do you mean?"

"He's going to control the narrative by cutting the video."

I could not decide what shocked me more—the fact that Logan could possibly do something so appalling, or that Michael sounded so mature. "Wait . . . he can do that?"

It was Michael's turn to look surprised. "You didn't know that?"

"No."

He tsked and shook his head, gifting me a pitying look. "Mom, it's not hard."

"Oh, my God—well, I don't know why your father did this, but I doubt he would actually show the video to anybody." As the words left my lips, I knew them to be, at best, wishful—and my stomach knew it too.

* * *

"Mom, what's going on down there?" Christine sounded panicked.

"What do you mean?" I asked, even though I already knew.

"Dad sent a video of you screaming at him. What did he do? I know you wouldn't be acting like that if he hadn't done something to upset you," Nathan piped in, his tone mirroring Christine's.

"What?" I blanched. Logan had not wasted any time. I had expected him to message them about the incident, but not this quickly, and certainly not with the inclusion of the video.

"Yeah, Mom. I'm sending it to you right now," Nathan said.

I gawked at the clip, horrified—somewhat because I had never seen what I looked like angry—but more so because Logan had stooped to a new low. I knew he could be spiteful. But this? This was ridiculous. My next thought went to who else he could possibly have sent it to.

I had no words.

"Mom, there's more," Nathan informed me. "I'm sending you the text messages that came with the video."

My head swam as I read out loud:

> I will no longer be going by the house. I was kicked out of the house I built and am still paying for. I wasn't even allowed to see Michael. I'm the one keeping a roof over their heads. I pay health insurance, school fees, massive medical bills, and child support for Michael, yet I am treated like a nobody.
>
> False accusations of abuse continue to be hurled at me. The house did not appear by magic. Your mom did not contribute a penny to its construction. I put her name on the title as a courtesy . . . and she turns around and accuses me falsely and kicks me out like a dog—

Totally mortified, I kept reading lie after egregious lie. I shook my head when mention was made of a mortgage more than once. Most of the funds for the building of the house had been gifted to us by Constance, yet over the years, she and Logan had both managed to throw a non-existent mortgage in my face every chance they had gotten. It was not unlike the money for the retaining wall that Eustace had gifted us and then, according to Logan, had demanded we reimburse him once our marriage was well on its way to being in the toilet.

I did not care about the money I had spent that Logan had conveniently neglected to mention. Instead, my focus was his text messages and how similar the content was to what Lowell had said to his wife in my dream. I had overheard a conversation about something that had not yet happened—in a conversation that had not yet taken place. I could hardly believe this had happened again, much less had gotten confirmed so soon. I was going to be drunk on this for quite some time.

"Mom, I'm so sorry this is happening to you," Christine said, sounding mopey, and I felt bad for her.

"It's okay, guys. Try not to worry too much about this. Everything is going to work out." My voice was gentle and consoling although my insides were tossed salad.

Michael, who had remained quiet the entire time, piped in. "How long is the video clip, Mom?"

My brows furrowed. "What?"

"The video clip Dad sent to Nathan. Was it a minute long?"

I checked the video, and my mouth fell open. "How could you possibly know that?"

"Because the one-minute video is a thing. I told you it's how you control the narrative." Michael chuckled. "I *warned* you this was what Dad was going to do. This is why you shouldn't allow him to aggravate you because you're always going to be the one who looks bad in the end."

My face burned.

I had just been schooled.

* * *

I could not sleep that night. I tossed and turned for a while before I decided to do some work to take my mind off Logan. After a few hours, I had gotten next to nothing done, and my back was killing me. Frustrated, I knelt on the edge of the bed with my feet dangling over the side and leaned over my laptop.

No sooner had I done that than icy-cold fingers grabbed my right shoulder hard, immediately cooling and numbing the skin underneath. The freezing cold radiated outward from the hand—spreading across my shoulder, rushing towards my back, and crawling down my arm. And it wasn't only my skin. I could feel the cold diverging—like cracks in broken ice—under my skin and within my veins. Shocked, I simply stayed there—stiff and barely breathing—with my heart hammering hard—not sure what to do. It wasn't until I felt the cold beginning to advance up my neck that I realized I was soon to be in serious trouble. I tried but could not raise my arm. Unable to straighten my elbow, I swung my forearm up and urgently began to pray. The hand immediately relinquished its crippling grip, taking with it the cold, but leaving severe pain in its stead.

I jumped up to look at my shoulder in the mirror and was mortified at the extent of the swelling. I could not stretch my arm out completely or raise it past my head. I iced my shoulder, took some anti-inflammatory medication, and crawled into bed. I was determined to keep sleep at bay—even if it meant I had to *cotch* my eyelids up with toothpicks. I did not have to resort to such drastic measures, though, because I could not slow the wheels spinning in my head. I played the incident over and over, and although I knew the hand was no longer touching my shoulder, for hours the sensation remained.

* * *

My shoulder still hurt well into the morning and looked even worse than the night before. It was only ten o'clock, and I was over the day already. I was also over the craziness that was my life. I needed a vacation from myself. I could not believe I had been attacked again. Someone had told me once that, instead of asking, 'why me', I should ask, 'why not me'. Really?

My cell phone rang, and I jumped.

Christine.

My stomach clenched. "Hey, *girlie*." Although I knew nothing good could come from this early a call from Christine, I tried to keep any traces of apprehension from my voice. "What's up?"

"Hey, Mom," she said, dragging her words.

Oh, Lawd, I thought *Now, I* know *I don't want to hear this*. My stomach fluttered nervously. However, I maintained control when I spoke. "Everything okay?"

"No, I had a dream about you a week ago, but I didn't say anything because I wasn't sure what to make of it, and I didn't want to jump to conclusions. I don't even know if it means anything now, but with everything that has been happening . . . I don't know . . . I feel that maybe it does."

"Well, we won't know until you tell me." My voice was calm, but I was cringing inside.

"I dreamt that you went outside to open the gate for Miss Annalise although she hadn't come yet. But instead of Miss Annalise, Dad was at the gate. As soon as you let him, a sinister figure appeared out of nowhere and started chasing you. It was dark, like a shadow, and I couldn't make out any of its features. But as I watched, I became confused because then it was Dad chasing you—then it was both of them chasing you—like they were one and the same. I don't know how to explain it."

"What!" I screeched, tons of questions bum-rushing my mind. What was a demon doing with Logan? Why were they chasing me? What all did this have to do with the demons in the closet? I fought to bring focus back to Christine.

"You were screaming for me to stay inside, but I was so scared for you that I didn't listen. As I ran outside, I held up both my hands."

I frowned. "Why? You usually use your right hand."

"I don't know. It's not something I've ever had to stop and think about . . . maybe I did that because I was super scared . . . and desperate. But anyway, as I did that, I was instantly *poofed* back inside the house. I tried to get back to you because I could see that they were gaining on

106

you, but I couldn't go back outside. It was like there was a forcefield keeping me inside or something. Mom, it was so horrible. I couldn't do anything to help you." Christine's fear was palpable. "What was weird was that all of a sudden, you were the one chasing them. That's when I woke up."

"Listen, it's okay. It's pretty cool that I managed to turn that around. The dream is tied to what happened to me last night but—"

Christine did not let me finish. "What happened to you last night?"

I slapped my palm hard against my forehead. *Stupid, stupid, stupid!* I chided myself. "Can I tell you later, please?" I did not see the point in worrying her further. My story would keep.

"Hmm . . . sure you don't want to tell me now?" Her tone had lightened.

"Nah."

"Oh." She sounded disappointed, and I imagined her shoulders sagging.

"Look, later we can talk about what happened to me, but until then, know that your dream means that I'm going to have to deal with the demons that come after me, myself—which I kinda sorta figured already."

"You did?"

"Uh-huh." I sighed. "Look, Chrissy, don't worry about me. I know that whatever is happening is going to be for my benefit at the end of the day. I consider it training—well—more like bootcamp." As I spoke, I realized that not only was I comforting Christine, but I was also comforting myself.

"What about Dad?" Christine's voice was laced with concern.

I hesitated. "I honestly don't know, but one thing I do know—and that is—it will all work out in the end."

"Okay," Christine said softly, not sounding at all convinced.

Logan's Army

For who can stand against the God of Heaven's armies?

—God in a message to Nathan, meant for Logan

Roughly three weeks later, *I dreamed that I took the kids to the mall because there was a leak in our house, and I did not want us to get in the plumber's way. The food court on the upper level was extremely overcrowded, so we had to sit at separate tables.*

"Who is at the house?" a male voice asked over the noise.

I could not hear the reply.

"What is he doing there?"

I frowned. The voice sounded familiar. It was one I had not heard in umpteen years, and one I certainly did not care to hear again. I spun around and glared at its owner, one of Logan's college buddies.

Nostrils flaring, Stewart—who was practically standing over Nathan—held up his hands in a shrug and said, "What? What yuh looking at, Jabez? Nobody cyaan talk to your kids?"

My back went board stiff at his acrid tone. I had no beef with him but had cut him off because there was just something about him. Still, that alone did not warrant this disrespect. I could ask him what his deal was, but I was not about to—no point wasting good energy. Jumping up from the table, I hollered at the kids, "Come on, guys. Let's go."

As the kids and I pushed through the crowd and headed towards the staircase, Stewart yelled, "Dutty gyal Jabez, I'm talking to you."

A profuse heat rapidly burned its way up my neck, coming to settle in my lobes, at the 'dirty girl' insult. Although I had heard my name, I wondered still, Is me Stewart really talking to? God, yuh si this? Imagine, I'm ignoring this bredda, yet he's hell-bent on starting something. Then, when mi start cuss, I'm the one in trouble.

Wanting to put as much distance as I could between Stewart and me, I held on tight to Michael's hand and quickened my steps, looking over my shoulder periodically to ensure that Nathan and Christine were close. "Come on, come on," I whispered impatiently at the people, in front of me, crawling at a pace that would put snails to shame. I could feel heat from the bodies of the people coming up at my back. I needed oxygen fast. I nudged two women out of my way and squeezed in between two others.

"You're a wicked woman. Yuh want to keep Logan's kids away from him and take his house? Think yuh getting away with that?" When I said nothing, he goaded, "Oi, dutty gyal. Is you mi talking to." He sounded extremely close.

I glanced over my shoulder and gasped.

Logan.

I spun back around and frantically began clawing at people. As soon as I cleared the stairs, I made a mad dash for the exit, dragging Michael behind me. When I had put a little distance between the building and me, I spun around to see where Stewart and Logan were. They had stopped just outside the doors.

Logan simply stood there while Stewart continued his rant. "Gyal, you are nothing. Do you think you're going to get away with any of this? I'm going to personally make sure that you don't—if it's the last thing I do."

Spectators were now gathered. I could have walked away—but not really. Somewhere between the exit and the parking lot, I had donned my boxing gloves. "Yuh going to stop me?" I laughed raucously. "You and what *army?" I spotted Logan a contemptuous glance before shooting daggers at Stewart. "What? Suh, Logan can't even talk for himself he had to bring along a toothless bulldog?"*

Shot fired.

Stewart railed up, huffing and puffing so hard his chest noticeably rose and fell. When he made a move as if to charge at me, Logan stepped around him and grabbed his shoulders.

Smug that I had gotten such a strong reaction, and feeling emboldened because he was being restrained, I decided to egg Stewart on. Wiggling my fingers, I taunted, "Come nuh. What yuh going to do? Beat me? Is that why your wife left yuh?" I had no idea what had happened between him and his wife, but I was enjoying the look of incredulity on his face. It served him right for talking trash about me. "Yuh think you're the only one who can talk things, eh?"

Stewart howled, his words indistinct—but then, I was not really listening because my focus was elsewhere.

"Logan," I hollered, "yuh better hold on to yuh guard dog." When he did not respond, I reached into my purse for my cell phone. "On second thought, release him. That way people can see what it is you do. You tell your friends all kinds of things about me, and then let them fight your battles for you." I held the phone up—past caring about the crowd that was growing bigger by the second—and hit the 'record' button.

I turned my attention to Stewart, who was struggling in earnest against the hands holding him. "Oi, john cruh," I hurled the Jamaican name for a turkey vulture (john crow) at him, which was a grave insult and one I had never used my entire life. But just now, I had shouted it with gusto. After all, he had thrown the first huge and ugly stone.

I could only hope mine had hurt as deeply. And from Stewart's roar, it was obvious that it had. It was obvious, too, that Logan was having to put his back into holding on to him.

Extremely satisfied, I kept my mouth running. "Come nuh! Do you think I'm afraid o' yuh? Eeh, john cruh? Come nuh! Come if yuh bad."

I jumped as an ear-splitting rumbling, analogous to the collapse of a thousand mountains, came out of nowhere. It immediately halted my tirade. The skies hushed for a few seconds before a thunderous boom reverberated across them, violently shaking the ground. People began screaming and scattering like ants in a stirred-up nest. They were scared, and they had a right because there was a storm a-brewing, and it had a name—God.

I gasped and looked around—my heart racing, my stomach churning, my nerve endings firing up—and I knew I should run. However, my feet felt like they were being held in place by mortar. The kids, who were all standing behind me, seemed calm. Bully for them!

I, on the other hand, was awaiting the lightning strike I knew was coming. I cautioned softly, "You guys really shouldn't be standing so close to me." The thunder began clapping in rapid succession, each sound overlapping the next.

As my eyes fluttered open, the sound grew more intense, more persistent. The rattling of my windows and the vibrating of my balcony door had me scrambling to see what was happening outside. When I yanked the curtains open, my mouth gaped wide. The sky, a pristine-breath-taking blue, was unmarred by even a speck of cloud. My heart started thumping in earnest.

I called Annalise to find out if she had heard the thunder.

"Yes, teacher," she said, her voice raspy. "It was so loud that it frightened me out of mi sleep."

"Right? It frightened me out of mine too. And the weird thing is it's not raining over here. Is it raining over there?"

"No."

"How is that? There's not a single dark cloud anywhere—not as far as my eyes can see." I sounded breathy, like I had just run a marathon.

"Teacher, how yuh sound like something happen suh?" Annalise asked, her voice filled with concern.

"It's nothing," I said quickly. "I'll talk to you later."

I hung up and groaned loudly.

I got away with nothing—not even in my dreams.

* * *

That afternoon, Logan stopped by. Instead of using his keys, he knocked on the door. Evidently, he was staying true to his word that he was never coming back inside the house, which suited me fine because I was tired of the drama. Michael went outside to talk to him and—after about five minutes—came and asked for my car keys. He said that Logan wanted them so that he could have someone take a look at the car. It struck me as odd because the car had not been working for at least four months. So, why now? I could not see Logan being altruistic in light of our recent hostile exchange. The Logan I knew remembered everything and forgave nothing.

I gave the keys to Michael anyway, and as he was heading out the door, my phone rang. I answered. "Hey, Mommy."

"Guess who just called me." She sounded vexed.

"I don't know. Who?"

"Guess."

Impatient, I pursed my lips. "Mother, I don't know. Just tell me."

"The one Lowell," she said disdainfully.

I knitted my brows. "Why? What did he want?"

"Nuh to put me in my place."

"What?" I instantly went into fight mode because the last thing I wanted was for anybody to harass or disrespect my mother. "Why is *he* calling you out of the blue?"

"Oh, he started off by talking about you and how you are disrespectful to Logan. He said you swore at Logan the last time he was at the house. I told him I could believe that because—if you get mad enough—that's definitely something you would do. I told him that you are sweet as long as nobody crosses you. I asked him what Logan did to upset you. Of course, Logan did nothing at all."

"Pfft," I gave out, rolling my eyes. "Yeah, 'cause Logan is a saint."

"I told him that for all the years you were married, you never *once* complained about any of your problems or said a bad word about Logan, and that I wouldn't know there was trouble in your marriage if Logan hadn't called me himself."

"Yeah," I sneered, "and when he did, I felt like you were taking his side."

"Yes, at first, and I'm sorry about that. I didn't know your side. It wasn't until you started opening up that I realized what you were going through."

"You know what I don't get? What is Logan hoping to accomplish here? You're supposed to turn against your own daughter?"

"Seems so. I guess that's why he had Lowell call me. Lowell said that you're a liar and a pretender—that you don't have Lupus—that one minute you seem to be dying and the next, you're up and about."

"What? Oh, my God. This is *un-believable*. I guess I'm doctoring my own bloodwork and prescribing my own medicine. Wow."

"I guess so. He also said that, according to Logan, you don't pay any bills. All the expenses are on him. He—"

I cut her off. "That's a lie. I won't even get into all the bills. But I'll tell you this—Logan was responsible for the water bill, and I just got a statement that shows it hasn't been paid for *five* years. I'm going to have to pay it or risk having the service cut off. He also changed out the electricity meter from a post-paid to a prepaid one while I was in Florida. So now, if I don't put credit on it, we sit in darkness. Who does that to his family? And that son-of-a-@&%# Lowell was the one who arranged it."

My mother gasped, and I knew it was because of my language.

"I'm sorry, Mommy, but this is *ticking* me off. And to think—Lowell called *Logan* a *maama man,* yet he's the one murmuring and complaining to you about me. So, now who's the *maama man*?"

"I didn't know about the electricity and the water. Why am I just hearing this? After everything, you're still protecting Logan?" She sounded hurt.

"I don't believe that I should throw Logan under the bus even though things have fallen apart. Apparently, he doesn't share that sentiment. Also apparent is that whatever I do affects Lowell as well because he's a part of this marriage. Question is—what does he expect you to do about his grouse? Beat mi?"

My mother chuckled. "Nuh mussi suh."

"Yeah," I laughed, "I'd like to see you try. But seriously—why did you say Lowell called to put you in your place?"

"He said that I'm claiming that I've had to help you guys out over the years, and that—according to Logan—that's a lie. He also said that I'm staking a claim in your house—the house that Logan built with his sweat, blood, and t—"

I started cracking up. "Really? This is funny. Mommy, you don't have to tell me anything else because this is nonsense. You allowed us to live in your house for years. We had two babies there"—I held my fingers up, forgetting she could not see me—". . . two. What bills did Logan pay? He should be ashamed of himself for calling your name in his mouth to people."

"I really can't believe this is Logan." She sounded so sad. "I treated him like a son and loved him so much. I'm really disappointed."

"Suh what *I* must seh?"

We both burst out laughing.

* * *

That night, *I dreamed that I found myself in Constance and Eustace's house. I was not happy with Logan because I had asked him to come with me to buy food, and because of Constance, he had said no. I put my sandals on, and although I was right by the front door, I opted to go round to the back.*

I passed through the kitchen and was almost at the door when I heard a mocking, "Miss Jabez, I'm making some food. You're welcome to have some, or you can make yourself a sandwich." I startled because I had not noticed Constance there. She was standing over the stove, stirring the contents of a cast-iron Dutch pot (dutchie), with a large spoon.

"No thanks," I said, trying to hide my shock that she had actually made me an offering—never mind her tone. I stepped outside and closed my eyes as I tilted my head back slightly, breathing in the cool, fresh air. It was such a relief to escape the denseness of the air inside. As I was about to step off, I rolled my eyes and sucked my teeth. I had forgotten my purse.

I really did not want to go back inside and risk running into Constance again. I slowly inched the door open, just wide enough to peek inside the kitchen. She was nowhere to be seen. Thank God, *I thought and quietly made my way through. As I neared the bedroom Logan and I used to sleep in when we visited, I heard Constance talking to someone. I stopped behind the wall in the passageway only because I had heard my name. I cocked my ears, trying to identify the other party to the conversation but couldn't, so I sidled along the wall and carefully poked my head around the corner.*

My heart almost stopped when I saw that Constance was talking to the only niece she had that I truly liked and got along with. It bowled me over as the niece—not only hung on Constance's every malicious word—but passed her own disparaging remarks. I squeezed my eyes tight to lock in the tears but quickly lost that battle.

* * *

Although I knew I should not care about the opinion of others, I did. I had tried my best to stay out of people's way, and I wanted to know why—all of a sudden—everybody was against me. For the rest of the week, I felt down—the dreams of Stewart and of Logan's cousin bothering me way more than they should. To make matters worse, I had run into a long-time-mutual friend, whom Logan and I had known since we were kids, and he had barely answered me when I had said hello. That Friday night, as I lay in bed unable to sleep, I went to The One with all the answers.

He did not speak to me directly, but when I eventually fell asleep, *I dreamed that I was walking home. As I got closer to my house, I saw Logan sitting on a neighbor's concrete planter, surrounded by about thirty people. The ones immediately around him were craning their necks to gawk at something on his cell phone. One person noticed me and called the attention of several others to me. Some whispered and giggled behind their hands, and some were rude enough to point and wrinkle their noses in disdain. My face burned as I hurried by. I could not bolt myself inside my house fast enough.*

I had sat down at the kitchen counter only a short time when Analise, who was by the front door, called out to me. "Teacher, there's a van at the gate."

My spirit immediately grew cross, and I sucked my teeth. "Seriously? Do you know who it is?

"No." She dropped the curtain and made her way to the kitchen.

I was not expecting anyone, nor was I in the mood for company. Sucking my teeth again, I made my way to the door, hoping that whoever was out there had already left. I pulled back the curtain tentatively and frowned at the grey pickup truck crawling at snail's pace in front of my gate. I did not recognize the truck nor its driver, so I had zero intention of going outside. Just as I was about to drop the curtain, the driver tossed a crocus bag out of his window. The bag flew over the wall in between two columns and landed square in the yard. I gasped as the mouth of the bag opened and potatoes started rolling out. They continued tumbling out of the sack until the lawn and driveway were no longer discernible.

Nonplussed, I yanked the front door open, but by the time I stormed onto the veranda, the truck and its mysterious driver were gone. I stood, hands akimbo, exceedingly vexed. I heard a sound and looked around to see Analise coming up behind me.

117

"Look at this mess!" I fumed. "That man has got some nerve."

"Here, teacher," Analise said calmly, handing me one of the plastic shopping bags she was holding. My brows furrowed as I stood there looking at her, dumbfounded. What did she expect us to do with a few shopping bags? Unfazed, Annalise stepped off. "Come, teacher. Mek wi pick up the potatoes."

I grumbled as we worked, shin deep in produce. Annalise was crazy. After we had filled all the bags, the yard looked yet untouched. We would need a team of people, dozens of crates, and a forklift to clean up the mess.

I looked over at the sack and scratched my head. How can one sack hold this many potatoes? How can it still be full? How is that even possible? *I wondered.* This doesn't make sense. Why would someone do this? Who would do this?

Confused and annoyed, I willed myself to wake.

However, once my eyes were open, my focus was entirely on the first part of the dream as abject humiliation trumped an untidy yard. "God, what was Logan showing people? I hope it wasn't the video of me," I lamented, a feeling of dread churning in my stomach. When I got no response, I threw the covers off and got out of bed because I felt crowded by it somehow—the mattress, the sheets, the comforter, the blanket, the pillows.

"Jeshua," I used a mashup of my intercessor's two names (Jesus and Yeshua), "was it the video of me? . . . because if it was, I'd flat-out *die*. I need your help! Please, I'm *begging* you. Stop Logan from doing this. I know I lost my temper, but You *know* I don't deserve to be humiliated like this because *he* provoked *me*."

Talking to Jeshua was like talking to no other. He was more like a friend . . . or maybe a brother.

I was wearing the shine off the tile, anxiety oozing from my every pore. "What if Logan puts this on social media, Jeshua?" My eyes filled up with tears. "You know how I feel about being publicly humiliated. I wouldn't be able to live it down. Jeshua, mi know mi give nuff, nuff trouble, and mi give nuff, nuff talking, and mi deserve some tough love—but not like this. I *promise* I won't lose my temper like that next time I talk to Logan—no matter which button him push. I promise that I'll try to . . ."

I rambled on for quite some time, making many a promise.

* * *

After what had to be at least three hours, I looked outside because I thought I heard Annalise at the gate. What I saw, instead, was that the car had been moved from the garage and was sitting in the yard.

Quite perplexed, I wondered, *When did Logan come here? It couldn't have been late last night because I was up, and it couldn't have been since I woke up—because I would have heard him.*

I shook my head, and a grating laugh escaped my lips as it dawned on me what had happened. Logan, ever the strategist, had come very early—when he knew I had to be asleep—and had tried to move the car, only to have it shut off on him. I knew this clandestine operation undoubtedly meant one thing—I was never getting the keys back.

As I began my tirade, bitterly ruing the day I met Logan, I had a vision of myself sitting in a brand-spanking-new SUV—in my favorite color. I was grinning from ear-to-ear as the salesman explained the features of the car. The vision faded the moment the lock on the gate began rattling. As I was making my way downstairs to let Annalise in, my phone rang. I took off running.

"Hey, mi soon come," I greeted Annalise breathlessly before turning right back around to go answer the phone. "Hey Abby." I could barely get the words out.

"Hey—how yuh sound suh out o' breath?" she joked light-heartedly.

I giggled and took a little while to answer. "I had . . . to run . . . to get . . . the phone. Annalise . . . just come."

Abby chuckled. "Okay. I'm not staying long, then. I just wanted to tell you about a vision I had as I was heading to the kitchen."

My heart, already beating hard and fast from all that running, picked up a bit of speed. "What? You just had a vision? That's crazy! I had one too—only a few minutes ago—but tell me yours first." I was about to burst from my excitement.

"It's so weird, but I saw you and George at a car dealership. You guys were walking around the lot, and he was helping you pick out a car."

I squealed. "Really? Did you see the color?"

"No," Abigail said, her tone quizzical.

"Well, you're not going to believe this, but I saw myself at a dealership, sitting in a car I was thinking of buying or had already bought—I'm not sure which."

"Wow! Isn't this crazy-cool?"

"Are you kidding me?" I asked, incredulously. "This is so beyond amazing. I keep saying it, and I'm going to say it again. I'm *really* happy to be who I am."

"Me too. I wouldn't want to be anyone else—or anywhere else, for that matter."

"Me neither." I could hardly contain the grin threatening to split my face it was so wide. "Anyhoo . . . I'm going to go talk to Annalise. Laters."

"Okay. Catch you later," she said, ringing off.

As I headed to the kitchen, I thought about how amazing it was that God had brought Abigail and me together. He had done so in a pretty cool way, and as events unfolded over the years, it had become obvious that our lives were intrinsically interwoven. We just did not know why. It had also become evident—shortly after Annalise had come to work with me—that she, too, had been dropped in my life for reasons far bigger than I could even imagine.

"Hey," I called out to Annalise as I took up residence on my usual perch.

"Morning, teacher," she said, not hitching as she busied herself with the food prep. "Suh, tell mi something—why di car innah di driveway?"

"Well, apparently the owner came for it, and it shut off on him," I said, my tone caustic. "Can you imagine? I would wake up and the car would be gone."

Annalise scoffed. "Suh yuh worried about dat?"

I shrugged.

Annalise scrutinized my poker face, and I could see she was not buying my act. "Teacher, I hope yuh nah worry 'bout dat—because a while ago, when I was walking in from the road, I saw yuh driving a brand-new vehicle."

I almost fell off the stool. "You're kidding me! Really?"

"Yes, teacher," she said emphatically, "one of dem *tall up* vehicle like Miss Abigail's."

"An SUV?" My voice was at least an octave higher than normal. "Did you see the color?"

"No, no color."

"Wow! Well, the color doesn't even matter. What matters is that Abigail and I got the same thing you did. That's what she called to tell me just now. Do you know how astonishing it is that all three of us got the same thing at around the same time? Isn't that insane?"

"*Bwoy*, teacher. When God ah bless yuh, *nobody* cyaan stand in yuh way."

"That's so true. Some people don't realize that though, including Logan and his family. The problem with them is they don't know the God *I* serve . . . Oh, I have to tell you about the dream I had last night."

Annalise listened intently as I relayed the events of the dream before she expressed her concern. "Teacher, a lot of people are recording their fights and putting them up on social media, so yuh shouldn't be surprised if yours end up on there. I only hope that that nuh happen to yuh. Look at this." She pulled up a clip of an argument between a woman and her husband that the woman had posted.

"Oh, my God! This is horrible! I don't want to believe Logan would do something so hateful, but the dream says otherwise. You know, some things I would never do, and this is one of them. As a matter of fact, you know me. You're always quarrelling that I never record anything. The thing, though, is that the morning we had the blow-up, I had turned on the voice recorder before going into the garage."

Annalise's mouth fell open, and her eyes grew wide. "Yuh have a recording? How yuh manage that?"

"It could only be God. Nobody knows about it yet, and I don't intend to send it to anybody. I'm glad I have it, though—just in case."

"Yes, because yuh never know. Yuh might need it. Suh, what yuh think the potatoes mean?"

I shrugged. "I have no idea."

Annalise picked up her cell phone. "Suh, yuh nuh Google it, teacher?".

I shook my head. "No, when I want to know the meaning of a dream, I don't go to Google; I go to God."

Annalise frowned. "Yuh hear somebody calling?"

"I'm not sure," I said, but Annalise was already moving towards the front door. I got up and followed her.

"It's Enzo," she called over her shoulder. I stood in the doorway as she let him through the gate. He came down the driveway balancing a huge bunch of green bananas on his shoulder.

I smiled. "Hey, Enzo."

"Morning," he said, addressing us both before turning his attention to me. "Nurse, Sugah send this for yuh."

Before I could answer, Annalise chimed in. "How many times must I tell you shi nuh name 'nurse'?" Although Annalise sounded gruff, I could discern the playfulness in her tone.

Enzo, though, was not accustomed to her yet. With a diffident smile, he said, "I keep forgetting."

"But mi tell yuh plenty times," Annalise chided.

I laughed. "It's okay, Enzo. People call me nurse all the time.

Don't know why, but they do."

"That's true." Annalise pointed to her left. "Put it in di garage. I'm going for di knife suh you can han' it up for me," she said before disappearing inside.

If Enzo cut the bunch into smaller hands, it would make it easier for her to simply grab a hand or two to cook, instead of having to contend with the whole thing. Besides, it would allow the stain to drain off as green bananas are quite *stainy-stainy*.

"Tell Sugah I said thanks," I said to Enzo as Annalise came through the door. I had seen Sugah earlier in the week when I was out in the yard, and he had asked, quite casually, if I liked green bananas. I thought he had asked to make conversation because we had started up a discussion about food. I really had not expected him to gift me a bunch. I had no complaints, however, because it went great with ackee and saltfish, which Annalise was about to prepare.

Enzo did not look up from his task. "Yes, teacher."

"Eeh hee." Annalise was wearing a pleased-puss look on her face at his use of my right pet name. "That wasn't suh hard."

Laughing, I moved off. "Later," I called out over my shoulder before Enzo could respond.

* * *

Two days later—as if Mondays were not manic enough—I became inundated with texts about the fight Logan and I had had. The first, and only call I answered, came from one of my sisters. It did not make me feel any better talking to her because, while she understood and would always have my back, I would not get the opportunity to explain my side to other people. Besides, how many of them would care anyway?

When I hung up from her, I set about wearing a hole in the rug at the foot of my bed. "Jeshua, *why*? Look how mi beg yuh not to let Logan release this clip. He gets away with *so* much, but as *soon* as *I* slip, I'm in a bag o' trouble." I was reeling from the unfairness of it all until I remembered the dream of Logan's flogging, and right away I was awash with intense satisfaction. "Anyway, it's good that Logan's *totally* going to get what he deserves, one day one day. You don't know how glad I am that you're going to allow him to be punished."

It is not punishment, God said.

All the smugness that had swelled up in me deflated like someone had taken a pin to it. "What?"

It is not punishment, God said again.

Seriously? I thought to myself but said, "God, I don't understand. What do you mean that the chaining isn't punishment? What is it then?"

It is the state of Logan's spiritual condition.

"What?" This was so out of left field it took me a while to close my mouth. "Seriously, Jehovah?" I sighed. "I mean, I feel bad because this would basically mean I've been mad at Logan for what he can't help." I sighed again. "While I'm grateful you cleared that up for me, honestly, it doesn't make me feel any better." I slumped onto the edge of the bed and massaged my forehead. "There's something I don't get. I dreamed that Logan would show the video, and he did. But what's with the potatoes?"

I showed you what Logan is doing to you.

"Okaaay," I said, extremely impatient.

And I showed you what I am going to do for you.

Straight away, that mollified me, and what Logan had done suddenly seemed paltry. I thought of what God had said, in Malachi 3:10, about throwing open the windows of Heaven and pouring out so much blessing that there will not be room enough to store it, and I grinned a grin so wide, it could only be rivalled by the Cheshire Cat's.

Carelessly, I threw myself back onto my pillow, spreading both arms wide. "Yes!" I squealed.

There was not much that could spoil my day after that.

Bread

Their destiny is destruction, their god is their stomach,
And their glory is in their shame.
Their mind is set on earthly things.

Philippians 3:19 (NIV)

For the next couple days, I reminded myself of the potato dream every phone call or text message I got regarding the video clip. Most of the times, it worked to put my mind at ease. However—once in a while—trepidation set in, and I did not want to leave the house. Either way, I was obsessing about it.

I was in the middle of praying for myself when God instructed, *Pray for Nathan.*

I knew, at once, to what God was referencing, and I felt guilty. This was something He had told me to wait on, and I had gone ahead—months ago—and prayed anyway. A test had shown that Nathan had a growth on his thyroid that needed to be biopsied. God had said I could pray for him, but after the biopsy. The procedure had shown that Nathan had, not one, but two nodules. I had waited months for God to indicate when I should pray, but He had not. Desperate, I had gone to my sister who follows me, and we reasoned that—even a minute after the biopsy—was after the biopsy; therefore, it was alright for me to pray. However, each time I had called Nathan, the lumps were still there. Now, to hear God tell me to pray, confirmed that I had messed up. There was no guesswork where God was concerned, and I knew better. I knew that I needed only ask if I was unsure, yet I had not.

The gift of healing was the one gift of the Spirit I had not yet grown comfortable with. I was not sure what to do as Nathan was still at school, and I had touched everybody else I had prayed healing for. As I was directionally challenged and could not figure out where South Florida was in relation to where I was standing, I lifted my right hand in no particular direction.

I was only two sentences into my prayer when a vivid image of Nathan's nodules popped up in front of me. It was like watching a 3D projection in high definition. With my eyes goggling, I inhaled sharply and brought my left hand up to cover my mouth as the bright pink nodules gradually began turning black. Once all the color had been eaten away, they instantly began shrivelling.

When they were no larger than peas, I whispered through my fingers, "God, what is happening? What are they doing?"

Necrotizing, He explained.

He might as well have spoken French because, in that moment, there was no connection made between what was said and what was witnessed. Baffled, I simply said, "Okay."

I had long stopped praying, but that seemed to have no bearing on the process that had already begun. I watched, enthralled, as the nodules continued shrinking until they had become nothing but tiny particles of dust, floating together, then drifting apart, only to disappear in a red river.

"Thank you, Jehovah. That was *so* crazy-cool," I whispered as the vision disappeared. I could not get to my phone fast enough. My heart bubbling with anticipation, I dialled Nathan's number. "Hey. Do me a favor. Feel the lumps on your neck. Are they still there?" I had breathlessly breezed through that, not bothering to explain myself.

"Why? What's wrong, Mom?" he asked, sounding extremely concerned.

I immediately felt kind of ridiculous frightening him like that. "I'm sorry, Nate. It's nothing to be worried about. I just prayed for you."

"Oh, okay." There was a longer than expected pause. "Yes, they are still there."

My heart sank a little. "Oh—okay. Well, I need you to check them every day. Promise me you will."

"Sure, Mom. I will." Nathan agreed, but his tone held a hint of confusion—or maybe it was scepticism—I was not sure which.

* * *

I was ecstatic by the time Friday rolled by. I had called Nathan every few hours since I had prayed for him—I could not help myself—and he had said the nodules were getting smaller. I had even called my mom and asked her to check as well—not that I did not believe Nathan.

The last I checked, they were the size of peas. Nervous, I held the phone tight and whispered, "Okay, God. Let this be it." Nathan picked up on the second ring. I smiled. "Hey, you. You know what time it is."

He chuckled. "Hold on, Mom." I held my breath. After what seemed like forever—and right when I thought I might expire from lack of oxygen—he came back to the phone. "I don't feel anything. I *think* they're gone." He had made that all sound like one big question.

"What do you mean 'you think'? They are either there, or they're not there. Check again." I was fighting for control of my anxiety, and it was hard to keep the annoyance from my tone.

I paced as I waited for him to get back to me. "They're really gone, Mom," he said far more confidently.

"Are you *sure sure*?"

"Yes, Mom. I'm sure." He sounded a tad excited.

"*Waiwaiwaiwai*-wait," I said breathlessly—once I had stopped shrieking and jumping up and down. "Check them again."

"Are you serious?" he asked, incredulous.

"Yes!"

"They're really gone, Mom." He sounded somewhat less excited and a bit put out by my insistence, but I did not care.

"Oh, my God. I can't believe it! . . . I mean—I can—but you know what I mean." Nathan had remained quiet. I took a deep breath, put my phone in my pocket, and held out my hands to steady myself. "Okay, okay. Call your grandmother so she can check your neck for me . . . wait! Are you guys done packing?"

"Yes, we're just putting in last minute stuff."

"Okay, great. Don't miss your plane. Tell Chrissy hi, and you guys call me when you get to the airport. Now, go get your grandmother."

"Are you for *real*, Mother?"

"Yes! Hurry up!"

"Oh, brother," Nathan said under his breath.

"Hey, Mommy," I said, once my mom got on. "Check Nathan's neck for me." I had not said 'please' or asked how she was doing. I would apologize for that later.

She took a while to come back to the phone. "They're gone!" she said, her voice teeming with excitement and wonder. "I checked and double checked. Jabez, there's nothing there."

"Oh, my God! This is so crazy-cool!" I shrieked, trying my best to control the volume so as not to deafen my mom.

"Yes, it is. God is good."

"This is the *best* day," I said with a jaw-busting grin.

* * *

Annnnd . . . because every day was a test within a test, that night, *I dreamed that my mother-in-law was at my house. We were smack in the middle of an all-out war.*

"What do you know about what goes on in my house?" I screamed at Constance.

"I know plenty."

"Yeah, that's right. You don't mind yuh own business," I retorted

acidly.

Her face grew beet red. "My son is my business and so are my grandchildren.

I heard a clanking noise but ignored it. There was no way Constance was having the last word. "No, they're not. And therein lies the problem. You know nothing about boundaries. You are clueless about what is your business and what is not."

"So that is why you're spiting me. That is why I can't even get to see my own grandchildren."

I glared at her. "Are you kidding me? Who's stopping you?"

"You are. It's like you have them caged up." She scrunched up her nose like she smelled something off-putting. "Controlling."

I laughed a raw, ugly laugh. "Said the pot to the kettle."

"It's no wonder my son couldn't live with you. You are the reason your marriage failed. You. You have no one to blame but yourself!"

Fuse lit.

My face grew instantly hot. I doubled my fists and stepped to her. "How dare you!" I screamed in her face. "That's the problem. You know everything, yet you know nothing. You are the reason my marriage failed. You, not me. You have done nothing but persistently poison Logan's mind against me. If I had to listen to you diminish me every single day, I'd hate me too."

What is that clanging noise? *I wondered but quickly ignored it. "Get out and leave me in peace! Look how far mi stay from yuh, and yet yuh* always *putting yourself in my way."*

There it was again—that insistent clanking.

I struggled to process what I was hearing.

Annalise, *I thought, opening my eyes.*

There was tremendous pressure in my chest, and my heart was racing. I was still stewing from my go-round with Constance; plus, I was beat. I had gotten only a couple hours sleep, and most of that time seemed to have been spent arguing with Constance.

As soon as I let Annalise in, I excused myself and crawled back into bed. Although I ached all over and had no energy, it took me a long while to fall asleep.

When I did, *I dreamed that I was at a printshop. I walked up to the young woman behind the counter and held up a pamphlet.*

"Excuse me, Miss," I said, addressing her as politely as I could to mask my annoyance at her failure to acknowledge me.

Apparently taking exception to having her telephone conversation interrupted, she looked daggers at me and said quite insolently, "Yes?"

I jiggled the pamphlet. "I need a hundred and fifty copies of this, please."

"When do you need them for?"

"Today." I hated dealing with people like her, and I wanted to tell her as much but bit my tongue.

She sniggered. "Well, that's *not going to happen."*

"When can I get them back, then?" I asked, unable to keep the bite out of my tone.

"In a week."

"That's too late!" I cried.

She shrugged. "Take it or leave it."

My temper boiled. "Look here, am I begging *you a favor? I'm a paying customer. Do your bloody job."*

Her lips curled, and I braced myself. "Gurl, let mi call you back," she said to her phone buddy, and without so much as a glance in my direction, she began stapling some papers.

"Tell you what," I sighed, no fight left in me, "just give me twenty-five copies. I'll wait."

Abruptly dropping the stapler onto the counter, she pulled a purse out of a drawer and said, "Yuh cyaan get dem now."

I scowled. "Why is that?"

"I'm going to lunch," she said in an exaggerated singsong as she sashayed from the room, unceremoniously dismissing me.

I caught a movement out of the corner of my eye as a woman, who had been engaged in conversation not too far from where I was stand-

ing, started walking towards me.

"Ma'am, what seems to be the problem? How may I help you?" she called out to me. I surmised, from her air of authority and no-nonsense-professional tone, that she was a supervisor—or perhaps the owner. I waved the pamphlet high in the air as I expressed my disgust at the shop's poor customer service. She looked embarrassed. "I'm really sorry. Our employees know better. I'll deal with her when she gets back." That appeased me. "You can have the twenty-five copies now, and the rest in about two hours."

"Hmm." I paused a moment. "Tell you what—I'll come back for everything later, thanks."

She smiled and held out her hand. "That's fine—if that's what you'd prefer." She looked at me quizzically. "Ma'am, you have to let it go."

I did not realize until she said that that I was holding the pamphlet so tightly I was crushing it. "I'm sorry," I whispered, but I could not seem to open my fist. I felt an awful gnawing in my stomach as she tugged gently, and the more she tugged, the more intense the feeling in my stomach.

"If you don't let go, I won't be able to print it for you," she said coaxingly. Her brows creased slightly. "Are you alright?" When I did not answer, she made lingering eye contact with the woman she had been talking to. "Get her a glass of water."

Lightly resting a hand on my shoulder, she guided me to a nearby chair. Resignedly, I plopped down in it—too tired to protest. I did not resist, either, when she prised the pamphlet from my fingers. It was as she rested it on the counter, I realized what it was.

"Oh, my God," I said, jumping up and stumbling slowly over to the counter. I picked up the funeral program and gawked at it. I could not see whose it was. The words were not discernible, and neither was the face.

It was as if the temperature in the room had suddenly plunged. My teeth began chattering, and tiny bumps raised up on my skin. I held on to the counter and took a few deep breaths to steady myself.

I scrubbed my eyes hard and looked at the blurred-out face again. "God, who is it?" I begged to know, my voice heavy with the weight of my desperation. When I got no response, I begged again. "God, please. I need to see who this is." When the picture remained blurred, my breath started coming in quick and shallow. Frightened I might stop breathing, I desperately gulped for air, keeping focus on the program even when my head began to feel light. No matter how hard I concentrated and stared, I could not see to whom the program belonged.

"God, please," I managed to wheeze.

I was abruptly kicked out of the printshop as well as out of the dream. When I opened my eyes, it felt as though the twelve-foot ceiling was sitting on my face, and my chest wall was caving in on itself. "Jehovah," I whispered. "Who was that? I need to know, please."

He said nothing.

This was the second time something like this was happening to me. Of late, it was like my brain had decided I needed to be protected. The last time my memories were blocked, all I could recall when I woke up was a date. When the date had finally come, I understood why my brain had shielded me from it. My father was supposed to die. Thankfully, by God's grace, he had not.

Oh, God, I thought, *if the only other time this ever happened was because someone close to me was supposed to die, then who was on the program? What if it's one of my kids?*

I could not breathe. My lungs burned as though the air in them was corrosive. My heart felt like it was vibrating violently. A piercing pain spread down my back, arms, and legs as though I was lying on a bed of *macca*. It all became too much. I flung the comforter off and bolted downstairs.

* * *

I had been unloading on Annalise no more than half an hour when a horn began relentlessly tooting outside. "Oh, Lord. I hope that's not my gate," I grumbled. Because if it was, it could be only one person. When the driver would not ease up on the horn, I rolled my eyes and sighed heavily because I knew I was right.

I got up from my stool and discreetly peeled the curtain back. I sucked my teeth when I saw Constance's car. Eustace was in the driver's seat. I wanted nothing more than to leave them out there, but that would have been 'unchristian'.

I released the curtain and said to Annalise, "It's Logan's parents. I'm going upstairs to put on some clothes although I'm not sure I'm letting them in." I heard the gate sliding and spun around to glare at her. "Did you leave the lock open?"

"Yes, teacher."

"Seriously?"

Now, I really have no choice.

Great.

I hurried upstairs, grumbling under my breath the entire time. I worked with super speed, and even then, it was not fast enough. They were already knocking on the front door by the time I got my clothes out of the drawer. They would not even wait a few seconds between knocks to allow someone to get to the door. Rolling my eyes, I yanked on some pants. I chuckled as it dawned on me that Annalise had made no move to let them in.

"Hello," Constance yelled, banging some more.

Seriously? I fumed to myself. *Where does she think she is— Coronation Market?* My neighbors and I were considerate of each other on weekends. Nobody mowed their lawns early or did anything else that made considerable noise. I gritted my teeth as she called out again. The kids were sleeping, and she was going to wake them. No matter how many times I had told Constance we did not rise early on weekends, she made it a point of duty to show up before eight o'clock.

As I made my way downstairs, I hollered, "Coming!" Constance must not have heard me because she kept knocking and calling.

I pushed the door open, and before I could utter a word, Constance said, "I'm here to see my grandkids." Her expression was severe—her eyes cold and piercing, her brows knitted into copious folds and creases, and her mouth set in a taut line. Constance had come fixing for a fight.

I *almost* wanted to laugh—almost. "Pfft! Good morning," I said as 'warmly' as I could before I calcified my tone. "They're sleeping." I met her eyes dead on, my glare equally as frosty.

"Miss Jabez," she said with that mocking, exaggerated emphasis on my name that I loathed, "I said I'm here to see my grandchildren." She tugged on the door, forcing me to tighten my grip on the knob.

I widened my eyes and dressed back. "And *I* said that they are sleeping."

"So, when can I see them?"

"This evening would be fine." I had managed to keep my tone even keel despite the anger roiling up inside me.

"I can't come back this evening."

Sounds like a 'you' problem to me, I thought, but said quite flippantly, "Well, you can come back another day. Make sure to call first."

"I keep calling Michael's cellular phone and getting no answer." Her words were loaded.

Suh what does that have to do wid me? I wanted to scream at her. "Well, his phone is not working." I kept my voice flat and my tone dry.

She arched her brows. "Since when?" And there it was—the implication that, somehow, I was lying.

"It's been a while—which you already know—because I have told that to you *and* to Logan *several* times over. Try contacting Christine and Michael on WhatsApp."

"My WhatsApp's not working." She retorted, as if I should have already known.

Jehovaaah! I screamed in my head. *Why? Why is she still here?*

"Well, you can call my cell phone and ask for any one of the kids. You have my number."

"No, I don't."

Funny, because right up to before Logan moved out, you were blowing up my phone whenever you weren't able to get a hold of him. My number has not changed, and even if you lost it, you could have asked Logan for it—simple. "Fine, I'll give it to you," I said, about to turn around to fetch pen and paper.

Constance motioned to the veranda chairs. "Can you sit and talk for a few minutes?" Her tone had changed and was now honeysuckle sweet.

I paused, reluctant, given how our last conversation had ended. Before pushing up the door and stepping down on to the veranda, I hollered for Annalise to get something for me to write on. As I was about to sit, I took notice of Eustace, who was still in his vehicle with the driver's side window rolled down. He had his arms resting in the window and his chin resting on his arms as if he were waiting for a matinee to begin. I acknowledged him, but he ignored me. I inwardly shrugged and turned my attention to Annalise, who had returned, pen and paper in hand. I wrote my number down and shoved the slip of paper at Constance before taking a seat. I folded my arms and waited.

After a few awkward seconds of silence, Constance said, "Jabez, I *need* to be able to get a hold of my grandchildren."

I gritted my teeth and began counting to ten.

I got to two.

"I don't get it. Why. Are you. Belabouring. The point. It's like you're not understanding what I'm saying or something. You have a problem, right? You need to speak to the kids and they're sleeping. I gave you a number so you can reach them when they're *not* sleeping. Pretty simple."

"Miss Jabez, all I'm telling you is that I need to see my grandchildren," Constance insisted as though I had not spoken at all.

I gritted my teeth. *But, Jesus!* I thought, sitting straight up—every muscle in my body tensing. *Am I being Punk'd?* I braced both hands on the arms of my chair, leaned forward dramatically, and looked around. *I'm being Punk'd. That* has *to be it.* I waited a few seconds— just in case—before spinning around on her.

"So, who stopping yuh?" I paused, narrowing my eyes. "Why are you here? Is it because Nathan and Christine are home? Well, Michael has been here this *entire* time, and he hasn't seen you or Logan *once*. And now that Nate and Chrissy are back from school, we suddenly have a problem?"

Constance drew back, waved her hand, and shouted, "No. No. Don't bring up Logan to me. That's between the two of you. That's not *my* business."

Pfft. Since when? I almost bit out, but held my tongue. "Look, Constance. This is ridiculous. What's so urgent that it can't wait till later? I already *told* you now is not a good time, and it doesn't matter how many times you ask, the answer is still no."

"Miss Jabez, as family, we—"

"Whoa! Hold up!" I held up a hand. "We"—I waved a finger back and forth between us and said, without compunction—"are *not* family." We were family only when she saw fit, and I was tired of it.

She actually rested a hand over her heart, managing to appear wounded. "Jabez, why are you being so aggressive? Hear how you're behaving." Her voice was unnaturally sedate. "It's like I can't speak without you jumping down my throat."

Why di devil send Constance over yah, Jehovah? I fumed. *Please tell me—why am I still looking at her?* I wished I possessed the equanimity it took to deal with someone as deliberately opposing as Constance. However, I honestly believed that *nobody* on Earth possessed that. That took strength belonging to God, and God alone.

"You came to me. I do my *best* to stay far away from you. This right here"—I poked a finger at the dividing space—"this is the reason I said no when you were trying to get Logan to build our house in your back yard. And you have a *nerve* talking about *my* behaviour. You honestly can't see yourself." I had to get away from her—and fast. My knee-jerk reaction when Constance upset me was to blow my top, and I was determined to not let her *draw mi tongue*. I got up and made my way to the front door. "Excuse me for a minute."

"Yes, Miss *Jabez*," Constance spat out as my hand touched the doorknob. "That's what you've been waiting to do since I got here—shut door innah mi face."

And there it was—the real reason Constance was stomping on my peace—not the kids—the house. I started, dropping my arm and looking up at the gate to see if anybody was passing by. *This is some hogwash*, I thought (Well, truth be told, my reference was to another animal entirely and had nothing to do with swill).

"Are you for real? This is what I cannot *stand* about you," I hissed.

Constance chuckled, shaking her head. She *actually chuckled*—a frivolous sound—light and airy, save for the sprinkling of derision. "Miss Jabez, all I know is that *I* care about my grandchildren's happiness and wellbeing."

I drew back as if she had slapped me. "Hmph, and I don't?"

She crinkled her nose. "I don't know that."

Fuse lit.

I wanted nothing more than to throw down fire like Elijah—a gift I had dreamed of since I was a kid. But if there existed a solitary reason why God would never give me that power, I was staring right at her. And so, I settled on a less fantastical weapon.

"Ah . . . and there it is—the reason I *hate* being around you. You're always so condescending." My face burned, and my hands shook violently. "You dare imply that you care more about my kids than I do? You feel you get to say whatever comes to your mouth? Well—"

Shut your mouth, The Holy Spirit admonished firmly, cutting me off. *Do not say it.* I recoiled, clamping my mouth shut abruptly, absolute dread stirring in my belly.

I had been about to blurt, *Well, don't worry. Yuh mouth soon lock*, revealing something God had shown me would happen to Constance.

In the vision, I was at the foot of her bed. She was lying on her back, and tears were running down her face as she struggled desperately to speak. All she could manage were moaning sounds in her throat.

God, I'm so sorry. My hands were not the only things shaking. My knees were practically knocking together. I had almost messed up—big time. It was unconscionable for me to use my visions, or any gift for that matter, to advance a personal vendetta. I did not get to reveal a prophecy before time for the express purpose of spiting someone or making myself into a *don gorgon* (someone to be respected or feared).

God had made it clear to me, several times before, that I did not get to say or do whatever I wanted, simply because I could. Once, He led me to the story of David in 1 Samuel 30. David's wives had been kidnapped, and although he was devastated, he did not impulsively charge off to save his family. He went to God to seek permission, and God gave it. After I had read the account, I had thought about what David would have done had God said no. It was a huge reminder to me that God's will supersedes all. After that, every time I had gotten a dream or vision, I had tried to remember to ask God if I should tell it. Hard, though it was, the rules did not change simply because I was dealing with Constance.

I curled my fingers to stem the shaking and took a few steadying breaths. I was dying to escape Constance and had to force myself to speak slowly. "Okay, so, you have my number, and I'll let the kids know you stopped by."

As I reached to open the door, Constance said, "Wait, I have something for the kids? Am I allowed to give it to them?"

Seriously, I thought, rolling my eyes on the inside. "Sure." I did not trust myself to say anything else.

Eustace did not so much as *spit on me* when he handed the two shopping bags to Constance. But that was okay. I had been ignored in public—a few times prior to this—by both him and Constance, which had humiliated me at first. However, I had since accustomed myself and, in the progress, grown a heavily armored, highly impenetrable skin.

"It's just some snacks," Constance said softly, her tone reminding me of a fire that had been smothered.

I never wished harder—in my life—that I had been able to keep my temper in check. My throat felt like it was clogged with goop.

"Thanks," I managed to choke out before galumphing inside.

* * *

I headed straight upstairs as soon as I dropped off the bags in the kitchen because if I had stayed to talk to Annalise, I would have surely sinned my soul.

"Jeshua, seriously? Why does Constance always end up making me look bad? Talking 'bout shi care about my kids and implying that I don't. Why? Because she brings over a couple bags of snacks twice a year? Twice a year, Jeshua! Like, where does she get off? She doesn't even know how my kids eat. Christine has had her extractions almost a year now, and she still hasn't gotten her braces because I can't afford it. I have no transportation to take the kids anywhere because her son came for the car keys. What is her son currently contributing to this household? I have no choice but to buy things on credit because I don't get to come up with creative excuses to give my kids. I guess if I were kissing up to her and her husband, the kids would have what they need. Is that it?"

Pick up the Bible, God said.

"*Oh no,*" I thought. *Jabez, you* never *learn. How many times are you going to end up exactly where you are right now?*

It did seem that, of late, I was in trouble more often than not, and I truly wanted that to change. However, I struggled to deal with Logan and his parents more than I struggled with anyone. I would eventually forgive Constance and Eustace for this day, but it would be a process. It would only take reminding myself everyday of Jesus' edict to love everybody same as I loved myself and answering His question in Luke

6:32 about what credit it is to me if I love only those who love me.

I sighed heavily. "Okay, God." I sat down on my bed, picked up my Bible, and held it in my hands. I was having a mishmash of feelings, and none of them started with the letter, 'l'.

Open it, He instructed.

I didn't flip through it; I opened it, and immediately before me was Genesis 14. As I began reading, I frowned. What all did an ancient war among kingdoms have to do with me? I kept reading anyhow, and when I got to verse 21, I saw the why of it.

Abraham's nephew Lot had been taken captive along with the people of Sodom and the people of Gomorrah. All their possessions and food had been taken as well. After Abraham took men to rescue his nephew and the others and reclaim all the goods, the king of Sodom said to Abraham, "Give me the people and keep the goods for yourself." However, Abraham said to the king of Sodom, "With raised hand I have sworn an oath to the Lord, God Most High, Creator of heaven and earth, that I will accept nothing belonging to you, not even a thread or the strap of a sandal, so that you will never be able to say, 'I have made Abraham rich'" (NIV).

By the time I got to the end of the passage, my face and ears were burning. God and I also had a covenant. That covenant was in my name—given to me when I was only five months old, shortly after my mother had given me over to Him. Why, then, was I mad about whether Constance truly considered her grandkids? What did it matter what was withheld from them? Why did it matter what her intentions were when she decided to get in her car at the crack of dawn to drive over to my house? One of my biggest problems was that I got distracted easily. Every time I found myself in the middle of a raging storm, my kneejerk response was to focus on the wrong things . . . the rain, the lightning, the thunder, the waves, the gale . . . everything, except Christ.

I read the passage once more and shook my head.

This was so like God.

I rant.

He plants a mirror in front of my face.
He plants a mirror in front of my face.
I take a keen look at the person in it.
I sighed. "I understand, Jehovah. I understand."
It was going to be a long day.

* * *

That night, I dreamed *I was at a gathering outside a house. I knew neither the owner nor the occasion. The yard was abuzz with gossip— not that I could hear the conversations, but there was something about the way the women were huddled—all conspiratorial-like—their facial expressions and body language speaking volumes. I did not recognize anyone, which made an uncomfortable situation more uncomfortable. I decided to go in search of a familiar face although what I really wanted to do was leave. It was as I was passing the cluster nearest to me that I realized I was the evening's hot topic.*

I kept telling myself—for about two seconds—to keep walking. However, with me, wisdom seldom ruled over feelings, so I drew brakes and spun around. "Do any *of you know me?" I yelled, doubling my fists to stop my hands from shaking. They all froze—some gifting me with withering looks, others throwing furtive glances at each other. But of course, no one dared answer. "So how? How can you say such horrible things about me, and y'all don't know me? And if any of what you people were saying was even close to the truth, it would be bad— and not too bad. But* none *of it is true. And do you guys even care?" Nobody was looking at me now.*

Recognizing I was wasting my breath, I charged over to another cluster, and then another, and then another—all in an attempt to stem the scurrilous attacks on me. I fought back tears because nobody cared to hear what I had to say. I could not speak fast enough or loud enough.

What was on the invitations? *I mused,* "YOU'RE INVITED TO THE BIGGEST BASH EVER! BRING YOUR OWN TEA"? Oh, my

God! This is why I can't stand people. *I inhaled deeply, wanting nothing more than to spit fire, but had to satisfy myself with an ear-splitting scream instead.*

Suddenly, someone grabbed my hand and gently tugged, tilting me off balance and forcing me to take a step back. Angrily, I whipped my head around, only to lock eyes with The Messenger—an angel who had brought me messages before in several dreams. Sometimes he came by himself, but at other times, he came with The Protector. When they were together, The Messenger did not even regard me, much less speak to me. He always showed deference to The Protector—standing at attention until he was given instructions.

I tried to yank my hand from his, but The Messenger tightened his grip. His expression was stern, sterner than I had ever seen it. I pursed my lips, yanking my hand much harder. His grip tightened as he gently tugged again. I had no choice but to go where he led. When we had gotten far enough from the others, he abruptly stopped and spun around to face me. Grabbing me by the shoulders, he gently shook me.

"Yuh have any battle ah fight?" he asked firmly. I gawked at him, dumbfounded at his use of my dialect. Before now, my messages had all been in English, except one. That, he had delivered on a piece of paper with words written in French. He did not wait for my response. "Yuh act as though yuh have any battle ah fight. Yuh have any battle ah fight?"

I scowled and tried to pull away, but he did not release me. My face and ears grew extremely hot, and I wanted to scream. "Of course, I have a battle to fight. What kind of stupid question is that? You don't hear them? Have you heard what they've been saying about me? I have to defend myself."

The angel gave me an and-how-is-that-working-out-for-you look before he said calmly, "Yuh nuh have no battle ah fight."

Tears welled up behind my eyes. "Yes, I do, and you're not helping me. W-why aren't you helping me? Isn't that what you're here for—to help me? So, why aren't you helping me then?" My lips quivered as the tears began to flow.

He let go of my shoulders and gently grasped both my hands. "I am. I am here to tell you to be still."

My tears instantly dried up. I wrenched my hands from his to angrily slap the wet off my face. "That's it?" I asked, incredulously. "You're not going to defend me? Even though you know that everything they're saying is not true?"

His eyes twinkled brightly—kinda reminded me of sparklers. Funny. I had never paid attention to his eyes before. He took hold of my hands again. "I am here to tell you to be still, and to lead you beside still waters."

Oh, my God! *I screamed in my head.* Seriously? *I could not believe he was solicitous enough to lead me to still waters but not to defend my character. Everything was growing white around me, and I could hardly see. I felt like my insides were going to implode. I jerked my hands back extremely hard, and instantly, I was free—not because I was strong enough—but because the angel had loosened his grip. I staggered backwards a little and had to fight to maintain balance.*

"Still waters?" I shouted, looking around. "Still waters, where?"

The Messenger calmly named a place I'd never heard of, and as he did, an image of a large, stagnant body of water—surrounded by nothing but forestry and mountain—flashed before me.

I shook my head violently and took several unsteady steps backwards, desperate to create some distance between us. "Seriously? I'm not going. Still water dutty. Do you know *what lies beneath still water?"*

The angel's eyes twinkled even brighter, and the corners of his mouth turned up ever so slightly. "Things that go chomp?"

"You got jokes?" I gasped and glared at him. He knew I was afraid of water because, in one dream, The Protector had had a hard time convincing me to get into a body of water so that I could be saved. He, on the other hand, had simply stood there saying nothing. I guess it made sense he knew I was afraid of crocodiles too because I had just

thought it. Somewhere deep in my spirit, I knew he was trying to set my mind at ease. However, I did not care. "I'm not going anywhere. Yuh hear mi? I'm going No-Where." I was screaming at the top of my lungs.

I abruptly opened my eyes and sat up, my chest burning from my rage. However, the more aware I became, the burning sensation became less and less about rage.

"Stupid. Stupid. Stupid!" I punctuated each word with a slap to my forehead. "Jeshua, what did I do? I can't believe I talked to an angel like that. You must be *so* mad at me, but I'm going to fix this. I just need a chance to talk to The Messenger—a chance to apologize. *Please.*"

I squeezed my eyes tight in the hope of falling back asleep. However, after about fifteen minutes, I gave up. I should have known better than to try under this stressful a circumstance because I usually found it hard to fall asleep when I was relaxed, much less. Besides, there was no guarantee I would end up back in the same dream.

As agents of God, angels are due the utmost respect. Yet, every time they had come, I had done something wrong—except be churlish. That was entirely new. I had been mad at the angel for sticking to his assignment—like he owed me, like I was the one he answered to. I was well past my place and a fine example of how inimical familiarity is to respect.

I could not blow this off because it had happened in a dream. What I did in the Spiritual Realm mattered. I had two types of dreams—the ones where I simply slept and my dreams were about regular stuff, and the ones where I walked in the Spiritual Realm and my dreams were experiences. I knew God would forgive me for what I had done because He was merciful like that. However, the thought that He might punish me, by never again sending me the Messager, had my stomach in knots. I did not know if I could handle not seeing him ever again.

I rolled over, buried my face in my pillow, and screamed long and hard. When I did not feel any better, I did it again . . . and again . . .

Fig

Do nothing out of selfish ambition or vain conceit
But in humility consider others better than yourselves.

Philippians 2:3 (NIV)

I rubbed the left side of my head and winced at the sharpened pain. My head felt like a watermelon with a ticking timebomb inside it. I had been suffering with migraine headaches for the longest time—stabbing-blinding-brain-eating headaches. However, of late, they had become more focused and brutal. I found it hard to so much as lift my head off the bed some days. If I did not know better, I would think that it was God punishing me for what had happened with The Messenger. It had been several weeks since the fiasco, and I had no doubt that I was forgiven because once God forgave, He kept no record. The problem was that sometimes I found it hard to forgive myself.

I missed Nathan and Christine. Usually, Christine would rub my temples while Nathan massaged my hand. I worked the hard knot between my thumb and index fingers, which never worked when I did it, but I did it anyway—every headache—on the off chance it might work. It was at least distracting, and distracting was usually good—but not on this day. My eyes stung, and my throat ached on account of my fighting back tears.

"Jehovah, you *have* to help me, please . . . because if this pain doesn't stop, I might lose my mind."

Call Myrna, He said, referring to a woman who used to frequent Hope Springs Eternal Missionary Church—the church I attended on and off for about six years after moving back to Jamaica from South Florida. I scrunched up my nose because I had hermit tendencies and, at times, would rather eat my tongue than talk to people—much less ask for help.

"Seriously, Jehovah? Myrna?" The piercing pain in my head intensified. Instinct had me reaching up to touch it, but I quickly recoiled when I remembered the added pain that had caused. "But you know I hardly talk to her. I don't even know if she likes me. Besides, I haven't been to church in forever, and I can count on one hand the number of times I've run into her in the street. I can't call her out of the blue asking for a favor. I don't want to be the person who calls someone only when she wants something. Just like I find that objectionable, she might find it objectionable."

I was doing it again—allowing my fear of what someone thought or might think get in my way. However, I could not seem to help myself.

"Aargh!" I said, both my hands flying up to cover my face. "Jehovah, can I *please* ask someone else—someone I actually talk to? Someone who knows me well and wouldn't mind? I don't think she's the best person to ask. I really don't. I'm not complaining—I'm just saying." At least five people immediately came to mind, but I did not dare suggest them. Instead, I bit my tongue and waited. After a few moments of silence, I sighed. "Fine. I'll call her."

I felt totally bummed because I knew that what I had just done was by no means cool, and I had known it before I opened my mouth; yet, I had done it anyway. I had asked God who to call and then had tried to get Him to change his mind—Him. God. The One with whom there is no variableness, no shadow of turning. Him.

It did not help that He brought to mind, in that moment, what He had asked Job: "Who is this that obscures my plans with words without knowledge?" Truth was, I knew nothing. I had no idea what this woman would think or say, but God knew. I did not know why He had told me to call her instead of someone else, but He knew. I also remembered what He said in Isaiah 58:8-9: "For my thoughts are not your thoughts, neither are your ways my ways. As the Heavens are higher than the earth, so are my ways higher than your ways and my thoughts than your thoughts" (NIV).

I flopped down so hard on my bed it bounced me up and down, jostling my brain inside my skull. "Ouch! Ouch! Ouch!" I held my head for a while, squeezing it hard to keep my brain from scrambling. My stomach was fairing no better. It rarely did when I had a migraine. When it no longer felt like I might toss my breakfast, I reached for my phone. However, chicken that I was, I sent Myrna a message instead of calling her.

I imagined Jesus shaking His head at my stubbornness as I lay back, flung my arms out, and opened my hand—letting the phone fly.

"I know, Jeshua. I know," I murmured, closing my eyes against the offending light.

* * *

By the time Annalise came a couple days later, I was feeling much better. Although my head still hurt a little, the dull remnants of the once ferocious headache were tolerable. I was tired of being in the bed. Christine had not been there to keep me company, and Michael had only checked on me at mealtime. I plopped down on my perch and rested my chin in my palms while I watched Annalise work. We chitchatted about the kids—I about mine, she about hers.

"Teacher, what do you think about tongues?" Annalise asked, changing the subject.

Oh, Lord—tongues, I thought. Even though I knew Annalise and I

147

could talk about anything spiritual, I did not like speaking to Charismatics about tongues because most of the ones I had discussed this subject with were touchy about it. I also did not like to be made to feel like I was not holy enough to make it into Heaven because I had not been *filled.*

Honestly, if it were anybody else, I would have used my headache to kill the conversation. I fidgeted in my seat a little. "Why?"

"Just wondering."

"Have you ever spoken in tongues?"

She nodded. "Yes."

"Well," I held up my hands in a shrug, "I haven't."

"In my church, you have to be filled and speak in tongues as the Spirit gives you utterance to be able to enter Heaven because if you do not have the Spirit, you are none of His."

"First off, I think it's pretty cool that you have the gift of speaking in tongues, but that is what it is—a gift. Having the Spirit does not equate to speaking in tongues. When you accept Christ—as soon as you accept Christ—you are sealed with the Holy Spirit. Jesus promised Him to us when He was leaving. He said that He would send another Comforter and that the disciples would recognize Him because He already lives *with* them and would soon be living *in* them. So, once you are saved, you have the Holy Spirit. You don't have to *tarry* for Him."

"Yes, but my church believes that once you truly have the Holy Spirit, you will speak in tongues. Suh, speaking in tongues is the evidence then," Annalise explained.

This was good. Headache all but forgotten, I shifted in my seat, becoming animated. "Look, I don't believe that everybody has to speak in tongues because the Bible doesn't say that everybody has to speak in tongues. The Holy Spirit is not a gift you have to beg for—but is, *himself,* the *giver* of gifts—and one of the gifts He gives is speaking in unknown tongues."

"Yeah, but on the day of Pentecost, *all* the disciples spoke in tongues." Annalise said.

I smiled. "Yes, but that was kinda like a Holy-Ghost-welcome party. A mighty rushing wind? Flames landing on their heads? How cool is that? I would love to have seen that. What happened at Pentecost was just proof that Jesus kept His promise because sometimes people need to see—or in this case hear—to believe."

Annalise nodded. "Well, that's true."

"You know what I think is pretty cool? . . . that the people passing by recognized their own languages. The Bible says that there were many tongues spoken from every nation under the sun. That's a lot of tongues. There were only twelve disciples so they each had to be speaking several tongues—tongues that were *unknown* to them but *known* to the people passing down below. Many of the passersby believed and accepted Christ because, except for Him, that would have been impossible." I paused to catch my breath. "Anyway, why don't we read about the gifts of the Spirit, so you can see what I'm talking about for yourself."

Annalise opened a Bible app on her cell phone and read 1 Corinthians 12:1-11. When she was done, I chimed in, "See? The Holy Spirit gives His gifts to Believers as He sees fit. The Bible doesn't say that He gives *every* gift to *every* Believer—although that isn't impossible. But the passage says *some* get the gift of speaking in tongues—not *all*. Can everybody heal?"

Annalise shook her head. "No."

"Does everybody prophesy?

"No."

"Does everybody have the gift of discerning of spirits?"

"No."

"Suh why does everybody have to speak in tongues?"

Annalise shrugged. "Mi nuh know, teacher. That's what di church believe. They expect you to be filled and speak in tongues or yuh nuh ready."

"Ah lie dem ah tell!" I guffawed. "I want to see if, at Judgement, *any* of them can tell God not to let in *dis* yah gyal yah"—I beat my chest vigorously—"because shi nevah speak innah tongues." (They are lying! I want to see if, at Judgement, *any* of them can tell God not to let in *this* girl because she never spoke in tongues.)

Annalise chuckled. "How yuh sound like yuh sure yuh getting into Heaven, teacher."

I smiled. "Because I *am* sure. Let me tell you something—People are focusing on the *wrong* things. What about the lives they are living? They need to focus on that. The Bible says that some people are going to hear God say, 'Depart from me,' but it won't be because of tongues. He will say to them—after they've rattled off the ton load of things they did in His name—that when He was hungry, they did not feed Him. When He was thirsty, they gave Him naught to drink. When He was naked, they did not clothe Him. When He was sick, they did not look after Him, and when He was in prison, they never visited Him. Many people put God down once service is over and they get outside the church, and Sunday morning, they pick Him up at the door on their way back in."

"True dat, teacher. I see plenty o' dat."

I nodded. "Yup. When saying so, I try my best not to watch what anybody else is doing. I'm busy trying to live right, and I have a lot of things to fix in myself. It's about your personal relationship with God because—it's like Collette is always saying—everybody has to know Him for him/herself."

"True, teacher."

I frowned. "Tell me something—when tongues are spoken in your church, does anybody interpret?" I asked, not to condescend, but out of sheer curiosity. I grew up in a quiet church, where you would be looked at funny if your amen went over a certain decibel level, so *getting innah Spirit* and speaking in tongues was a definite no-no. However, I had visited churches where tongues were spoken, and I had never heard anyone interpret.

Annalise shook her head. "No, sah."

I raised my eyebrows. "How is that? I'm not saying somebody has

150

to interpret every time—but never? I don't get that. The gift of interpretation of tongues is given for a reason. Suh, what does anybody get from sitting and listening to it?"

Annalise shrugged. "The first time somebody speaks in tongues, the pastor's wife usually confirms if the tongue is real, but shi nuh interpret."

"Okay. Well, I'm just asking." I slapped the counter. "Anyway, mi nuh grudge *nobaddy* fi dem gifts. You can keep yours 'cause I'm happy with mine."

Annalise laughed. "Same me, teacher."

* * *

That Monday, I opened my eyes to God saying, *Pray for my sheep.*

I frowned. "Okaaay. But what do you mean pray for your sheep? What sheep? And what am I supposed to say?"

Instead of answering, God brought up—before me—an enclosure. Sheep grazing outside the open gate came into focus first. They were grazing away, so content to be indulging, that they did not realize—or maybe they did not care—that they were no longer within the fold.

God then brought into focus the sheep, inside the enclosure, that were trampling other sheep to get to a bush that was food. They stomped on the backs of others, not caring that they were causing them harm. Their focus was their own needs. The sheep that were being trampled were battered and bloody, and some had even gotten caught in the dense thicket. I was appalled, but I did not get to tarry there.

God drew my attention to some others that were barely plodding along, their movements heavy and measured. They seemed weary and about to give up. I could identify with these sheep. They had worked hard and were somehow feeling low, dejected, discouraged—maybe for different reasons—but they were all struggling to hold on. Those sheep stirred something deep inside me, but God did not allow me to wallow with them there.

Instead, He brought into focus some sheep that were charging forward, their enthusiasm palpable. Spirted, driven, and focused, they marched on like soldiers. A string of nostalgia curled rings around my heart. I was once those sheep. I wanted that back—that unflagging ardor, that unfading joy, that infallible faith. I watched them for a while until they shimmied, gently fading away.

The notion that God was asking the girl with the Peter Spirit to pray for His sheep was not lost on me. I smiled and set out—for once in a long while—to do exactly as I was asked without giving God lip.

As soon as I was done praying, He said, *Pick up the Bible*. I held it in my hand and waited. *Open it*.

When I did, immediately before me was Matthew 10:6-8: "Go rather to the lost sheep of Israel. As you go, proclaim this message: 'The kingdom of Heaven has come near.' Heal the sick, raise the dead, cleanse those who have leprosy, drive out demons. Freely you have received; freely give" (NIV).

I frowned. "Jehovah, what does this have to do with me? I don't have a problem praying for healing for people. I don't have a problem praying for cleansing for those afflicted with contagious diseases. But I know for *absolutely* sure that I *suck* at casting out demons. Look at what I did to my daughter. I could have killed her." I saw and heard Christine's head slam against the concrete driveway the night I made an audacious attempt to handle something I had no business messing with. I shuddered. "And death?" Cringing, I shot up off the bed, dropped the Bible, and started backing away from it. "*Nah-nah-nah-nah*. You *know* how I feel about death. I have been afraid of death my whole life. I want *nothing* at all to do with it."

My mom chose that moment to call, and normally I would have waited until I was through talking with God to answer the phone. However, I could not snatch the phone up fast enough. We talked for a long while, and when we were done, I started on my chores. I cranked some Praise and Worship music up loud—belting out song after song for hours—in hopes that I would not have to finish that conversation God had started.

* * *

Abigail called that afternoon. "Guess who I just saw in the bank?" she asked. She did not sound quite like herself, but I could not read if that meant it was someone I would be interested in or someone I could care less about.

"Hmm. I don't know. Tell me," I said rather impatiently.

She did not make me suffer. "Lowell."

I immediately set my nose a way—like I was smelling something odious. "Really? I drawled.

"Yes, and I'm not going to lie to you. I was tempted to ignore him."

"Pfft. Tempted? I would not have had to be tempted. Ignoring him would have come easy," I said, my tone acidulous.

"To tell you the truth," Abby said calmly, "at first, I *did* ignore him. I held my head straight and pretended that I didn't see him, but God chastised me . . . so, I went over and said hi to him."

I gasped. "You did what?"

"I went over and said hi," she repeated in answer to my nonquestion.

"What was his reaction?"

"He seemed surprised, but he answered. He was pleasant enough but not overly friendly."

"Mm-hmm," I said, tuning Abigail out and going inside my head. *That Judas. I was* not *going to call to him. I only hope I never see his trifling behind again.* God had shown me in dream a few weeks back that Lowell was going to apologize to me one day. Frankly, since then, I had been hoping against all hope that I would never be so unfortunate as to run into him because God knew I could not pretend.

There is no redemption in righteousness, God admonished.

I frowned, not understanding at first what that had to do with Lowell, and then it sank in. *Oh, my God, this is about me.* My stomach turned over as I gained clarity. *If God forgives you when you go to Him, why do you believe Lowell unworthy of the same mercy? Do you think yourself more righteous because you're not nearly as despicably duplicitous? God's Word says there is none righteousness—not a single human being anywhere. How many times has Abigail had to remind you that every test is not only twofold, but is in itself a lesson— a lesson for the other person, and a lesson for you? Someone who is already righteous doesn't need to be redeemed, but all are in need of redemption. Therefore, if Lowell humbles himself and apologizes, that would be him coming to a place of redemption. If you turn him away without forgiving him, where is* your *redemption?*

I swallowed hard, trying to dislodge the lump in my throat, as my focus returned to Abigail. "So, what was talking to him like?" It hurt to talk.

"It was a little bit awkward, but at least I did not shy away from doing what I was supposed to do. At the end of the day, if Lowell had snubbed me, that would have been on him. I can't—"

Saved by the bell, I thought and cut in, "Abby, let me call you back. I'm getting another call." It was not that I did not want to talk to Abigail; I did not want to talk about Lowell anymore as the situation brought to the fore how much work I still had to do on myself.

A cousin who lived in England and with whom I had not spoken in years—until about a month prior—was on the line. After we had inquired about each other's families, he said, "Listen, don't think me strange, but I got a message from the Lord for you. He said there is something He has for you to do—and it's huge—but you're afraid."

Goosepimples covered my arms, and nervousness caused my stomach to feel weak. "What? Oh, my God!" This could not be about this morning. I had not told a soul what had transpired. "Do you know what He's talking about?"

"No, I don't. That's all the Lord told me. But He told me just now that you know."

I did not think it was possible for my stomach to grow weaker, but it had. I nodded but remembered he could not see me. "Yes, I do. Oh, my God!" I was glad he could not see the horror on my face.

"Well, He said He can't use you the way He wants to if you are afraid."

There was something about the way my cousin spoke—emphatic, passionate. I shivered. "Okay," I said, my voice as shaky as my knees.

"I want you to hear this—The Lord said, 'Fear not, for I am with you. Be not dismayed, for I am your God. I will strengthen you, and I will help you.' You are not on your own. Whatever He asks you to do, He equips you to do. Do you understand what I'm saying to you?"

My heart was beating so loudly in my ear I could hardly hear myself when I answered. "Yeah, I do."

"Hold on. The Lord is telling me something else. He says you are going to know things—things that other people don't know—things that people are going to wonder how you know."

My breath caught in my throat, but I managed to force out the next words. "What things?"

"I really can't tell you—He has not said. The important thing is to be ready. My God! I wish I could tell you how huge this is! So many people, especially young people, are going to be drawn to you. I don't know what to tell you, except be ready."

"Okay," I said softly, feeling chilled to the bone. "Thanks so much. You have no idea how much I needed to hear this."

"Listen, Jabez, I'm at work, and I have to get back. I'll call you tomorrow if that's alright. God bless you and your kids. Say hi to your mum."

"Okay, *cuz*. Tomorrow is fine. God bless you and your family as well. And I will definitely say hi to Mommy when I call her later."

When he rang off, all kinds of thoughts began swirling about in my head.

* * *

When Myrna arrived near the end of the week, I was nervous. At first, the conversation was stilted, but as we continued chitchatting, the mood lightened. After about ten minutes, I suggested we get on with the business of praying for my head because she was on her way to work.

When I handed her the bottle of olive oil, she said, "You didn't have to call me. You could have anointed yourself."

Ooh. Okay. My cheeks reddened a little because I had already felt like I was inconveniencing her. I got defensive. "I know that—but like I said when I got in touch with you—God told me to ask you to anoint me, and that's exac—"

"That's the thing with Christians. A lot of us don't realize the authority we have, so we ask people to do things we can do ourselves."

Seriously? I thought, but said, "I know I could have anointed myself because God has told me to anoint myself before, which I did. However, I called you because God said to, and I have to be obedient." I tried to keep the grit from my voice. "I once had a dream in which a sinister spirit was trying to get in through my mother's front door. When I woke up, God told me to anoint the door. When I told my mom, she asked me to anoint the other doors and windows as well, but I told her I couldn't do that because God had given me instructions regarding one door only."

Myrna raised her eyebrows a little. "This is what I'm talking about. Why didn't you do what your mother asked?" Her tone caused my cheeks to burn hotter.

"Because it is *not* what God instructed me to do." I was struggling to keep my breathing even. "He didn't tell me to do all the doors and windows, so I didn't do all the doors and windows."

"Your mother, the owner of the house, asked you. If she is asking, then why can't you honor that request? You must learn to exercise your God-given authority. You should have done all the doors and windows per her request."

I gnashed my teeth and screamed in my head, *But I did not have God's permission.* "Well, I know you have to get to work," I said, walking over to her. "I don't want to keep you from your job." I wondered if she had heard the tremor in my voice.

"It's fine. I'm on the road today, anyway." She slathered a healthy dose of olive oil onto my forehead before placing her hand atop my head. By this time, I really did not want her touching me and had to fight to remain still while she prayed.

"Thank you so much for taking time out of your busy schedule," I said as soon as she said amen. Although some of my irritation had sloughed off during her prayer, I was not into any more talking. I moved towards the door.

"Tell me something," she said, stopping me in my tracks, "do you pray in tongues?"

Oh, my God, I rolled my eyes—on the inside. *This again?* "No, I don't."

I knew what she was going to say before the words tumbled from her lips. "Well, you should." When I stood there stiffly and said nothing, she was encouraged to continue. "My girls have been praying in tongues since they were three and five. My God! You should hear those girls *pray*."

So was not expecting that. She had prayed in tongues just now, and I expected she was going to talk to me about herself. "Wow. Really." I said flatly—miles off from the animated conversation going on in my head. *Is this supposed to be encouraging to me? You don't know how to pray right. My kids pray better than you. Really?*

I forced my focus back to what she was saying. "You *need* to ask for the gift of tongues."

"Mmm."

"Tongues is a secret language between us and God that He alone understands. Do you know that when we pray, the enemy can hear us? It's important to speak in tongues so that demons cannot intercept and sabotage our prayers. Tongues is a gift every Believer should have, so *ask* for it." She was forceful and very passionate in her conviction, and it was clear this was *not* a conversation.

"That's interesting," I said, as she began making her way to the door. "Anyway—thank you again for coming, Myrna. I know you're busy, so I appreciate your taking the time."

As soon as I locked the gate and waved at Myrna, who had answered a business call and was sitting in her car, I charged upstairs to my bedroom.

"Argh! *Really,* Jehovah! Myrna." I began pacing. "Myrna is who You told me to call? I don't get it. First off, I got lectured about how I could have anointed myself. Then, I had to hear that I wasn't praying right. Seriously, Jehovah? And to add insult to injury, I had to stand there and listen to her tell me her girls pray better than me? Worse still, they have been praying right since they were babies?" I held up three fingers. "Three years old, God! Three!" For some reason 'three' bothered me *way* more than 'five' did.

I stopped abruptly, inhaled deeply, raised both my hands above my head, and pinched my fingers together before steadily lowering my arms and slowly blowing the air out through my mouth.

Did not work.

"What is with people, huh? What's with people and this belief that everybody should be speaking in tongues? I feel like garbage. I wish You had not asked me to call her. You know what *irks* me? The Bible says that the Spirit gives different gifts to different people. I'm not making it *my* business whom He gives what. And You know why? I. Don't. *Care.* That's between them and Him. It has nothing at all to do with me. So why is it that people keep harping on about what the Spirit chooses to give to me? I don't go telling people they should get the gift of prophecy, or the gift of healing, or the gift of discerning of spirits simply because I have them. As a matter of fact, Paul said he would rather speak five intelligible words than a million words in an unknown tongue. On top of that, he gave a ton load of reasons why it's better to ask for the gift of prophecy than to ask for the gift of speaking in tongues. I don't go around asking people if they have the gift of prophecy—and if they don't—disparage them for that."

God said, *Pick up the Bible.* The stillness of His voice was like refreshing rain on a raging fire. It quieted my spirit instantaneously.

I was not in the mood for a scolding, though, so I crawled at snail's pace towards my nightstand. I picked up the Bible and held it in my unsteady hands.

Open it, God instructed.

I did not flip through it. I simply opened it, and immediately before me were the words, "Though I speak with the tongues of men and angels, but have not love, I have become sounding brass or a clanging cymbal. And though I have the gift of prophecy, and understand all mysteries and all knowledge, and though I have all faith, so that I could remove mountains, but have not love, I am nothing. And though I bestow all my goods to feed the poor, and though I give my body to be burned, but have not love, it profits me nothing" (1 Corinthians 13:1-3, NKJV).

The words, in this passage, were breadcrumbs, leading me to where I needed to be. All of a sudden, I was not focused on Myrna anymore—or anyone else for that matter. I was focused on me. That was what was fantastic about communing with God. That one-on-one relationship was everything.

* * *

By the time Annalise arrived that Saturday, I was still in the best of spirits although my body felt as though it had been run through a meat grinder. That was the thing with Lupus. One moment I would be feeling great, and in a matter of seconds, I would be in the middle of the worst flare-up no amount of medicine could help. Going to the hospital in my hometown was a no-no. I always felt it was where people went to die. I'd rather die at home, thank you very much. The better hospital was at least twenty-five minutes away, and that hospital was D-class at best. Not to knock the staff in any way, but it was a government hospital, and the funds—to offer anybody decent, much less top-of-the-line medical care—simply were non-existent.

I took up my usual position and stance in the kitchen as Annalise worked. I really wanted to sleep, but there was no way I was getting back in that bed. I used my ring fingers to keep my lids up. I watched as Annalise walked back and forth, going from the counter to the sink, from the sink to the refrigerator, then back to the counter. I imagined I looked like that cat clock with the eyes going from left to right—then from right to left—and I hid a smile. The more we talked, the livelier I became.

"Teacher," Annalise stopped in the middle of cutting up some seasoning that was going into the salt mackerel, "yuh know seh, Sunday gone, the little boy next door brought over some sweetie. He only had three, so he kept one for himself. He gave one to Karina and told her to share with Ciara, and then he gave the last one to Raheem."

I rolled my eyes because I knew I was about to hear the next episode in this ongoing saga. Candy sharing and kids? *Crawses.* Annalise had taken in Karina because her mother, Annalise's friend, was unable to care for her. Although Karina was only four-years old, she tore through the house like a Category 4 hurricane most days. One might wonder about the extent of the damage a four-year-old could possibly do, but that is for another story.

"Oh, Lawd," I said, and braced myself.

"I thought everything was okay until I saw Ciara crying. When I asked her what was wrong, she said that Karina ate the entire sweetie. Teacher, mi was so upset. I asked Karina if anybody in the house has ever been anything but kind to her. Shi shake her head and start cry. I decided to teach her a lesson, suh I went into the kitchen and plate breakfast fi Raheem and Ciara, but none fi Karina. When Karina realized I didn't share a plate for her, that's when di wailing start. To my shock, as soon as mi put Ciara's plate in front of her, she forked up some of her food and start feed Karina."

I opened my eyes wide. "What?" So not where I expected this story to go.

"Yes, teacher. Mi get mad and tell Ciara not to share any of her food with Karina because I need to teach her a lesson. Ciara start *one-piece-ah* bawling and said, 'I can't do that . . . not because she didn't share with me . . . I have to share with her,' and she kept on feeding Karina."

"What?" I was now sitting up at attention. "No."

"Yes," Annalise said emphatically, "and it don't stop there."

"Wait. Suh, you nevah give Karina any breakfast at all?"

Annalise chuckled. "Of course, mi give her, teacher. She got it shortly after they started eating. It did share out already."

"Oh. Okay." I knew Annalise would not have withheld food, but I asked anyway and was relieved to find out I was right.

"After breakfast, mi give Karina a strong talking to and give Raheem some money to get Ciara some sweetie. Teacher, would you believe that when Ciara get di candy, shi unwrap it and hold it up to Karina mouth for her to take the first bite?"

My mouth fell open. "She did what?"

"Teacher, I couldn't believe it either. After what Karina did to Ciara—after shi nuh treat her right—Ciara repay her wid nothing but kindness. Yuh ever see anything like that?"

If I could have picked an ideal what-would-Jesus-do moment, this would have been it. My heart welled up. I had a special storehouse for my ill feelings, and it was hard to keep it empty. Yet, what I had struggled with, for years, had come as nothing to a seven-year-old. For her, loving was not hard. She was not conflicted about it. She had not ruminated on it. She had not obsessed about it. She had simply acted on it.

Wow! A seven-year-old. Pretty cool, Jeshua—pretty cool. I turned my attention to Annalise. "You know there is an important lesson here, right?"

"Yes, teacher. Mi see it."

The Line

About a month later, I dreamed that *I pressed my back against a cold wall, trying to blend into the shadows. Those in the line did not know him, but his was a face I would never forget. He was The Deceiver, and he was in the business of selling destruction shrouded in hope. The last time I saw him was at a cliff's edge. He had promised healing then, and people had clamored for it. He was throwing people a lifeline now, and they were lining up for it.*

Beneath the hope in the air, however, was an undertow of desperation and fear. Half the people in the line were shabbily clad, some wearing caked on grime like a second skin. Severe hunger told on some, their hollow eyes set deep in their sallow faces, white squall outlining their cracked lips. The majority stood patiently, but a few were becoming surly, their dispositions as foul as their mouths. Those had already started pushing and shoving. A few stragglers hung back reservedly—in the line, but not in the line—wearing their desperation as well as they wore their tailored clothing.

The town looked like a ghost town—stores gutted and graffitied, cars abandoned and destroyed, garbage strewn about and scavenged. The queue had grown exponentially—with about thirty people joining in the few seconds I had been standing there. At that rate, it soon would be wrapped around the block.

I knew I should get going, but curiosity overruled any instinct for self-preservation. I craned my neck as the man at the front of the line stepped forward. I could not hear what was being said to him. However, I saw him nod his head. The Deceiver picked up a mask that was as thin as paper, as delicate as spun glass, and as intricate as woven web—the complication in its design meant to confound, but I discerned it instantly. I shivered, pushed back harder against the wall, and held my breath. The piazza offered me cover, but somehow, I knew The Deceiver knew I was standing there even though he had not once turned his head. My heart was pounding to the beat of a thousand conga drums. I could only pray he was not hearing that.

You're such an idiot, *I chided myself, keeping deathly still. However, after a few moments and no alarm was raised, I exhaled but remained still.*

When The Deceiver placed the mask on the man's face, it seemed to come alive and meld with his flesh. I slapped a hand over my mouth to stifle a shriek. This was not in keeping with what I thought getting the mark would be like. I had always thought it would be like taking a branding iron to the forehead. However, it was inconspicuous, seamless, perfect.

As soon as the man left the line, the next person stepped forward. My stomach churned as I watched him head in my direction. Oh, my God! Oh, my God! Don't come this way! Don't come this way! *I screamed in my head.* Oh, my God. I'm going to be sick.

As he passed by me, he turned his head slightly and glared at me with so much hate I felt I was suffocating. I gulped and held my back ramrod stiff, but I did not avert my eyes. Heart pounding erratically, I tracked him, not daring to turn my head. When he was outside my peripheral vision, then and only then, did I dare move. Still very aware of The Deceiver, I cautiously watched until the man was a safe distance away. I pushed myself up off the wall, and throwing one last look at the growing line, set off in the same direction as the man. I had no idea where I was going, and it was not like I was following him, but I needed to get away, and I did not want to walk past the line. Although the sun was punishingly hot overhead, I was chilled to the bone. I hugged myself, running my palms up and down my arms.

People were heading towards the line in droves, and although it would have been in my best interest to mind my own business, I could not. "Turn around. You're being tricked!" I urged, careful not to shout too loudly. I glanced nervously over my shoulder, but there was no indication the Deceiver had heard me, so I kept at it. "That man is not who or what you think he is. You're all marching to your doom. There's no coming back from this! Don't get in the line!" Nobody seemed to be hearing me. Yet, I persisted.

I was growing increasingly frustrated as, like sheep to the slaughter, people kept blindly filing past me, so I decided it was worth the risk to raise my voice a little louder. I started to get attention then, but not the kind I had hoped for. I had to jump out of the way to avoid getting intentionally mowed over by a large group of men. Others looked daggers at me, some of the looks so hateful that I would have been reduced to ashes if looks could kill. One woman spat at the ground near my feet as she sidestepped me without slowing down.

"Get out of the way! You're the one who's doomed," one man bellowed. "No mark, no food."

"Yeah," another shouted.

Someone else started chanting, "No mark, no food," and others joined the rhythmic chorus: "No mark, no food. No mark, no food."

A little way off, a very small group of maybe five or six approached. One man's eyes met mine. I immediately discerned that there was something different about him. I started off towards him, but he frowned, shaking his head. That stopped me in my tracks. Normally, I did not trust easily and assumed people were bad until they proved otherwise. He hung back a bit before breaking away from the group.

"C-can you tell when someone is wearing the mask?" I asked as soon as he reached me.

The man glanced about, surreptitiously scanning the crowds before leaning in. "Yes. I take it you can?"

I looked around before I nodded, nervously shifting my weight from one foot to the next.

His expression became severe. "Don't tell that to anyone if you want to live. Come, I'll take you somewhere safe."

I shook my head. "T-that's okay." There was no way I was going anywhere with a stranger. I was many things, but stupid I was not.

Bringing a hand up to gently touch my arm, The Stranger said firmly, "You cannot stay here." I recoiled because I did not like people touching me, but he did not seem to notice, much less take offense. "Things have already gotten extremely bad in other towns. People without the mask are being hunted."

My stomach lurched. "I have to warn people."

He shook his head, his expression glum. "It's too late for that. Come, let me take you off the street."

I hesitated and looked towards the town. The crowd was growing increasingly rambunctious, and I had no idea where to go to stay safe.

I nodded. "Okay."

His expression lightened. I could tell he was pleased. "Follow close behind, and don't speak to anyone."

I struggled to keep up with The Stranger, whose legs were like a giraffe's, making him well over six-feet tall. He kept going at a steady clip, not once turning around to ensure I was behind him. At times, I found myself running to catch up, only to fall behind shortly thereafter. Although we had not walked very far, by the time we got near the line, I was huffing like I had run the 100 meters. Surprisingly, the line was not as long as I had expected. Evidently, The Deceiver worked fast.

As we were going around the last woman in line, I grabbed her arm and urged, "Get out of the line if you want to live!"

She yanked her arm away violently and hissed, "Leave me alone. My kids are starving. Yuh have food to give mi?"

I shook my head, my heart weighty. "No, I—"

"Exactly!" the woman shouted, her eyes wild. "That's why yuh have no talk! Mind yuh own damn business."

"Let's go," The Stranger said brusquely, grabbing my hand and jerking it gently, but firmly. "You're drawing attention to yourself."

"Wait!" the woman in front of the last woman in line called out. She was desperately flapping her wrist as though she were flagging down a country bus. I stopped, my breath catching in my throat. I knew her. And knew her well. She was an old friend with whom I had lost touch. I had not seen her in—maybe—ten years, but she looked the same.

She was immaculately dressed—her hair cut and beautifully styled, her face powdered flawless, her ears adorned in baubles that matched her turquoise blouse. The only color on her face was the faint kiss of the rose-pink in her lip gloss. A delicate, gold necklace clung to her neck, its tiny-silver-horseshoe pendant dangling low on her chest. Her French manicure showed off long, slender fingers so dainty they deserved to be immortalized in a catalogue. We had joked about that once.

The Stranger tugged at my hand, but I ignored him. "Yes?" I had said that so softly it was barely a whisper. I had wanted to say her name, but it stuck in my craw like a fistful of asham *(parched-ground-up-sugar-sweetened-corn dust). I touched my throat with my free hand in an effort to stem the excruciating fullness from the huge ball of grit in it.*

"Excuse me, Miss. Do you know who that man is?" my old friend inquired, glancing back at the Deceiver, an extremely worried look on her face. I looked her directly in the eyes, searching for a glint of recognition, but her expression remained blank. A low feeling socked me in the gut.

Miss?

She had called me 'miss'?

My spirit grew exceedingly sad because I knew I was seeing her for the last time. My stomach felt the way it usually did whenever someone close to me died. "Everybody will haffi know him fi demself," (Everybody will have to know him for him/herself) was all I could choke out. I was not sure she had heard me. But, deep down, I knew it did not even matter.

The stranger at my side gave my hand another tug, and this time, I heeded. We had not walked for long—maybe about a block and a half—when he dropped my hand.

"Didn't I tell you not to talk to anybody?" He spat out.

I scowled. "Those people are going to die. My friend is going to die. So, don't you tell me I should not have said anything because I had to try." I was close to tears.

He sighed. "That's the problem with you. You don't listen."

My face crinkled in exasperation at his audacity. "Pfft. What? What yuh know about me?" As the words left my lips, I got the feeling that he not only knew me but knew me well, and that he was not helping me out of the goodness of his heart but was doing his duty.

Before I could begin interrogating him, The Stranger bent down at a manhole with some unusual and intricate patterning. "We're here."

"Here, where?" I asked looking around.

Instead of answering me, he inserted all his fingers—except his thumbs—into two notches in the middle of the covering and pulled up and outward. He rested both halves of the hatch on the ground, stepped back, and looked at me. I moved forward and stood at the mouth of the hole. I could see the top of a metal ladder that descended into what looked like a bottomless pit.

I stepped back, gave him a yuh-must-be-crazy look, and stylishly swept a hand towards the hole like I was a model showcasing a prize on a gameshow. "After you." My voice was shaky, so to cover my nervousness, I flashed him a weak smile. God help me if this man turns out to be an axe murder, *I thought wryly.*

The Stranger's eyes twinkled, and he said gently, "I am not an ax murderer."

I harrumphed, rolled my eyes, and thought, Said the ax murderer, right before my eyes widened and met his. Oh, my God! I had not said that out loud. My mouth fell wide open.

The corners of his mouth turned up ever so slightly. "I will go first—since you insist."

I closed my mouth, opened it, and snapped it shut again. I had questions, but he had already started his descent. As I watched his head disappear, my chest tightened. I was not sure I would be able to climb down that hole, but things were getting weird, and I was going to need a hiding place. And since I didn't know any . . .

Turning my back to the opening, I held on to a handle on each half of the hatch as The Stranger had done. I froze momentarily, trying to plot how I was going to negotiate my descent. After a long while, I gingerly lowered one foot onto the first rung of the ladder, my fists maintaining a death grip on the handles. After sucking in a few deep breaths, I hesitantly rested the other foot on the same rung.

"Hurry! And close the hatch," The Stranger called up. His voice reverberated off the walls and seemed to be coming from everywhere and nowhere. "The point of a hiding place is that it is secret."

"I-I can't c-close the hatch. A-are y-you kidding me?" My arms and legs were trembling so violently I could not bring myself to let go of the handles long enough to lower myself to the next rung, much less swing a hatch.

"It's alright," he called up, his voice reassuring. "I'll do it."

"Okay." My voice was as weak as my stomach felt.

The next few minutes seemed like a lifetime. When my feet finally touched the ground, I almost fell to my knees to smother it with kisses. And I might have, were it not for the eyes on me.

I raised a hand slowly as a momentary hush fell over the room. "Hi," I croaked, taking stock of the number of heads crammed into the small space. I turned to The Stranger—who had come to stand beside *me—my eyes and tone pleading. "Please. I can't stay here."*

He rested a hand on my shoulder and said soothingly, "Breathe."

I tried to, but my fear of heights was no competition for my claustrophobia. I shook my head and wrung free. "I can't."

"Wait!" he called after me as I made a mad dash for the ladder.

Ignoring him, I began climbing like my life depended on it.

Once I cleared the hole, I stopped to catch my breath. I began looking around frantically, trying to decide where to go.

I felt The Stranger come up behind me. Turning to face him, I said apologetically, "I know you're trying to help me, but I'll die if I stay down there."

"And you might die if you don't." His face showed compassion not reflected in his tone.

I did not argue because he was right. I sighed, my spirit heavy. Not wanting him to think me ungrateful, I muttered, "Thanks for trying to help me."

He gave a nod but did not respond.

With my heart beating in my ears, I turned and headed down the road. After I had gone a few steps, I glanced over my shoulder. The Stranger had disappeared. There was nothing quite like feeling utterly alone in the world. Gutted, I kept moving.

I had only been walking a short time when someone screamed, "Over here!" I looked to my right to see a woman with the mask, standing at the mouth of an alleyway, frantically pointing at me. "Here's one of them over here!"

One of them? *I thought, highly offended.* Like I'm some kind of alien species?

I heard the roar of a mob and realized I was in trouble.

"Wake up," I heard me whispering to myself. "Wake up. Now!"

I quickened my steps and glanced back at the woman. She had blood in her eyes. She began jabbing her index finger as if to pin me in place. Every so often she threw a glance over her shoulder to check for her back-up.

"Oh my God," I lamented. "I messed up big time."
The roar of the crowd filled my ears. They were gaining ground.
I opened my eyes.

* * *

I rolled my eyes and slapped my daughter on the arm to get her attention. She removed her earbuds and scowled at me. "Oww! What did you hit me for?"

"Seriously? That did *not* hurt. Do you know how *long* I've been calling you? Ten minutes."

Christine raised her eyebrows. "I didn't hear you. And why do you always exaggerate the time?" I often did that because we were late to *everything*. The kids hated it, but it was effective.

I guffawed and shook my head. "Ah, bwoy."

"Whaaat?"

"Nothing."

It was her turn to roll her eyes. "Seriously, Mom," she said, bringing the earbuds up to her ear.

"Wait. Something's been bothering me." I suspected she was tired of hearing about the line dream because that was all I could talk about since I woke up. However, I persisted. "God keeps bringing me back to the necklace my old friend was wearing, and I don't know why. I'm going to Google 'horseshoe'."

"Mom, I thought you weren't supposed to go to Google for your dreams."

Chastened, I said sheepishly, "Yeah, I know, but it's not like I'm Googling the dream itself, just one item."

"Justifying much?" She began fiddling with her phone, swiping through videos.

So annoying.

I sucked my teeth and turned my attention to the computer. I ended up checking several sites because I could not believe what I was seeing.

"Oh my God. This is crazy," I finally said. "It says here a horseshoe is a symbol of good luck or a charm used to ward off the devil."

Christine pepped up, giving me her full attention. "What?"

"Can you believe the irony of it?" I stared at the screen in wonderment. "Wearing a charm to protect you against the devil while waiting in line to get the mark of the beast?"

Christine's eyes grew wide. "Wow. That *is* ironic."

"It's so crazy that people wear charms thinking that can protect them."

"Mom, you're missing the point." The lightness in her tone was gone. "This is not only about the horseshoe. You're taking this too literally. It is symbolic of everything people do that they believe will save them and keep them out of Hell. They go to church, they give to charity, they feed the hungry . . . which are good things. But these things are meaningless without a personal relationship with God."

I got goosebumps hearing her say it. "Oh, my God. That's so true. This is so much bigger than this one woman. Sometimes we focus on the wrong things and, in the process, lose our way."

"Yes." Christine's eyes were glossed over as though she were lost in thought. "It's sad."

"It is. I can't believe I was so obsessed with who was in the line when why she was there is more important. Still, I can't shake how I feel. I feel really conflicted because I want to tell her . . . out of a sense of duty, I guess. What do you think?"

She did not answer, and I thought maybe she had not heard me, but then she said, "I think maybe I'll get a tattoo of a little red cross right here on the inside of my wrist."

I spun around and glowered at her. "Seriously?"

Christine giggled. "Just kidding." Her expression abruptly changed, growing serious. "Mom, I know it's hard because this is someone you know, and somehow you feel you have to try and save everybody. But you know you can't ever talk to her about this without talking to God first, and if He says no, you have to accept that."

I nodded, my lips curling into a smile, which I tried to hide from her. As she put her earbuds back in, dismissing me, I remembered what Jesus said in Luke 10:21, "I praise you, Father, Lord of Heaven and Earth, because you have hidden these things from the wise and learned, and revealed them to little children. Yes, Father, for this was your good pleasure" (NIV).

Christine was not little anymore—but still.

* * *

I tried to hold off going to God about what to do regarding my old friend because I was afraid. I thought that at least this way, I could hold out hope. However, I could only stand the suspense a couple days.

"Jehovah, this is totally up to you. What do I do?" I asked, my heart filled with anticipation.

You have given her all the messages she is to get from you, He said.

My heart sank. "Yes, but what about *this* dream? This dream is worse than anything I've ever told her. Maybe this is the thing that will make her listen."

You have given her all the messages she is to get from you.

"Okay, I understand that, but—"

She did not recognize you, God reminded me.

"I know. That was so freaky," I whispered, picturing the blank look on the woman's face. "How was that?"

The wheat and the tares will be allowed to grow together until the Harvest. At Harvesttime, they will be separated.

My chest was on fire. "Okay, Jehovah," I muttered, "but I'm not going to pretend that I'm happy at all because you already know what's in my heart. So, I'm confessing out loud how I feel. I'm totally gutted."

Every man gets the same chance. Whether it be a day or a hundred years. Whoever is dead is dead already.

I buried my face in my palms and wept.

Ezekiel 12½

Not having a righteousness of my own that comes from the law,
But that which is through faith in Christ.

Philippians 3:9 (NIV)

S eriously!" I fumed as I read the affidavits Logan's lawyer had filed with the court. The documents were riddled with information that was irrelevant as well as misleading, all designed to make me look bad, of course. By the time I was done reading, I was close to tears. The past few weeks were some of the hardest because I had run into my old friend from the line dream. Talking to her was extremely distressing. I had forced a smile and talked about mundane issues—the fire ant problem at my house, the persistent drought island-wide, the shambolic collection of garbage in the community—when all I wanted to do was holler at her to go to God about her life. I could be unwittingly disobedient, and at times, blatantly wilful, but I knew better than to cross God regarding this. As I walked away from her, guilt had almost brought me to my knees, and that guilt was still eating at me. And now this?

I would wish to disappear to a deserted island, but I knew I would not last an hour. I was not outdoorsy by any stretch of the imagination. I lived on an island, yes, but there was nothing better to me than sitting under the shade of a tree, at the beach, reading a book. I had joined the hiking club in high school only because it did not require brainwork. After all, how hard could it be to do something I did naturally every day? Plus, it would afford me time away from the boarding school I considered prison. If I had a bucket list, hiking up to Blue Mountain Peak would have been at the top because of the adventure books I had read growing up. It had taken one weekend hike up the mountain for roughing it in the great outdoors to forever lose its allure—walking in the clouds aside.

I began drafting a letter to Logan. However, after about twenty minutes, I saved it to allow myself time to cool down to avoid having to beg God pardon later.

"God I'm tired of this," I grumbled, slamming my laptop shut.

I marched straight for Michael's closet because it was the only closet that had floorspace—well, except for Logan's, and I definitely was *not* going to talk to God in *that*. I had no explanation for my choice of meeting place because I always thought the closet in Matthew 6:6 to be figurative, and I was already alone in my room.

Because I could not bear to be cooped up inside, I plopped down onto the floor just outside the door, banging my knees hard on the tile. After howling and rolling around in pain for a bit, I knelt, placed my palms flat on the floor, extended my arms in front of me as far as they could go so my head was cradled, and began talking to God.

Well into the third hour of drudging up and sieving through years of dregs, I had grown exhausted. My forehead was beaded with sweat, and my throat was achy and dry. My lower back felt as though it were being ripped open by birthing pains. The tiles, like shards of glass, were cutting into my knees, and the parts of my legs that I could feel were mostly pins and needles. My cheeks were wet with tears I had been unaware of shedding. I should get up. However, my heart was still full. To ease my discomfort, I slowly, and with a great deal of effort, stretched my body out until I was lying prostrate. The grit of the grout bit into my forehead, but I was beyond caring. After all, what was a little more pain on top of pain that was already plenty?

"God," I cried from a place deep in my belly, "I feel totally set upon, and I don't know what to do about it. Why is everything a fight? Why can't I have peace in my life? Every time I think there is going to be an end to the madness, Logan and his parents come up with something else. I just want to be left alone. I have stayed out of these people's way, and yet they've continued to plague me. This has been going on forever now. What am I supposed to do? Am I to stand still and let them trample on me? Grind me to dust? *Why*? What have I done to deserve that?"

As those were not questions to which I expected answers, I kept going. "Every time I'm tempted to go at Logan hard, I remember what The Messenger said, and I back off. Well, honestly, that's not the only reason. I'd probably try and do something if I knew what to do . . . but I don't. I have no other help but You. You, Oh Lord, are my only recourse, and well You know it, but You want me to ask . . . so here I am, Most High Judge . . . on my face . . . at your feet, begging for your justice. I have no interest in man's justice because man's justice is garbage. Look at what is happening with the hearings . . . continuance after continuance, delay after delay. All the judges have been doing is kowtowing to Logan." I paused a moment to think about what I hoped Logan would do with all the pieces of long rope every judge had gifted him to date, and my face grew hot. "Okay, so I don't really mean that. I'm sorry."

The aching in my eyes was almost unbearable as tears began to flow once again. "I don't mean to be cruel, but I am tired of these people, Jehovah—every last one of them. They take pleasure in autopsying my character, besmirching my name—telling people that I'm crazy because of my dreams, calling me a witch, claiming that I'm speaking out against churches, claiming that everything I say that I'm getting from You is actually from the devil, saying that the things You show me will never come true because I'm making them up—I guess because they sometimes take long to manifest—well, whatever the reason, I'm tired of all of it. I know I shouldn't care what they say about me, but I do. I don't know how to *not* care. I. Have. Tried. Believe me."

The tears were flowing uncontrollably now. "Tell me . . . how are they allowed to say whatever they want to say and do whatever they want to do, and all I get do is stand still? Stand still? That's it? Moses told the Israelites, 'The Egyptians you see today, you will see no more forever.' What about me, Jehovah? Will the time ever come when I have to deal with these people no more forever? I have been waiting and waiting for You to do something, and I don't see what you're doing. God, where is your salvation? Where is your justice? How can people who claim to know You behave like this? How can they say they serve You, yet act as though You don't exist? People take You for a joke! That's what it is. The whole world takes You for a joke. Every time people who claim to serve You live their lives like You don't exist, they are taking You for a joke. How much longer will You allow this to go on? You *need* to show people who You are."

A low rumbling began somewhere far off in the distance. Gasping, I sat up as it got louder and louder, barrelling closer and closer. The ground vibrated softly underneath me. The windows began to rattle—softly at first—before the rattling built in earnest to a crescendo, the thunder now almost deafening and seeming to come from every conceivable direction.

"Oh, my God—oh, my God—oh, my God," I whispered, scrambling backwards into a far corner of the closet and huddling against two stacked tubs of toys. The rolling and shaking went on for maybe ten seconds although, in the moment, it seemed like forever. After it finally stopped, I stayed where I was for a couple minutes because I was shaking too hard to move. As soon as I was able, I raced over to a window. The sky was beautiful and clear—no surprise there. I checked my yard and the neighboring yards. Nothing seemed amiss—no surprise there either. I ran to Nathan's room and yanked the door open to check on Michael, who had taken up residence in Nathan's room since he left. He was still asleep.

I ran to my bedroom and called Abby. "Hey," I said breathlessly when she answered. "I can't explain now . . . but quick question. Did you feel the ground shaking?"

"No."

A ton of questions were compressed into that one word, but I had no time for any of them. "You're sure? Not even a little bit . . . like maybe we just had an earthquake."

"No, why?" Her voice was now thick with concern.

"Nothing . . . well, something. But I'll have to call you back."

"Okay," she said, sounding a tad disappointed, but I quickly rang off before I let my guilt about that keep me on the phone.

"God, what was that?" My heart was jackhammering against my chest. I would have felt so much better if we had had a quake. I knew my ranting had been a bit over the top, but I had always felt comfortable saying exactly how I felt. "Are you mad at me?"

No answer.

"Jehovah, I don't understand what just happened. I need to know if you're mad at me." I was shaking now—well, maybe I had not really stopped but never realized it. "If you are—can you please tell me so I can say that I'm sorry?"

No answer.

My head felt light, and my stomach felt like I had eaten bricks for breakfast. "Well, I'm just going to go ahead and say sorry anyway . . . because with my track record, more than likely I *did* say something wrong."

No answer.

I spent almost a whole hour on my face.

* * *

The next morning, my mother called me. I was in a sore mood and did not want to talk, but I answered her anyway.

"Hey, yuh up?" she asked.

179

I rolled my eyes. "Really, Mother," I said, my tone sarcastic. "Am I not talking to you?"

I expected her to laugh, but she hadn't. "I know. I mean—did I wake you?" She sounded serious.

She had woken me up, but I was not going to tell her that now. I frowned and sat up. "What's wrong? Are you feeling sick?"

"No." There was something in her tone that caused fear to take hold of my heart anyway.

"Mommy, what is it?" I asked forcefully.

"Something strange happened to me early this morning. You know those night terrors I've been having since the chemotherapy?"

"Yes."

"Well, I had one, and the thing is I don't remember what I was dreaming about."

I sighed. "You usually don't. So, why are calling me about it then?"

"I know I usually don't remember anything and have to ask you guys what I was saying, but this time was different. When I woke up, I was still screaming."

I frowned. "Really? Do you remember what you were saying?"

"Yes. Ezekiel 12½. Over and over and over again."

I threw back the comforter and flew out of bed. "What? Ezekiel doesn't have 12½ chapters." I shook my head and chided myself, *Dumb-dumb, what are you saying? No book in the Bible has a half-ah chapter.* "Wait—are you sure that's what you were saying?"

"Yes. I figured it didn't mean anything. But then, I kept getting this urge to call you. I ignored it at first because I figured you were probably sleeping, but it wouldn't go away."

I began pacing. "This makes no sense."

"I know."

I suddenly stopped mid-pace. "Mommy, Ezekiel 12½ is for me."

My mother gasped. "What? How do you know that?"

My heart skipped about a little. "I don't know—but I do." As I said that, an equation popped up in front of me. "Get your Bible and tell me how many verses Ezekiel 12 has."

"I have my Bible right here beside me," she said, her voice breathy. I began pacing again, but she was not long. "It has twenty-eight verses."

I stilled. "Okay, read from verse fourteen."

"Why?"

"I just saw twelve divided by two equals six."

"That makes no sense," my mother said, sounding sceptical.

"I know it doesn't to you, but it makes sense to me. I can't explain how." I tried not to sound short with my mother. "Mommy, just read. Please."

The hairs on my neck back tickled my skin as she began to read:

> The Word of the Lord came to the prophet Ezekiel saying:
> "I will scatter to the winds all those that are around him to help him—his staff and all his troops—and I will draw out the sword after them.
> And they shall know that I am the Lord.
>
> But I will spare a few of them from the sword, from the famine, and from the pestilence so that they may admit to all their wrongdoing whereabouts they end up.
> And they shall know that I am the Lord.
>
> Son of man, tremble as you eat your food, and shudder in fear as you drink your water and say to the people,
> 'This is what the Sovereign Lord says:
> They will eat their food in anxiety and drink their water in despair, for all they own will be destroyed and their land will be left empty.'
> And they shall know that I am the Lord.
>
> Son of man, what is the proverb that they have, saying, 'The days

go by and every vision comes to nothing?'
Say to them, 'This is what the Sovereign Lord says:
I am going to put an end to this proverb, and they will no longer
use it.'

Say to them, 'The days are near when every vision will be
fulfilled. For there will be no more false visions or flattering
divinations among them. But I the Lord will speak what I will, and
it shall be fulfilled without delay. For in your days, you rebellious
people, I will fulfil whatever I say, declares the Sovereign Lord.'

Son of man, they are saying, 'The vision he sees is for many years
from now, and he prophesies about the distant future.'
Therefore, say unto them, 'This is what the Sovereign Lord says:
None of my words will be delayed any longer; whatever I say will
be fulfilled, declares the Sovereign Lord.'"

My heart was spasming so hard my chest hurt. "Oh, God," I gasped, bringing a hand up to clutch my chest.

"What's wrong?" my mom asked, sounding highly concerned.

"This is crazy. Oh, my God. Oh, my God. Do you understand what this is saying?" As the question tumbled from my lips, I knew the absurdity of it because I did not even know, and it was meant for me.

My mom hesitated, probably trying to digest what she had just read, and then said, "No, not really. What is this about?"

"I think this is about yesterday."

"What happened yesterday?" She sounded frightened and confused.

"Later, Mommy. I can't talk about it now," I spat out quickly. I could sort of see it, but I was not sure, and the last thing I wanted to do was to jump to any conclusions. "Let me talk to God first."

* * *

When my mother called back half an hour later—twenty-nine minutes later than I expected—I still was not certain what the message really meant. All I had were my own maybes, and maybes were not good enough. I was frustrated that no matter how I tried to get answers, God had remained silent.

"Mommy," I said impatiently, "I still don't have any answers. Can I call you back?"

"Wait!" my mother called out, her tone desperate. "Check your texts. I just sent you a message."

I was not sure I could deal with anything else at the moment, but curiosity would always win out for me. "Okay, I'll check now," I assured her and hung up.

My mom's message said that she had wanted to read Ezekiel 12½ again. However, when she flipped open the Bible to search for it, the Bible opened to Proverbs 24 instead. She had sent a picture of the page showing verses16-20. They read:

> "A just man falleth seven times, and riseth up again: but the wicked shall fall into mischief. Rejoice not when thine enemy falleth, and let not thine heart be glad when he stumbleth: Lest the Lord see it, and it displease Him, and He turn away His wrath from him. Fret not thyself because of evil men, neither be thou envious at the wicked; For there shall be no reward to the evil man; the candle of the wicked shall be put out" (KJV).

My hand was trembling so much I had to put down the phone. I started pacing. After putting significant wear on the rug, I stopped short, took a few deep breaths, and held out my hands as one would to say, 'hold up or wait a minute'. "Okay, God . . . okay." I took a few more deep breaths. "I *really* don't know what you're saying, and you're not talking to me. What *exactly* are you saying?" My desperation was through the roof. "When I came to you in the closet, I was frustrated. I was at wit's end, and I needed to vent. I did not mean for anybody to get hurt, so I'm begging you . . . *please* . . . if you're saying what I think you're saying, when you draw out your sword, let them see your justice—but let them also see your mercy."

Pick up the Bible, God said.

Oh, bwoy, I thought, *What did I do now?* I did not feel my legs move, and it wasn't until I was waiting for God to tell me to open my Bible that I realized I was holding my tablet instead.

Oh crap! I thought. However, too shaky to get out of bed again, I held up the tablet. "Uh, God, I have my tablet." When my announcement was met with silence, I felt a little silly. This was not how it worked between us. I needed my Bible, but then again, maybe I did not. "Where do I go?"

The Book of Job, He said.

Okay, then, I thought. *This is pretty cool.* I typed Job 1 in BibleGateway and waited.

Keep going.

I forwarded to Job 2 and stopped.

Keep going.

We kept this up until I got to Job 9. *Stop,* He instructed, and when I did, He said, *Scroll up.*

I'm really digging this, I thought as I scrolled up slowly.

Stop, He said when verse 11 was at the top of the screen.

I began reading: "When He passes me, I cannot see Him; when He goes by, I cannot perceive Him. If He snatches away, who can stop Him? Who can say to Him, 'What are you doing?'" Bug-eyed, I brought my hands to my mouth. My heart felt ready to make an emergency exit from the cradle of my chest. I was going to pass out. It was a good thing I was already sitting. "God does not restrain His anger; even the cohorts of Rahab cowered at His feet."

Stop, He said, halting my reading at verse 13.

"Jehovah, I-I don't know what to say, except that I-I'm *really, really* sorry. I know better. I know better than to have the audacity to tell you what's in people's hearts or dictate what you should do about it. I'm so sorry. I-I don't dare propose to know your mind . . . or your will . . . or your heart. The only thing I know for sure is that your heart is good and so are your intentions towards us." I wanted to cry so badly my eyes hurt from the sheer intensity of it, but somehow, shedding tears seemed trite. "I know I messed up by saying what I did in the closet. And I messed up further by trying to fix it. I know that you show mercy to whom you choose to show mercy, but just like I want mercy for myself, I was begging for mercy for others."

I am not unjust, He said.

"I know," I whispered, tears slithering down my cheeks.

* * *

As soon as I opened my eyes the next morning, God said, *You are to fast and pray for Logan.*

I was greatly relieved He was asking something of me; I just was not happy about what. However, I was determined to start the day off on good footing. "Okay, God. For how long?"

Seven days.

Groaning, I rolled on to my side and threw my arm over my ear—as was my habit when I did not want to hear what God was telling me. "*Seven days*, Jehovah? Seriously? It's Logan. I cannot pray for him for one day much less seven whole days. Can I please pray for somebody else? Anybody else—as long as it's not Logan. Please. Even though you already know my heart, I am confessing this. First off, I don't know what to pray, and . . . honestly, even if I did . . . I wouldn't mean it."

What if you asked Nathan to sweep the floor, and instead, he did the laundry? God asked.

I sat up and frowned. "Why would he do that?"

What if you asked him to do the laundry, and instead, he took out the garbage?

185

My brow furrowed deeper. "I'd be upset if I asked him to do one thing, and he did something else. I'd be upset he wasn't listening. I'd feel that what I wanted didn't matter to him."

Imagine me.

I quailed, feeling as big as a flea. "I'm sorry, Jehovah," I sighed. "I'll do as you ask." And even though I would sooner pray for a total stranger, I dragged myself to Michael's room. "Jehovah, here I am. I don't know what I'm supposed to say, so you're going to have to tell me. What do you want me to say?"

I was being neither feisty nor flippant. I needed help, and I knew I could ask that of God because Romans 8:26-27 says, "We do not know what we ought to pray for, but the Spirit himself intercedes for us through wordless groans. And He who searches our hearts knows the mind of the Spirit, because the Spirit intercedes for God's people. This, He does, in accordance with the will of God" (NIV).

And so, I waited for the Holy Spirit to do His thing because I was not going to risk putting my foot in my mouth again.

Folly

I press on to take hold of that for which Christ Jesus took hold of me.

Philippians 3:12 (NIV)

You got green bananas at the market?" I had not put any on the list. However, Annalise sometimes bought things she thought I would want but had left off only because I had forgotten.

"No, Sugah send dem."

"Really? Tell him thanks for me," I said taking a seat in my usual spot.

Annalise immediately picked up her phone and dialed Sugah's number. I shook my head as they bantered playfully. She turned to me and said, "Teacher, Sugah want to know why I'm di one calling him."

I took the phone she handed me, cradling it. "Hey, Sugah."

"Yuh nuh waah talk to mi. I see how it is, Mama G." His voice was light and playful.

I laughed. "No, that's not it. *You're* the one who doesn't want to talk to *me*. That's why you haven't given me your number?"

"Sugah chuckled. "*Cho*, Mama G, man. Nutting like that. I thought Madam give it to yuh."

I looked over at Annalise, who was standing hand akimbo, and smiled. "No, she didn't—but I'll get it from her. Or better yet, I'll call you and hang up, so you can save mine, and then you call me and hang up, and I'll save yours."

"Awright."

"Thanks for the bananas."

"*Cho*, dat ah nuh nutting, Mama G, man."

To him, the bananas were not big deal, but to me, they were huge. I beamed, handing the phone to Annalise, who rang off rather quickly with the excuse she had stuff to do.

She and I talked about her kids and some stuff going on in her neighborhood before she changed the direction of the conversation. "Teacher, yuh think the things in Revelation are really going to happen?"

I frowned. "Do you?"

"I don't know—because from the time Jesus supposed to come back—him nuh reach yet."

"I've heard that argument a lot. But what people need to remember is that God's timing is not the same as ours. The Bible says that, to God, a day is like a thousand years. So, if I look at it that way"—I chuckled—"Jesus has been gone all of two days."

"It's funny yuh should bring up that Bible verse because the pastor—who was visiting our church last week—mentioned it. But he was talking about how when wi ask God for something, wi expect Him to answer right away."

"That's true."

"Bwoy, teacher, mi nuh know about Revelation, though, because all of it is a vision. Plus, a lot of it don't make sense."

"I know it's confusing. I don't understand a lot of what is in Revelation either. However, one thing I do know—Jesus *is* coming back, and when He does, those who belonged to Him when they died will be the first to rise, and then all who are still alive will be caught up to meet Him."

"Yuh believe suh, teacher? I don't know. Maybe Heaven is on

Earth, and death is in the grave."

I frowned. "What do you mean?"

"That when we die that's it. That this life is all we have."

I opened my eyes wide. "Really, suh no life after death? Well, when Jesus call yuh name, yuh nuh lie down weh yuh deh." (Really, so no life after death? Well, when Jesus calls your name, lie down where you are). I guffawed, and Annalise chuckled.

"Look," I got serious, "even if Revelation is hard to understand, we have to go off what Jesus himself said. Before He ascended into Heaven, He said that He was going to prepare a place for us—and that He would come again to get us—so that where He is, we'll be there as well. This wicked, wicked world could *never* be Heaven—because if that were the case—we would have no hope."

"That mek sense," Annalise said pensively.

"Besides, I've seen some of the very scary stuff Revelation talks about . . . and some of the not-so-scary stuff as well—like the dream I had that the kids and I were in a warzone somewhere. We could hear explosions and gunfire, and we could see flames blazing both nearby and off in the distance. The air was filled with smoke and ash. We could hardly see. People were running and screaming." I shuddered at the bloodcurdling sounds filling my head. "It was *awful*. I was looking around for somewhere to hide when Jesus appeared and started walking towards us. Can you imagine? *Jesus*"—I crossed my heart—"came for *me*."

I sighed dreamily, awestruck all over again, as I watched Jesus walk towards us. "It was the most *amazing* thing—to see Him coming through the thick cloud of dust and smoke. He told me to take His hand, and then He led us to a *massive* wooden gate—about the height of a two-story building. It had solid double doors with no latches or handles, and as we approached, it opened. Inside was the most breathtakingly *beautiful* place I've ever seen. You should see it. There were so many flowers—flowers of all shades and kinds—and each color had tons of shades. Like for the purple, each shade was only a little lighter or darker than the next—the spectrum going from"—I waved my arms to the left—"almost white with barely any purple"—I swung my arms to the right—"to extremely dark and saturated . . . almost to the point of looking black. And that's how it was for *every* color you can think of." I paused momentarily to marvel at the memory. "A postcard could never do it justice."

I surprised myself gushing so much over the garden. The death of my favorite cousin, when I was eleven years old, had triggered an unreasonable aversion to flowers. I had fought Logan tooth and nail about what plants to include in the landscaping when we had first moved into our house. I had not wanted a single blooming flower in the yard. We had agreed he could plant as many palm trees, evergreen bushes, and fruit trees as he wanted. Any flowers had to be planted beyond the perimeter wall, and he had to promise to keep them manicured so they would not be visible from inside the house. He had manged to sneak a red hibiscus plant amongst the bushes he had planted in the yard and—once it had eventually bloomed—had found my reaction beyond hilarious. At least he had had the good sense not to plant it at the front of the house.

There was so much more to the garden in the dream, but knowing I could never adequately describe its magnificence, I moved on. "The people walking around didn't seem afraid of the lion that was lying close to the front of the garden. The lamb, lying near to him, had no care in the world either, and nobody seemed worried about the kids who were sitting or lying around the lion. The coolest thing was when Jesus waved His hand for us to enter. That's when I woke up." I forced myself to stop yammering because Annalise—who was busy sautéing seasoning for the ackee and saltfish—had not hitched or looked up once.

"Then, teacher . . . I thought nobody could si God's face and live," she said, her tone sceptical.

The corners of my mouth turned up. I had not lost her at all. "Well, that's true. Because nobody is worthy. Besides, He *is* light and dwells in what the Bible calls unapproachable light. Moses only saw His back, and yet He had to hide Moses in the opening of a rock and shield him with His hand as He was walking by. If He hadn't, Moses probably would have burnt to toast because even though all Moses saw was God's back, his face was glowing when he came down from the mountain. Jesus is another story. Jesus—God in the flesh—came and walked among men. People could see Him and touch Him, so it's not unbelievable that He shows himself to us in dreams. I've already seen Him twice."

"So, what about in the cave?"

"When I saw God in the cave, I only saw an image projected on a wall. In that dream, He simply came to me in a form that an eleven-year-old could relate to, and because that wasn't His true form, I got to live. When I was supposed to die, I did not get to go ask God for more time for myself even though it was a dream. An angel had to do that."

Analise was frying ripe plantains, signaling that breakfast was almost ready. "I don't know, teacher, but sometimes the Bible seem so confusing—like it seh one thing one place, and seh something else in another place." She turned off the stove. "Breakfast ready. Yuh can share it out now, teacher."

I took a small sip of water. "I'm not eating. I'm supposed to be fasting." As if on cue, my stomach started growling obscenely. I groaned and pushed the stool back. "I need to go pray."

* * *

Every morning after that, I entered Michael's room and presented myself to God, and every morning, I said the same thing: "Okay, Jehovah. Here I am. What do you want me to say?"

Five days, four hours, and about ten minutes in, I was over it. I sighed and sat down on the bed. "God, I don't mean to complain . . . but . . . why am *I* the one doing this? Is Logan miserable? No. As far as I can tell, he is living his best life—all footloose and fancy-free—doing exactly as he pleases without any thought of me and how *I* am faring. And here I am—stuck—praying for him. Is he fasting and praying for me? No. Because I'm sure you haven't asked that of him. Is Logan losing sleep because of me? No. I'm sure he's sleeping just fine. What exactly have you required of him? What exactly are you holding his feet to the fire for? I'm not complaining—I'm just saying.". I sighed once more. "I am just *so* tired, Jeshua, and I really, *really* need some coffee."

I knew I was being more than petty, but what was spilling from my mouth was what I was feeling in my heart—and that's the thing about the heart; it is the keep that houses a person's truth. I knew I could not continue my fast like this—bogged down and resentful—so I immediately messaged Pastor James whom God had led me to when it had come time to baptize the kids. In response to my gripe, he wrote:

> Your anger, though justifiable, is only going to hurt you if you hold it for any length of time. You have had your trust betrayed and your investments overlooked; however, the anger must go, and the sooner the better. You are a woman of the Word, and as such, I expect you to obey it. Take note of the following:
>
> 1. Forgiveness:
> We are forgiven on the grounds of our ability to forgive (. . . and forgive us our trespasses as we forgive those that trespass against us . . .)
> 2. Fasting:
> Fasting with an unforgiving heart will avail nothing; it will only be a hunger strike. I just want you to be the servant God wants you to be.

Okaaay, I thought, So *not how I envisioned this conversation going.* However, truth be told, it had gone *exactly* as I knew it would—subconsciously anyway—and that was why I had not contacted anybody else. I was spiralling down the proverbial rabbit hole, and that called for the council of someone who would not coddle me. I did feel a little ridiculous, but more importantly, I felt well and truly chastised. Consequently, that feeling helped nudge me towards a renewed mind.

* * *

On the seventh and final day, I stayed in my bed.

I stretched languidly and smiled. I had made it. I had managed to chuck the weight the fast had dumped on my spirit and had come to a place of acceptance, seeing the fasting not as a laborious chore, but as my God-given duty. This I was able to do only because I had taken self out of the equation. Funny, the request God had made of me to pray for His sheep had factored largely into that.

Although it was the last day, I still had to pray, and even though I knew that if I stayed in bed, I would be dead asleep in under five minutes, I could not drag myself out of it. *I'll get up the minute I start feeling sleepy*, I promised myself.

I stretched once more and closed my eyes. As I prayed, I entered a white space I had been in once before in a dream. Everything was the same. There was a single table in the middle of the room, and on it were some small rectangular boxes wrapped with red gift paper.

As He had done in the dream, God said, *Pick one out for Logan.*

Obediently, I walked over, and without hesitation, picked up one of the boxes. My breath caught in my throat because—unlike in the dream—the gift had no price tag. I looked down at the table, only to find that none of the gifts had a price attached.

In the dream, all the gifts had had price tags, and the difference in price had been mere cents. Yet, I had repeatedly picked up and put back gifts, all because I had deemed them too expensive for Logan. As far as I had been concerned, he was not deserving. However, God had chided me for my actions by saying, "You do not give to Logan because of who Logan is; you give to Logan because of who I am."

Beaming, I opened my eyes as warmth permeated my body.

I had passed my test.

I will be doing a new thing, God said in the stillness.

I frowned. "Really? What new thing?"

Will you see it?

My heart fluttered a little. "I don't know. I hope so. But what do you mean? What are you going to be doing?"

I will be making a way in the wilderness and rivers in the desert.

I smiled. "Really? How?"

Watch for it.

My heart quickened. *Okaaay. Another puzzle. Great*, I thought.

* * *

When Annalise came the next day, I was in a mellow mood. We were laughing and chitchatting for a while when she abruptly stopped in the middle of what she was doing and got a distant look in her eyes.

Dread crept into my heart. *Oh, no,* I thought, holding my breath. It was too soon. I had not yet come down off my high.

"Teacher," she said, her tone serious, "The Spirit seh yuh have di gift of interpretation."

I drew back and looked at her as one would look over a pair of glasses. "Are you serious?"

"Yes, that's what di Spirit just seh."

I frowned. "Are you sure that's what you heard . . . I mean . . . I've been to lots of churches where people speak in tongues, and I've never been able to understand what was being said." I searched my mental logs. "Well . . . except this one time . . . umpteen years ago. A lady was speaking in tongues, and I seemed to understand everything she was saying. But by the time she was done, I had convinced myself it was probably pure imagination. I never thought of it again because it has never happened since."

"It nuh matter if it happen long time; it happen," Annalise said, sounding quite resolute.

I frowned. "I don't know," I drawled. "If I really had this gift, wouldn't it have been manifested more than once?"

Annalise shrugged. "Teacher, mi know wah mi hear—and it's not every time I'm in church I speak in tongues either."

"Yeah, I get yuh. I'll have to wait and see, I guess." I was ready to drop the matter—and not because I had doubts about Annalise. She would not say she had gotten something she had not, but I needed confirmation. "Guess what! My mom's coming for Christmas, so I was thinking maybe I'd have Boxing Day dinner and invite a few people."

"Sounds good." Talk of having a get together had pepped her up because feasts were right up her alley, and the bigger the better. "So how many people were you thinking?"

I waved my head from side to side. "Hmm. I don't know. Maybe thirty—thirty-five."

Annalise raised her eyebrows. "That's a lot of people for you."

"I know," I said, a look of feigned horror on my face, "but I can't remember the last time my mom was here for Christmas, and I don't know when she'll be back for another one. Plus, she's been through a lot with her health, and the kids have been struggling with the breakup of the family, so I think it'll be good for everybody—even me."

"True. Suh what would be on the menu?" I could see the wheels already turning in her head and knew she was way ahead of me.

I shrugged. "Dunno . . . I definitely want mannish water and curried goat. We can figure out the rest."

"Well, yuh have to figure it out soon because people are putting in their orders at the butcher's already."

I scoffed. "Why? Christmas is a couple months out."

"Trust me, teacher, this is *not* early—but anyway, if yuh don't get through with the butcher, there's a new meat shop we could go to."

"That's good to know because I can't take the stress. Oh, I'm going to ask Mommy if she'll bake. You *have* to taste her fruitcake." I cocked my ears. "I hear my phone. I'll be right back."

"Awright."

I pushed away from the counter and ran upstairs like fire was at my tail. "Hello," I said, panting hard into the phone.

Abigail chuckled. "How yuh sound suh out o' breath?"

I laughed. "You know me—never near my phone. I was downstairs talking to Annalise."

"Oh, okay. In that case, I'll call you back. I just wanted to tell you a dream I had last night."

"No, you'd better tell me now," I said hastily. "You know that if you don't, it's going to bug me the entire day."

Abigail laughed. "Well, I've been waiting *all* morning for you to wake up." She paused a little for me to finish giggling. "Anyway, I dreamed that I heard that Logan had died."

I inhaled sharply. "Oh, my God!"

"Wait, don't panic. Listen to the rest."

"Okay," I agreed, although I honestly did not want to hear.

"So, when I came over to the house to offer my condolences, I saw Logan sitting on a wall outside, looking pensive. When I told him I had heard he was dead, he said he was *supposed* to die, but he was given a second chance. There were a lot of people at the house, and I thought they were there because, like me, they had heard he was dead. But when I asked Logan about it, he said that he was going to marry his wife again, and he was getting the house ready because he wanted it to be perfect for her—he wanted to make her happy. When—"

"Wait, whoa! What? I'm sorry, but I don't know about this. I mean, don't get your feelings hurt or anything, but this does not line up with what we've gotten so far. This is not how the small chance Logan is getting is supposed to go."

"Don't you think I know that? I've been thinking the same thing since I woke up," Abigail said, sounding equally perturbed. "I'm simply telling you what I got."

"Mm . . . I understand that, but I don't know. Have you met Logan?" Such a redundant question as she and Logan had been friends since high school. "Make *me* happy? Logan is only concerned about one person's happiness—Logan's. I was never good enough because I was never ambitious enough. I'm responsible for ruining his life. If it rains, it's my fault. If the sun don't shine, it's my fault. He hates me like poison and avoids me like the plague. Need I go on?" I paused, but only for the drama of the effect. "Maybe he's going to get married again and then remarry his second wife because that dream could *not* be about me. There is no way, on God's green Earth, Logan would consider marrying me again. Besides, I'm not sure I'd want him either."

"Jaye, you can't—"

"Yeah?" I hollered loudly before saying, "Abby, Annalise is calling me."

"Okay. Later then," she said, a knowing smile in her voice.

"Yeah, laters."

* * *

Midweek, *I dreamed that I was struggling to lug an empty rickshaw along a bumpy road. One of the wheels hit a rock, and I lost my grip on the shafts I was using to drag the conveyance along. Before I could react, it began careening down a hill, heading straight for the ocean. I chased after it, but the faster I ran, the further ahead of me it barrelled. By the time I got to the bottom of the hill, it had disappeared beneath the frothy waves. Frantic, I toed off my shoes and waded in, giving no thought at all to my fear. When the water reached my waist, I plunged beneath the surface, flailing my arms and thrashing my legs about. Visibility was next to zero, so I was forced to rely on touch. I did not have to grope around for long before I hit metal. I yanked hard, but all that came up was a bar about two feet long. I swam ashore, dropped it on the sand, and immediately spun around. This time, I came up with a piece of metal that was even shorter. I wanted to give up, but I was determined to bring the rickshaw to the surface even if it meant doing it one piece at a time. I kept going in and coming up with small pieces I had no idea what to do with. I did this for what seemed like forever until my frustration began to mount.* Deciding it was time to end my torture, I opened my eyes.

This dream made no sense to me. Why a rickshaw? I had ever only seen one on television. Why didn't I simply let it sink? There was no way I could put it back together, so why had I been so determined to retrieve the pieces? I knew I could go to God for the answer, but I did not want to—at least not yet. I was afraid that the rickshaw was symbolic of something that was about to go incredibly wrong in my life, and I wanted to hold on to my peace a little longer.

* * *

Around midday, my cell phone rang. "Hi, Mom," Christine said in that draggy voice she used when she had something to tell me she knew I would not want to hear.

My heart sank, but I called on my inner *Cheery Mary*. "Hey, *babsey*. What's up?"

"Mom, you're on speaker phone. Nate's here."

"Hey, Mom," he said, his tone solemn.

I tensed. "What's wrong?"

"We both had dreams that you were in," Christine said.

"Oh?" was all I could manage to say.

"*Yeah.* It's so weird," she said.

"And serious," Nathan chimed in. "Both dreams were basically warnings for you."

"Oh, Lord," I sighed. "*What* did I do now?"

"Well, in my dream, you wouldn't listen to me—"

Nathan did not let her finish. "And in mine, you misled me."

I frowned. "Wow! It's as bad as all that." They sounded *bringle*—Nathan more so than Christine. I kind of felt a little set upon. Afterall, I had not *actually* done anything.

"Well, you can judge for yourself," Christine said. "In my dream, there was something evil knocking on the door. I did not see it, but I could sense it. Even though we were ignoring it, it kept hovering around. You got mad and said that you were going to go confront it. I told you not to bother because we were safe inside, but you would *not* listen, Mom. Before you could get to the front door, Nate grabbed you and told you to stop, but you yanked your arm away and opened the door anyway. As soon as you got outside, the noise stopped. When I asked if you saw anything, you said that whatever was out there was gone. I asked you if we were fine, and you said yes. I asked you if you were sure, and you assured me we were fine."

"Okaaay," I said, searching for something to say; however, I had no defense because that was me—indubitably. "So, what happened in your dream, Nate?"

"Mine's worse," he said, his tone a bit peppery. One thing with Nathan was he was fairly quiet, but if he got extremely upset (on rare an occasion), he could be a stick of dynamite. "In my dream, I was in my room, and I heard a tapping at the window—"

"Hold up!" I held up my hand, forgetting he could not see me. "How is that? Your room is on the second floor."

"I know—right? It freaked me out . . . so, I walked over to the window, and the curtains were moving as if the windows were open. The night was pitch black and although I did not see the being, I could feel it. It started talking to me in a language I could not understand, so I came and got you. You went into my room, and I stayed in yours. When you came back, you told me that the being said I needed to make a choice. When I asked you what kind of choice, you said it didn't specify. When I asked you if I should be worried, you told me you didn't think so. You assured me that angels did things like that— delivered cryptic messages and stuff. I asked—"

"That's so weird. I can't believe I said that."

"Yeah, but you did."

I furrowed my brows. "Why would I do that, though? That thing was evil."

"You know that? How?" Nathan asked incredulously.

I really was not in the mood to explain that while he was talking, I was seeing the entire thing play out and hearing everything the entity was saying. I shrugged. "It's hard to explain, but I do. The question is—why would I downplay that? I don't understand."

"When I asked if you were sure it was an angel, you said it could be, so I went back to my room. As soon as I stepped inside, the curtains flew out and wrapped around both my wrists. Then, the being said, 'You must choose between here and there.'"

I cringed at the image of Nathan standing with his arms splayed, completely trapped. "Oh, my God!"

"*Yeah.* I didn't think twice. I immediately told it I was choosing to stay here. As soon as I made my choice, the curtains let go all of a sudden, and the being left."

"Oh, Lord. That's crazy," I said, shaking my head. "What would have happened if you had made the wrong choice . . . and all because of me? That would have been so bad." I instantly started conjuring up the worst-case scenario.

"Yes, Mom," Christine jumped in. "It would have been a disaster. That's why we have to talk to you. These dreams are warnings for you. You *need* to change the way you handle situations, or we are *all* going to pay for it."

"Chrissy's right, Mom. You are stubborn," Nathan said, his tone spiced with a little bit more ire than I deemed reasonable. "Sometimes you don't listen to us about spiritual things. It's like you think you're always right, or you don't think that what we get from God in our dreams and stuff is as important as what you get."

My heart hurt from the knife stab. "Nate, I don't think that at all. I know that I can be stubborn. I can totally see myself doing what I did in Chrissy's dream, but I'm not dismissive. I promise you I pay attention to everything you guys tell me—every single thing—even though I might not make it obvious. Sometimes I don't address stuff right away because I, myself, don't understand, and I honestly don't know what to tell you." I sighed. "Bottomline is, I don't know how to process some of the things you get. That's why I tell you that we should wait and see sometimes—not because I don't think they are relevant or important."

"I know you think that, Mom, but you do dismiss us more than you realize, and you don't make it clear sometimes whether what you're telling us is what you get from God or what *you* are thinking," he said.

"Yes, I do," I said, quite briny.

"No, you don't—not always," Christine chimed in, her tone alerting me that her dukes were up. "Mom, sometimes you speculate regarding what things mean instead of simply saying you don't know. Plus, you're not forthcoming with everything you get because you think you're protecting us although we keep telling you you don't have to do that. Look at what happened in Nate's dream. You confused him."

"But he was able to make the right decision with God's help. His is the voice you guys should depend on—not mine. I'm not sure why I intentionally misled Nate in the dream, but that's something I would *never* do in real life. These are only dreams, guys. Why are you so upset?"

"This is what you do," she said tersely. "Every time we come to you about things you need to work on, you immediately go on the defensive and try to shut the conversation down quickly, so we go away. You don't take criticism well, Mom."

I sputtered and harrumphed but could say nothing.

"It's true, Mom. You don't," Nate said, joining in the horn-locking.

Seriously? I screamed in my head. *Is this a flipping intervention?* "Look," I said slowly—a feeble endeavor to carefully measure my words—"this is some *hogwash*! I listen to you guys—your dreams, your messages, your questions, your feelings—but I don't have all the answers. I can't do better than my best. I don't know what you guys want from me. The thing is that I muse out loud—it's what I do. I usually say maybe something means this or maybe it means that. Maybe sometimes I don't, but if that's the case, I don't even realize it. I'm sorry if I've confused you at times. I've said it already, and I'm not going to keep on it like some broken record. So, listen up." My tone was razor sharp. "I know I can be a little stubborn, which I'm working on, but I would *never* intentionally deceive you. I cannot even believe this garbage."

"Mom, you are taking this all wrong. Why are you mad? All we are saying is that you need to make it clear when it's you just thinking out loud," Nathan said, toning down the bite he earlier had in his voice. "We're not attacking you."

"Exactly! When it comes to spiritual stuff, you need to forget that we're your kids and remember that we are all the same," Christine chided.

Miffed, I promised gruffly, "Fine, I'll try to remember."

Now would have been a good time to turn the conversation away from the negative aspect of Nathan's dream to focus on its finer point. I had interpreted an unknown tongue—and one of a supernatural being, at that.

And it was not that my spirit was not willing.

But, oh, my wicked, wicked flesh.

* * *

When I let Annalise in that Saturday, I followed her into the kitchen, so excited to share my news about the interpretation of tongues confirmation that I was about ready to burst. However, before I could open my mouth, she said, "Teacher, I had a dream dat I saw Jesus last night."

I stopped dead in my tracks, my mouth dropping open. "What? Really? You saw Jesus in a dream?" There was no hope for it now—a Jesus sighting definitely trumping the gift of interpretation of tongues. "Ah lie!"

"Yes, teacher. Mi dream that I was lying in bed when mi si a movement out the window. Mi get up to check it out, and mi si Jesus with him arms around mi house. When mi si him, mi start to shout,

"Jesus is real! Jesus is coming soon! Jesus is real! Jesus is coming soon! Over and over again—at the top of mi lungs."

I smiled to myself and thought, *Jeshua, yuh not easy enuh. You had Annalise confess the very thing she was denying with her very own mouth! And not only that—she was declaring it for all to hear. This is good—really*, really *good.*

"But when I woke up, I wasn't sure that it was really him mi si."

I frowned. "Why not? You recognized Him in the dream. Suh, why doubt it once yuh wake up?"

"Teacher, mi just not sure."

"What did He look like?"

A warm fuzzy feeling spread through me as I listened intently to the details Annalise gave. "That *was* Jesus," I said, my voice tremoring with awe and my face splitting into a huge grin.

"What yuh think di dream means?"

"Well for one, the fact that Jesus was hugging your house is beyond cool. He is definitely with you and your household. It doesn't get any better than that. But I think this is more about Revelation. This is about what you said regarding whether the things in Revelation are true, especially as it pertains to Jesus coming back. It's pretty funny—not in a ha-ha kinda way—that *you*, who doubted, were the one confessing it to others. I can't get over how God works."

"I know this guy who, for years, has been saying that he would love to see Jesus, and he has never seen Him."

I shrugged. "Well, that's the way it is. Jesus shows himself only to whomever He chooses."

As we talked some more, I could not help but marvel at the great lengths God goes to in order to ensure people have access to the truth, even if it means putting in an appearance. When it was time to eat, I was not hungry in the slightest.

And my belly remained full the entire day.

Fine Wine

Your eyes saw my unformed body;
All the days ordained for me were written in your book
Before one of them came to be.

Psalm 139:16 (NIV)

lmost a week later, *I dreamed that I was walking outside on a clear day. I was unaware of where I was headed, yet I walked with a sense of purpose. Suddenly, a giant bookshelf lowered from the heavens and hung, suspended in midair, a few feet from me. Startled, I pulled up short, dazed by its magnificent etherealness. Not constructed from any discernable material, it shimmied in a there-yet-not-quite-there kind of way. Countless books rested on its shelves, each book having a spot of its own. I started slowly approaching it, mouth agape, when I saw a flash of movement out of the corner of my eye.*

The devil dashed ahead of me and grabbed a thick, brown leather book from one of the shelves. On its cover, which appeared old and worn, was written (in letters resembling Old English lettering) one word—Knowledge. The letters were raised and appeared to be formed from gold dust; however, the gold lacked luster and was a bit underwhelming to look at. Somehow, I knew that the devil had taken the one book meant for me, and I was not about to let him have it. Rage boiled up inside me, and I charged forward with no thought for my safety.

"Put it back!" I screamed, grabbing ahold of the book. "It's not yours."

However, the devil held fast. I yanked with all my might, but I was unable to budge the book. I leaned back until I was so far back, I was balancing solely on my heels. He began pulling, dragging me forward in the dirt.

"Stop!" I screamed. "You can't have it!" I did not recognize my own voice it was so shrill and piercing. Unfazed, the devil kept pulling, dragging me along. I tried to dig my heels into the dirt; however, it was no use.

My hands were beginning to grow tired, my arms feeling as though they were being stretched to capacity and would soon rip from their sockets. Nevertheless, I refused to give up. I squeezed even tighter until the burn in my fingers was so great, I might as well have been holding hot tar.

"Argh!" I groaned, my eyes burning with unshed tears. Sweat from my brow ran down into my eyes, stinging them further and making it near impossible to see, but still I held on.

After a while, my hands began slowly slipping, inch by agonizing inch. "Oh, God. No-no-no-no," I cried, as overwhelming desperation and fear welled up within me.

Groaning through my gritted my teeth, I muscled up, and held on even tighter. However, my hands kept slipping and were now almost off the book.

Unable to stick around for the devastating outcome, I opened my eyes. I was bathed in sweat from head to toe and felt chilled to the bones. I frowned, trying to process whether we were in the middle of an earthquake. It took a good few seconds for me to realize I was what was shaking.

"Oh, my God! What was that? Did the devil get the book? Jehovah, *please* tell me that the devil did not get the book." The pounding of my heart became so loud, I could hear it. I could not stand the thought that the devil might have gotten his hands on something he wasn't supposed to, and that it was my fault. "I'm totally confused. What was in that book anyway? Why was I getting a book called, *Knowledge*? Does it have anything to do with the information the demons in the closet claimed they came to get? Is it another gift? But I already get dreams about stuff that is to come, so does it mean I've had this book all along?"

All my questions went unanswered, causing intense frustration. How was I supposed to get on with my day having this huge thing looming over my head? Why was I seeing the devil in yet another dream? That he had shown up a third time was immensely disconcerting. All I wanted was to fly under the radar as I went about God's business, but evidently, that was unlikely.

"Jehovah, honestly . . . this is too much," I said, hauling my covers over my head.

* * *

The gate squeaked as it slid open.

Annalise.

I had been under the covers about twenty minutes, and I did not want to move. However, dragging myself out of bed, I clomped down the stairs to open the door.

"Morning, teacher."

"Hey. Wha' ah gwaan?"

"How yuh look suh?"

"I feel like garbage," I drawled, already turning away. "I'm going to go lie down."

"Okay."

I made a beeline for my bed while Annalise headed off to change into more comfortable clothing. I was not in bed two minutes when there came an insistent knock at the door.

"Mi can come?" Annalise called out.

"Yes. Di door's open."

She burst in, still in the clothes she had arrived in. "Teacher, mi just get a vision of yuh! You were downstairs writing something on di wall."

"Wait!" I said, jumping out of bed, garbage mood all but forgotten. "What wall? Show me."

Annalise led me to the room off the kitchen that I used for a classroom. "Yuh were in here"—she pointed to a spot near one of the desks—"and yuh were writing on this wall over here." She pointed to the widest wall, which had nothing stuck to it or hanging on it—a perfect canvas. "Yuh were writing with both hands."

I frowned. "At the same time?"

"Yes," she clarified.

My heart missed several beats. "Wow! That's crazy!" I had been naturally left-handed when I was little, but my mom had kept putting my pencils in my right hand until, after a while, she had retrained my brain. I had never told Annalise that.

Approaching the wall, she held up her hands. I watched with rapt attention as, like a maestro conducting an orchestra, she began gesticulating—moving her hands up, then down, and then swirling them around—starting from the middle of her chest and working her way outwards and away from her body.

"So, what was I writing?"

When she turned to face me, her eyes were open wide in wonderment. "That's the thing, teacher," she said, her tone matching her expression. "You were writing a lot of words and letters and symbols that I could not understand."

My blood ran cold. "What? That's insane! How? You didn't understand any of it?"

"Well," she said, her tone contemplative, "there was one thing I could make out clearly."

My heart sped up in sheer anticipation. "What was that?"

"*I Am.*"

"What?" I choked out, taking a giant step backwards. My voice sounded strange to me as though someone else had uttered the word.

"Teacher, all mi could mek out clearly were di words, *I Am*," she repeated—in case I was deaf.

I had to pick my mouth up off the floor. "Oh, my God! Do you know who *I Am* is?" She simply stared at me, her expression blank. "*I Am* is God!"

She raised her eyebrows. "Really?"

"Yes." I could scarcely speak.

"Wow," she said. "Teacher, mi nevah si anything like it. The—"

Jehovah, I thought, checking out, *what does this mean? Does this mean I got the book? Was that why I was writing weird stuff on the wall?* I sighed heavily at the silence. *Honestly, I wish you would give me a simple answer to a simple question. My heart seriously can*-not *take much more.*

* * *

That night, *I dreamed that I was waiting for an elevator along with several people. I was standing off to the side because I did not like people on top of me. One super tall guy, to the left of me, was annoying the garbage out of me because he was standing too close. I wanted to bolt, but instead, I took one baby step to the right in an attempt to be inconspicuous. He mimicked me.*

Miffed, I thought, Wah duh dis bredda? Just up underneath people armpit (*absurd because I was the one whose head reached him at his armpit*). *I took another baby step to my right, and so did he. Sucking my teeth, but without the sound effect—my mother taught me better than that—I took yet another baby step—an apparent waste of time because so did he. I scowled but stayed where I was this time.*

Just then, the elevator door opened, and a super tall, menacing man stalked off it. Moving towards the group of people across from me, he opened his mouth and gently blew. The man directly in front of him, held his neck before sliding to the floor, dead. Everybody gasped in unison; however, nobody moved. Like me, they were frozen in fear.

The elevator man turned to look first at me, then at the man flanking me. He opened his mouth and effortlessly blew. A needle-thin-dark-grey-metallic dart, about four inches long—it made no sense I could see—flew well over ten feet to hit my flanker in the chest. I gasped, my eyes glued to the dart. It did not pierce the man's shirt, but instead, remained suspended in thin air. In a split second, the outer layer began peeling back—curling like shaved chocolate—starting at the tip. It peeled gradually to reveal a razor-thin shaft underneath. Once the outer layer had stripped back completely, the shaft began disintegrating from the tip, becoming finely ground dust. This slowly continued—like fire burning along a piece of rope—until the head was undiscernible. The thin line of dust remained suspended in the air for a beat before sprinkling to the ground.

It was at that moment I realized what the men were and what was happening. I stood, poker-stiff, as the demon's eyes narrowed slightly at the angel before coming to rest on me. A strangled sound escaped my lips as his gaze, piercing and cold, met and held mine. The muscles around my heart squeezed tight, and a sharp pain spread throughout my chest. I desperately looked around, but everybody else was so preoccupied with the man, who had dropped dead, that no one was paying attention to me.

Oh, my God! *I thought.* He's here for me. *The tightening in my chest intensified, but as I was struggling to calm myself, it suddenly clicked that the demon could not lay a finger on me. If he could, he would have already done so. A calm settled in my spirit, and I relaxed a little. I saw on the demon's face the moment he knew that I knew he was a dud. His eyes darkened and the hate in them pierced me to my core. I shuddered but stood my ground. He spun around, in a fit of rage, on the group of people still standing there—because not one of them had had the good sense to run—and started rapidly spitting darts.*

As bodies began falling, the angel said, "Come." Turning, he pushed open a door behind us, I had not noticed, and led me into a stairwell and down some stairs. When we exited the building, he took my hand, and I started running. Funny, but the angel did not run at all, and somehow, he managed to remain ahead of me. As I ran, I kept looking over my shoulder, gasping when the demon exited the building and started walking in our direction.

"Do not keep looking back," the angel chided gently.

Hard, though it was, I obeyed, but not of my own accord. Every time I was tempted, he gave my hand a tiny squeeze. We kept going until we stopped in front of an imposing fortress with huge brick walls and iron gates. I gasped and turned to look at the angel. I had been here before—twice in other dreams.

"Go," he said, as I stood gawking.

I began turning my head round the other way, anxious to see if the demon was close. However, before I could look, the angel chided, "Do not look behind you. Go."

I did not want him to leave me. I turned back around to search his face quizzically. He did not have to say anything. I knew. Like the other angel who had led me here in one dream, he was not coming inside.

"Run," he said softly, but with an intensity that was palpable.

I faced forward and started running.

I opened my eyes and rolled them. "Seriously, Jehovah? *This* is a simple answer?"

* * *

The Boxing Day preparations were going well. I was genuinely excited, and it was not just about the party; it was about the people. I had almost finished finalizing the list, which included friends and family I had not seen in ages. I was especially excited about a cousin from England, my roommate from boarding school, and my older sister living in Jamaica but with whom I hardly spent much time anymore. I had a full house. Nathan, Christine, my sister who follows me, and my mom had already come from the U.S.; plus, Justin, Caleb's son, was there as well. I had rented a car for a few days because the preparations called for me to be on the road a lot, and having to call a taxi every few hours, simply would not do.

Annalise was coming over so we could go to the meat shop she had told me about, and I could not find my shades. At the very moment I stepped outside to search the car, Sugah walked by the gate.

He stopped, hailing me. "Morning, Mama G." He was all teeth.

"Hey, Sugah. Yuh good?"

"Mi *always* good, Mama G."

I smiled at his always-on positivity. "Good for you! Listen, I'm glad you're here. It saves me from having to call you later to invite you to Boxing Day dinner."

Sugar raised his eyebrows, but quickly relaxed his face, masking his surprise. "Sure, Mama G. Mi wi come. Want me to bring anything?"

I already knew I did not want him to bring anything, but I did not want him to know that. "Mmm . . . no," I said, after a contemplative pause. "I can't think of anything. But if I do, I'll let you know." I pointed a finger at him and narrowed my eyes. "Just don't tell me yuh coming, and yuh don't show up 'cause I know where yuh live."

He had a good belly laugh before he said, "Shame on you, Mama G, man. I wouldn't do that to yuh." His brows furrowed. "What happen to yuh car? Why yuh not driving it? Long time now mi see yuh taking taxi."

I hesitated because I did not like people in my business. However, he had never discussed anybody else's business with me, so figuring mine would also be safe with him, I said, "Logan took the keys."

Sugah scowled. "When yuh seh, 'tek di keys,' yuh mean *gone* with the keys?"

I could only nod because suddenly I felt like crying.

He dressed back and remained quiet for a few moments before he sucked his teeth, his countenance further darkening. "This is unbelievable. Mi nuh *like* men like dat. Suh, what if you or yuh son get sick in the night?"

I shrugged like I was indifferent, but my cheeks were flushed. "It is what it is. I keep praying that never happens. That's all I can do. I'm not going to worry about it or let Logan stress me out."

Frowning, he shook his head. "No, man. This not right. It doesn't matter that your husband done wid yuh. Him nuh know that if him spite you, him spiting him son? Mi nuh understand some men. Dem—" He suddenly stopped talking and, using the back of his hand, tapped my arm gently several times to ensure I didn't miss what he had to say next. "Mama G, hear me. Him going to come back. And when him come, he's going to ask for your forgiveness, and yuh must forgive him."

"What?" My voice was shrill, and I was gawking at him, bug-eyed.

Sugah took one look at the sheer shock on my face and interpreted it as dissent. His brow creased deeply. "*No*, man, Mama G. Yuh must forgive him, yuh hear?" His tone was firm, yet encouraging. When I said nothing, he dressed back a little and scrutinized my face. "Yuh wouldn't forgive him?"

"I-I—" was all I managed to say. I was shaking my head, but not in response to his question. I was having a somewhat hard time coming to grips with the fact that he had basically told me the same thing the woman in the doctor's surgery had.

"Yuh must *do* it, Mama G, man," he said, his tone coaxing. "And yuh see his parents"—he shook his head and scrunched his nose up in disgust—"dem a guh si who is God."

As he said that, *and they will know that I am the Lord*—a line from Ezekiel 12½—came to mind, and I shuddered. My teeth began chattering like a wind-up-denture toy. I ground them together and passed my palms repeatedly over my arms to warm myself.

"I can't even believe this," I whispered.

Sugah's brows creased slightly—a question on his face—but then he looked past me, his eyes lighting up, his seriousness morphing into playful mischief.

"Morning," I heard Annalise say.

Sugah looked her up and down. "Dear, yuh nuh si seh yuh shoes wah clean?"

Just as I was about to spin around, Annalise came up beside me, and the look on her face made me chuckle. Sugah was always teasing her that her shoes needed cleaning, and I did not have to look at them to know they were not dirty.

Annalise sucked her teeth. "Morning, teacher," she said, throwing a glance in my direction before pinning Sugah with a peppery glare. "Yuh can stay deh. Mi have things fi duh."

Sugah and I both started cackling.

Annalise stalked off towards the house. "Teacher, call mi when yuh ready," she called over her shoulder.

His eyes lighting up playfully, Sugah puckered his lips, gesturing with a jerky head motion in her direction, as if to say, 'look at her.'

I chortled and shook my head. "You two are something else. Anyway, I have to go. We're going into the town to do some shopping."

"Awright, Mama G. Si yuh Boxing Day."

"Yeah. See you." As I walked off, I felt a twinge of disappointment at not being able to continue our conversation because I had questions. Sugah and I had never discussed anything spiritual, and I wanted to know how he had come by the things he had said—although I already knew . . . but not exactly.

* * *

I steered with one hand and made a sweeping motion with the other. "This right here is what I hate about this town." We were inching forward in a long line of cars, going five miles per hour—and that was only every few minutes. If I would not have looked like a raving maniac, I would have started screaming. I gritted my teeth.

Annalise, who was used to the fact that I was not human before noon, chuckled. "What would you do if they hadn't made the street one-way?"

"I don't see where it makes any diff—" I slammed on my brakes to avoid hitting a man who had suddenly crossed in front of my car without so much as turning his head. "Oh, my God! These people!" I gripped the steering wheel tight and grumbled under my breath as no less than ten pedestrians followed him pee-pee-cluck-cluck like ducklings behind a duck. And not a one was in a hurry.

Annalise pointed. "Make a right over there, teacher."

A suck-teeth and eyeroll later, I was turning on a narrow, steep road sandwiched by two rows of haphazardly arranged commercial buildings. The only difference between it and the main road was having to dodge the piles of produce and haberdashery lining the streets. It seemed like wherever people found an empty spot, they squatted and set up shop—some on stubby-legged stools, some on buckets or baskets flipped on their heads. There were no parking spots to be found anywhere. However, I managed to secure one behind a plaza—and only after paying some man for it.

I made a sound of disgust in my throat as we approached the z-shaped queue extending and then curving out the door of the meat shop, which was *cotched* between two taller buildings. "Seriously? There's a line?" I exhaled heavily on a groan. *And Annalise had said we would miss the crowd. Ha!*

"It's not going to take long because dem work pretty fast." Annalise seemed unfazed, which was not surprising as she lived to shop. On top of that, she was a morning person. She was usually up in the mornings by the time I was crawling into bed.

Although I had on a sweater, I was cold. I rubbed my palms over my arms to try and generate some heat as I reluctantly fell in line beside Annalise. *They better work fast or else it's chicken for dinner*, I thought, ready to significantly shave the menu.

We were there, maybe five seconds, when I got a strong urging to go back to the car for my cell phone. I was tempted to stay put because

I was not married to my phone, but more so because I thought that, subconsciously, I was looking for any excuse to get out of the line. However, the urgent need to get my phone would not leave me.

"I'm going for my phone," I grumbled, walking off.

As I was about to cross the road, Analise called out, "Teacher, wait for me," stopping me in my tracks. "I'm coming for my sweater." I thought it a bit odd, as she was never cold, but I said nothing. "I don't know what happen, but I feel cold."

I wanted to suggest she hold our space in line as it did not make sense for both of us to go to the car. However, as badly as I did not want to once again find myself at the back of the queue, I kept my lips zipped.

In that short space of time, the parking lot was even more crowded with people looking for parking. Frustrated drivers were simply parking behind others and going about their business. It was a good thing we could see the car from the meat shop because I was not in the mood to walk from shop to shop asking who drove a certain make, model, or color car.

Just as I reached into the car for my phone, a loud commotion erupted. Dread gripped me because Christmastime seemed to give people free pass to temporarily lose their minds. The muscles in my back coiled as I glued my eyes to the road, poised to jump inside the car, needs be. I watched in absolute horror as a white delivery van flew downhill backwards—at breakneck speed—stopping only when it crashed into the concrete stump exactly where Annalise and I had just been standing.

We gave each other a do-you-see-what-I'm-seeing look as people shouted frantically, rushing the van. One man, I assumed to be the driver, yanked the driver's side door open and pulled up the emergency brake. My legs were shaking so violently I could not move even if I wanted to. Annalise stood frozen as well.

Eventually picking my mouth up off the ground, I said softly, "Oh, my God! We were just standing right there."

"Can you imagine, teacher? What if we nevah move?" Annalise, who was usually calm and collected, sounded rattled.

I could not tear my eyes away from the spot. "I don't even want to think about it. It's crazy how I couldn't shake the feeling I needed to get my phone."

"And I got cold all of a sudden. This is why yuh haffi listen to di Spirit," Annalise said, slamming her door shut. "Come, teacher. Let's guh get di meat."

Twenty minutes later, we left with nothing—no goat meat, no goat head or belly for the mannish water (goat soup), no fish, no pork, no beef, no shrimp. I could not be upset, however, because I had left with something far more valuable.

* * *

Not quite half an hour after we had gotten home, I heard a horn outside. One of Logan's friends was at the gate in a grey pickup truck. He and I did not really talk much, and our families never really hung out. However, we were friendly enough. He was a farmer and tended a field nearby. He usually travelled with a small group of workmen, but this group was markedly bigger. Because the bed of the truck was full of potatoes, the men were sitting all about, including on the ledge of the bed and on top of the tailgate.

Logan's friend and I exchanged pleasantries and inquired after each other's family. When I told him my mom was there, he got excited and insisted on saying hi as it had been umpteen years since he had last seen her. After he and my mom were done catching up, he handed me a black *scandal bag* filled with potatoes. I was not sure how plastic shopping bags, especially the black ones, came to be known as *scandal bags*, but that's what everybody called them.

My bad estimation skills aside, the bag felt at least thirty pounds heavy. I was extremely grateful because I had not bought potatoes for my salad, and the bag had more than I needed. My mind immediately went to who I could share them with. This was what I loved about island life. It was not unusual for me to get fruits and vegetables from other people's garden or get homemade dishes from family members or friends. And one thing I learned from my mom—you never return a container empty.

Before I could express my gratitude, a young man—who had escaped my notice because proper view of him was obscured by huge mounds of crocus bags—abruptly stood up from the floor of the truck bed and said to me, "Ah plenty more." His gaze was so intense, it creeped me out.

I frowned. "Pardon me."

"Ah plenty more."

My brows furrowed even more. "What?"

"Potato," he said with impatient insistence—like I should know what he meant, and I wished I did; however, I could only stare blankly at him. "Ah plenty more potato ah come." This triggered rounds of boisterous laughter and some taunting from the rest of the men—but acute awareness in me. My arms got goosebumpy, and a chill went up and down my back. The young man did not respond to the other men. Instead, his expression became wooden, and he sat down just as abruptly as he had gotten up.

Jeshua, what is this? I thought, shooting a startled look in my mother's direction, hoping to get her attention—only to find her already looking at me. I widened my eyes at her, and she raised her eyebrows at me. Everything was a blur after that, including the goodbye to Logan's friend.

As soon as the truck had pulled off and the men were no longer within earshot, I said, "Oh, my God! That was so freaky!"

"My God, that was odd!" my mother said at the same time.

"I know right?" I was still reeling from the shock.

"Do you know that young man?"

I shook my head. "Nope. Never blessed eyes on him in my life."

"Suh why would he stand up and say that—and only that—to you and then just sit down?"

"Don't you realize what this is, Mother?" I paused to calm myself a little because I felt ready to burst. "The potato dream!" Zero understanding registered on her face. "The dream where a grey pickup pulls up to the gate, and a man throws a sack of potatoes over the wall."

Her eyes widened. "Oh, yes! My goodness!"

"Isn't this crazy? The first thing I thought was that the guy was weird—mentally challenged even. He seemed so wooden, yet so passionate, even though there was no indication he understood what he was saying. What's so amazing is I shouldn't have been able to tie what he was saying to the dream based on how little he said. But somehow, I just knew."

"Well, however you got it, my dear, all I know is that God is good," my mother said, her voice full of wonder.

"Yup. I totally love the way God confirms things to me, but I don't think I'll ever get used to it." I picked up the *scandal bag* of potatoes and made for the house, my mother in tow.

As I walked towards the kitchen, a sense of foreboding welled up in me, and I pulled up short of the counter. "2020 is going to be a bad year," I said to no one in particular.

"Why yuh seh that, teacher?" Annalise asked, frowning.

An almost unbearable heaviness settled in my spirit, and I shook my head, fighting against it. "I don't know. I can't explain it. I just know that ah nuff people ah guh bawl innah 2020" (I just know that plenty people are going to bawl in 2020).

"Jesus, teacher!" Annalise said, her eyes wide. "Why?"

"I don't know why. Oh, my God—so many people—so much grief." I shivered. "I honestly don't know what it is. Maybe it's a natural disaster or something because it's *huge*. My God! It's going to be really, *really* bad."

The heaviness in my spirit settled in my belly as an innards-eating ache, an ache with which I was all too familiar—overwhelming grief.

Perpetuity

Being confident in this, that He who began a good work in you
Will carry it on to completion until the day of Christ Jesus.

Philippians 1:6 (NIV)

O n Boxing Day, I struggled to set aside the niggling feeling of doom and gloom that had taken up permanent residence in the pit of my belly. Once the dinner drew near, however, the feeling was ousted by excitement.

The menu was exactly as I had planned thanks to Annalise's mom and Abigail, who had both managed to source the meat I needed. Abigail had lent me a huge white tent, which I pitched at the entrance to the garage to create one big, cozy room. Justin had left a few hours before dinner started to go visit Constance and Eustace but had gotten back in time to help the kids set up the music and decorate the tent. More people showed up than I had anticipated because some of my guests had guests for the holidays and had brought them along. On any other day I might have felt overwhelmed, but the more the numbers increased, the more my excitement.

When I finally sat down to eat, it was with Annalise, her mom, and Sugah. I had chosen that seat with the expectation that the bantering between Sugah and Annalise would keep me entertained, and they certainly did not disappoint. I could not recall when I had last laughed that hard. As I looked around the tent and saw the good time being had by all, for the first time since Logan moved out, I felt something I thought had been lost to me forever—happiness.

After dinner, my mom left to spend a few days with her sister. A few of my guests slept over, but they were all gone by the next morning, except Annalise. She had slept over to help me clean up and was in no rush to go home because her kids were spending holiday on the coast.

* * *

The next day, about five minutes after getting up, I told Annalise I was going to lie down because overdoing it for Boxing Day was still telling on my body. It took me a while to fall asleep, and it seemed like as soon as I did, Annalise was knocking at the door.

"Yes?" I said gruffly, rolling over and folding my pillow over my ears.

"Teacher," Annalise called out again.

"Yes?" I said much louder.

"Teacher, yuh sleeping?"

I could not understand why she would not just open the door. "Coming!" I winced. It hurt to speak, and the light—pouring into the room through the thin curtains—was intent on pulling my eyes out of their sockets. I rolled out of bed, and the act of standing sent a jarring pain shooting across the left side of my head. Trying my best to look alive, I flung the door open. "Hey."

"Teacher, how yuh look like mi wake yuh up suh?"

"Because you did."

Annalise frowned. "Teacher, yuh nuh *just* open di window?"

Looking at her quizzically, I shook my head very carefully so as not to jostle my brain. "No."

"Don't seh dat . . . because if ah nuh you, ah who?"

One look at her face told me she was spooked, which in turn spooked me. "Annalise, I'm dead serious. I did *not* open a window.

222

How could I have, and you woke me up just a while ago? Which window did you hear?"

She pointed to a window it was my habit to open first thing after I got out of bed. "That one."

"Ah joke yuh mekking!" I walked over and yanked the curtain aside. "It's locked. Are you sure you heard it open?" I somehow knew her answer was going to be one I did not wish to hear.

"I'm sure," Annalise said firmly. "Di window is why I came off the phone. I was talking to Mommy, and when I heard di window slide, I told her I had to go because yuh wake up, and I needed to talk to yuh."

"No." I began shaking my head, not caring about my headache and whatever bit of sleepiness I had been clinging to. I made a mad dash to Nathan's room with Annalise at my heels. She waited outside while I tiptoed around the room, checking each window.

"All of them are closed, and Nate and Michael are fast asleep," I whispered, closing the door quietly behind me.

We checked Michael's room next, where Justin was fast asleep. No open windows there. I did not bother checking Christine's room because I could hear her snoring.

When we got back to my bedroom, Annalise said emphatically, "Teacher, mi know wah mi hear."

"Trust me, if you were anybody else, I would say maybe you imagined it. I believe you heard something." I frowned. "Wait, do you feel anything?"

Annalise did not hesitate. "No, I don't. Yuh feel anything?"

I shook my head. "No, I don't either, but I know something is not right." My head began to throb something fierce. "I can't deal with this right now. I'm going back to bed."

"Awright, teacher."

"Wake me when breakfast is ready, please," I called over my shoulder as Annalise closed the door.

* * *

Almost two hours later, I was still tossing and turning. I heard every utensil Annalise put in the sink, every pipe she turned on, every dish she picked up, every pot she stirred, every conversation she had, every door she opened—and closed.

"Urgh!" I flew up out of bed and went downstairs.

Annalise was putting the last of the ripe plantain in the frying pan. I asked no questions; I simply put the kettle on. We moved about in silence—plating food, pouring coffee, reheating food. Annalise had made fried pocket dumplings (dough rolled out on the counter and cut out with a cookie cutter, instead of traditionally palm rolled into a ball) and callaloo to go along with the plantains, which we were having with left over mac and cheese, potato salad, ham, roast beef, and fried fish. And as much as I wanted to enjoy my food, I could not.

"I can't let this go," I lamented. "I know you heard what you said you did, and it's driving me crazy because this could only mean one thing."

"That's *exactly* what I was thinking."

I scratched my head. "So, you still don't feel anything at all?"

"No, teacher."

"Me neither. That's so strange. At least one of us should be able to feel this spirit. This is new, and I don't like it one bit. Feeling it is usually bad and I hate that, but honestly, not feeling it and knowing it is there is so much worse."

Annalise nodded. "That's so true. This has never happened to me yet either."

"That's it. I've had enough of this." I pushed my stool back, held up my right hand and said forcefully, "Whatever in yah, wah nuh belong in yah, come out"—I swept my hand downwards—"*now!*"

A *crash* reverberated throughout the house.

I almost jumped out of my skin at what sounded like two large ceramic plates smashing together. I immediately looked at Annalise who was staring equally gape-mouthed at me.

I found my voice first. "Jesus! Annalise, ah wah dat?"

"A spirit just leave out, teacher. Pastor said sometimes when they're leaving, there's a loud sound." My mind immediately went to a dream that Christine had had in which cymbals had clashed when she had confronted a demon.

Nah, I thought, *this is crazy. It would be one thing if this were a dream, but . . .* Skin covered in tiny cold bumps, I walked over to where some dishes were drying on a rack, hoping that one of them had coincidentally fallen forward to smash against another at the exact moment I had spoken. However, even before I looked, I knew that, given the magnitude of the sound, that was impossible. I looked around for any other plausible explanation and found none.

Without saying a word to Annalise, I bolted for the stairs, taking them two at a time. I was almost at the top of the staircase when I was met by Nathan, Michael, and Justin.

"Mom, what did you break?" Michael asked, concern written all over his face.

I gawked at him. "Me? I came to ask what *you* guys broke." My gaze shifted to Nathan and Justin before coming to settle on Michael once again. "You guys didn't break anything?"

They all shook their heads to a chorus of *nos*.

"But y'all heard the sound—right?" I asked, conducting a saneness check.

They all nodded their heads to a chorus of *yesses*.

I held both hands out in front of me. "Okay," I said as I pumped the air. "Just making sure."

"Do you have any idea what that was?" Nathan said.

"I think I do, but I don't want to say anything until I'm sure. Don't worry, though, we will have an explanation soon enough."

"You're sure?" Nathan asked, his question reeking of skepticism.

"Yup. I am. Anyway"—I turned towards the staircase—"y'all can go back to sleep. I'll let you know when I have something for you." I shooed them. "Gwan! Go!"

The boys immediately complied, all except for Michael. "Maybe

Chrissy knocked something over. I'm gonna check," he said, adorably flashing me his pearly whites (rarely a good thing) as he took off in the direction of her bedroom. I charged after him, getting to the door in time to see him vigorously shaking her awake. She did not budge although her teeth were knocking together violently. Waking Christine was a feat as she slept sounder than a log. He shook her harder, yelling as though she were over in the next county. "*Chrisssy! Chrisssy!*"

"Mhmm," she groaned, batting at his hand. "Stop!"

Michael kept shaking her although she had responded to him, which he knew would serve to highly annoy her. I shook my head and smiled. "Chrissy, did you just break something?"

She plain bit his head off. "*Noooo!* How can I break something if I'm sleeping?" She batted at his hand again. "And quit shaking me."

Still rocking her, Michael yelled over his shoulder, "She didn't break anything, Mom."

I rolled my eyes. "Seriously? I heard her—on account of my standing right here." I scowled at him. "You need to stop."

Michael grinned and let her go. After I had closed the door softly behind him, he asked, "Still not going to tell me what's going on?"

"We'll talk later—okay?"

Satisfied for the moment, he nodded and headed back into Nathan's bedroom while I made a beeline for the kitchen to talk to Annalise. No sooner than I had pulled a stool out, Christine came into the kitchen. She muttered hi to Annalise and me, but her eyes and tone spoke volumes more.

"Teacher, mi cyaan believe what just happen," Annalise said pensively. "I knew I wasn't just imagining things." She shook her head. "Suppose you didn't say what yuh said? We would be here perplexed about di window all now."

"I know right!" I said, glancing over at Christine, who had suddenly stopped stirring her coffee and was now frowning at me. I narrowed my eyes and held her gaze. "But now I'm perplexed about the crashing sound. All the kids heard it, except Chrissy. She just woke up."

Christine's eyes screamed, *I need to talk to you—now,* as she picked up her mug and proceeded to breeze past us. I immediately excused myself and took off behind her.

"Hey," I called out as she was about to mount the staircase. She stopped and spun around. "Have something to tell me?" She nodded and continued up the stairs. I followed her into her bedroom and closed the door. "Talk to me."

She sat down and immediately began fiddling with her mug. "Mom, I had a weird dream." I waited for her to expound, but she simply kept fiddling.

"Okay," I said impatiently, taking a seat. "Go on." However, Christine was not to be hurried. She turned her mug this way and that, and even though it was killing me, I kept quiet and waited.

"I dreamt that a demon opened my bathroom window and came into my room," she said when she finally spoke.

I inhaled sharply, my skin feeling like it had been set upon by millions of microscopic crawlies. "Oh, my God! What! When? So, *that's* the sliding sound Annalise heard." I got up and started pacing. "I can't believe it—I mean, I can because this is my life—but still—I can't believe it!"

Christine frowned and tensed slightly. "I don't understand. What happened with Miss Annalise?"

I waved her on. "Forget about it. I'll explain later. Finish telling me your dream."

She set her mug down on the bedside table and did that funny thing she did with her lips when she was less than satisfied with something I had said. "Fine. So, when I saw him, I ran over to the window and opened it so that he could come out, but he slammed it shut on my fingers."

"What!" I sat down and grabbed her hands to examine them, turning them over several times. My reaction might have seemed a bit over the top to anyone watching. However, Christine had once woken up from a dream with her palm burned.

"My hand's fine mom." She gently tugged her hands away. "Anyway, after he slammed the window on my fingers, he started zipping all over the room. At first, all I wanted to do was get him out of here, but then I realized that he was the one I had seen before—the one that was none of my business—" She searched my face for the slightest flicker of understanding. "—the one I saw with dad when he was chasing you."

My face lit up. "Oh. Really?" But then it just as quickly fell. "I don't understand—how did it come to be here if, in your dream, it was attached to your dad somehow—and your dad hasn't been here?"

Christine shrugged. "Beats me. In the dream, I wasn't worried about how it came to be here. I just knew I did not have to be afraid of it because, while I could not trouble it, I knew it couldn't trouble me either. It wasn't here for me. So, I just sat back on my bed and watched as it zipped all over the room."

"Are you sure it was the same demon?"

"Yes . . . hard to forget because it was so strange. It was more like a shadow—I couldn't make out any of its features—and it was short—really short—just like the one chasing you with Dad."

My heart skipped a few beats, and my head swam a little. "Wait. You didn't tell me that one was short. How short?"

"I dunno—maybe just a little above my knee—or maybe half-way up my thigh."

My heart raced a little faster. "I think I've seen that demon in my dream—the one where the demon was zipping around in the church. It sounds too similar in looks and how it moves for this to be a coincidence."

"Mom, if that's the same one, that would be crazy."

"Would it? Anything's possible. We know that. Anyway, finish telling me the dream."

"There's not much more to tell. After like—forever, the demon just flung those windows open"—she pointed to the casement windows near her bed—"and left."

I gasped. "Just like that?" Christine nodded. "You didn't say anything?" She shook her head. My mouth fell open. "Oh my! That would be the crashing sound we all heard." She frowned. "The windows slamming against the wall would sound *exactly* like that." I knew I should fill her in, but something had suddenly occurred to me, and I shot up off the bed. "I have to talk to Justin."

I bolted from the room. I did not have to go far. Justin was just outside the door, sitting in the study. "Hey," I said. I was breathing fast, and the word sounded more like an exhale.

He looked up. "Hey."

"I need to ask you something really important. When you went up to your grandparents, was Logan there?"

"No," he said, shaking his head. "Why?"

I frowned. "That's weird. Were there other people there besides your grandparents?"

"Yeah, but not a lot."

"Did you touch anybody?"

Justin's expression became deeply contemplative. "No, not that I can remember."

"*Think*," I said desperately. "Think hard. Who might have touched you . . . shaken your hand, fist bumped you, hugged you . . . anything."

I discerned the moment realization hit him because his countenance changed from confusion to unadulterated horror. "This is about a demon, right? And it was able to come inside the house because of me."

"Yes," I confirmed brusquely, despite the fact that he had essentially answered his own question and did not need my help. "Who did you touch?"

"Only one person touched me—Uncle Logan's woman. She came over to me and gave me a hug."

My heart sank. "You've got to be kidding me!"

"Seriously?" Christine said at the same time, coming up behind me. When the other boys came flying out of Nathan's bedroom, it dawned on me that I must have come across more agitated than I had intended.

"I'm sorry Aunty Jaye." Justin sounded so remorseful I felt bad.

Lightening my tone, I said, "It's fine. You couldn't have known. You know how I feel about the other woman, but I can't tell you who to talk to. Am I happy about it? No—and I know you probably think this one hundred percent has to do with the fact that Logan left me for her. But—"

"No, I really don't," Justin interjected. "I know it's more than that."

"Good," I said, highly relieved. It would crush me if he thought me that petty. "Look, I don't understand any of this, but all will be revealed in time, I guess."

"I'm really sorry, Auntie Jaye."

"I know. It's fine. We're fine." I looked over my shoulder at Christine. "Go get the olive oil."

* * *

Around 9:30 the next night, my cell phone rang.

Sugah.

I tensed, immediately thinking that something must be wrong, because he had never called me that late. In my best *Cheery Mary* voice, I said, "Hey, Sugah."

"Hey, Mama G. Yuh awright?" Concern was heavy in his voice.

"Yeah, I'm fine. Why?"

"I just drove past yuh house. Di gate is open, and there's a yout' standing behind it."

"Oh, that's only Justin, Caleb's son. He's locking up for me. Yuh remember him? He was playing music Boxing Day."

"Oh, yes . . . Awright, Mama G. Just checking."

"Did yuh finish yuh food?" I asked, referring to the food Annalise had parcelled out for him on Boxing Day.

"How yuh mean, Mama G. Dat finish long time."

I chuckled. "I have your cake. I'll bring it up by the shop in the week—or you can come for it when you're ready."

"I'll come for it later in di week." He paused briefly before he teased, "Don't eat it though, enuh."

I burst out laughing. "Trust mi, I won't. My mother already warned me a million times to make sure yuh get your cake."

He chuckled. "Tell her thanks for me."

"I will."

"Awright, Mama G. Have a good night."

"You too, Sugah. And thanks for checking up on me."

"No, problem, Mama G."

* * *

Two days later, as my mom was dragging her suitcase through the front door, she called over her shoulder, "Don't forget Sugah's cake."

I laughed. "Seriously, Mother? How many times are you going to remind me?"

She pulled up short and pointed at me. "Look, mek sure that if nobody else nuh get cake, Sugah get cake."

I rolled my eyes. "Okay, Mother. For the umpteenth time, I'll make sure that if nobody else gets cake, Sugah gets cake." My mother had taken a shining to Sugah the instant she met him on Boxing Day. She had ensured that Annalise and I had sent him home with enough food to feed him and a small army.

As soon as the driver stepped out of the taxi, he asked, "Did you hear what happened to Sugah?"

My heart began thumping hard. "No, what happened to him?"

"Sugah didn't show up for work this morning, and when a couple co-workers went to check on him, he didn't answer the door. I passed the fire truck on my way here. Dem going to try and break down the door."

I gasped. "Oh, my God! Is he alive?"

"I don't know," the driver said solemnly.

I felt sick to my stomach. I hastily hugged my mom, Nathan, and Christine. "I'm going to go check to see if Sugah is okay. Call me when you guys get to the airport." I glanced over at Michael. "Lock the door, *boogsie*. I'll be right back."

"You're going dressed like that?" my mom hollered at me as I was going through the gate.

I looked down at my robe—thick enough to suit the harshest Alaskan winter—and rolled my eyes. "I have on clothes." I did not give her a chance at a retort. I waved at her and blew several kisses at the kids and set off.

"God, please. Don't let Sugah be dead," I whispered as I climbed the hill, but the closer I got to his house, the more suffocating the feeling of dread in my spirit.

Faces blurred and voices hummed as I approached the gate—all except Japheth's. He was staggering about and spouting garbage. I threw him a look that could curdle milk as I blew past him.

The moment I stepped into the yard, I saw myself get up from the chair in the printshop in my dream and walk over to the counter to pick up the funeral program lying there.

"Teacher," someone called out.

My breath stopped as the blurriness of the picture gradually began to clear.

"Teacher," someone called out again.

I kept my eyes glued to the program as the face came into focus. I gasped and looked up.

When my eyes locked with Enzo's, he shook his head, and I saw, rather than heard him say, "Sugah dead, teacher." His face crumpled as tears began streaming steadily down his face.

The Branches and the Vine

You did not choose me, but I chose you
And appointed you so that you might go and bear fruit—
Fruit that will last.

John 15:16 (NIV)

About two weeks later, *I dreamed that Annalise and I were sitting on a couch in Sugah's house. It was strange that I knew that because I had never been inside. We were sitting on a loveseat, and Sugah was sitting nearby on a small step-up. He was dressed in loose-fitting-white-linen trousers and a matching notched-neck-loose-fitting shirt with three-quarter sleeves. The extra-long-slim-brown cigarette he was smoking drew my interest because I had never seen a brown cigarette before. He treated it more like a spliff, though, holding it between the tips of his thumb and index fingers.*

The consummate spectator, he watched silently and intently as Annalise and I talked and laughed, his head going from one to the other, as one's head would in a tennis match. He occasionally shook his head and smiled at something one of us said, but he never joined in the conversation. All of a sudden, he got up and—without saying a word—began sauntering towards the front door.

"Sugah," I called after him, my tone desperate, "yuh leaving?"

He did not answer, nor did he turn around. He simply kept walking

233

as though I had not spoken. Pain squeezed my heart in its vice.

I pitched my voice louder. "Sugah, yuh leaving without saying goodbye?"

He did not hitch, answer, nor turn around.

My head felt like it had been replaced by an anvil, and my chest felt like I was breathing in bricks for air. With tears streaming down my face, I screamed, "Bye, Sugah! Bye Sugah! Sugah . . . bye!"

He did not answer, and in an instant, he was gone.

I sank down onto the couch, rested my head on Annalise's shoulder, and sobbed so hard I felt like my gut was being turned inside out. When I could finally speak, I groaned, "Annaliiise, I-I f-feel s-sick." No matter how hard I pulled air in, I could not pull hard enough. "Oh, my God. Annaliiise, I-I c-can't b-breathe."

"Yuh shouldn't have spoken to him, teacher. Why yuh talk to him?" she reprimanded gruffly.

"I just w-wanted to tell him g-goodbye."

"It doesn't matter the reason. You should not *have done that," she said with even more bite in her tone, brushing my excuse off as fiddling.*

When I opened my eyes, my pillowcase was wet. "I'm so tired, Jeshua"—I cried woefully—"tired of people dying around me—tired of not being able to do anything about it—tired of not getting to say goodbye."

I thought about Caleb, in that moment, and I buried my face in my pillow and bawled until my tears dried up.

* * *

A shadow hung over the new year. Besides Sugah's death, I was having back-to-back dreams of impending doom. In one dream, black birds were falling from the sky like rain. In another, I had to run out of my house with my kids because we had had an earthquake. In another, Nathan had ended up being held prisoner by a militant group—dubbed *Tribune*—that had taken over the whole country. In my attempt to rescue him, I had also been captured. To make matters worse, Kobe Bryant and his daughter died in a crash a few days after that, and millions mourned. As I watched the news coverage of the accident and the world's response, I was terrified out of my mind because I knew this grief and disbelief paled in comparison to the sorrow that was to come. Happily, the 7.7 magnitude earthquake Jamaica experienced, two days after that, had occurred at sea with no subsequent damage to the land. Neighboring islands, however, were not as fortunate.

Wherever I went, all the talk—the rest of the month of January—was of Sugah and the kind of person he was. Christine had said, on the day he died, that although she had met him once, there was something about him that had caused her to feel a profound sense of loss. That was the sentiment reverberating throughout the community.

I hated funerals, but I felt I had to go. Although I had three black dresses, I kept getting a strong urging to buy a purple dress, which I resisted until Annalise prodded me to give in to it. When I asked her if she had given any consideration to what she was going to wear, in true Apostolic style, she had settled on a black dress, purple belt, purple shoes, purple bag and purple hat.

* * *

I decided to wait until Annalise was at work to buy the dress because if Annalise knew nothing else, she knew what not to wear. As long as she was around, I was not allowed to leave the house without passing inspection. More often than not, she would scrunch up her nose, shake her head and say, "No, teacher. Yuh cyaan wear dat," and proceed to put together a different ensemble.

"Hey," I called out to Annalise as I came through the front door, holding up a large bag. "I got the dress . . . and another dress . . . and another dress . . . and a blouse . . . and a pair of heels."

She chuckled. "Nutting nuh wrong with that, teacher."

I smiled and rested the bag on the counter. "Yeah, well except for the bill. I reached into the bag. "Here's the dress for the funeral."

Annalise frowned. "But teacher, dat nuh purple."

"Well sue me for not knowing colors," I giggled. "That's why when I told the salesperson purple, she kept bringing me dresses closer to the color of your purse."

When Annalise asked where I had gotten the clothes and I told her, she said, "Then, that store nuh expensive?"

"Yes, it is. I paid through my teeth, but this is the only place in town I can shop without *me and di whole o' Jamaica* showing up to the funeral in the same dress."

Annalise laughed. "We definitely don't want that." She jerked her head towards the dress. "Mi like di gold pattern on it."

"Yeah, it's really pretty. Every time the salesperson brought the other dresses, I knew they weren't right. And then, I saw this hanging on the rack, and I knew it was the one. But it's driving me crazy not knowing what color it is." Grabbing my cell phone, I searched the internet. "Here it is." I showed her my screen. "It's called wine red."

"It's a really pretty color. Suh, guh try it on nuh."

I headed off to do something I hated. When I emerged from the powder room, Annalise's eyes lit up. "Turn around and let mi si." I spun a couple times. "Yes, teacher. *Dis* is di dress."

"Yes!" I said, doing a fist pump.

Annalise chuckled and then got serious. "Teacher, yuh know what I was thinking?" She paused contemplatively. "How God put people in our lives only for a season, and when di season up, dem have to go. Look how yuh brother-in-law used to look out for yuh and him dead. Sugah come along and start to look out for yuh, and now him dead. Before yuh mother leave, she said shi glad yuh have Sugah looking out for you. She said she feels better about yuh safety knowing he's just up di road. Now, where is Sugah?"

I sighed, "I know. I know we shouldn't take anybody's death hard because to everything there is a season and a time to *every* purpose under the sun, which means we all have an expiry date. But to just accept death like that? That's easier said than done."

"Teacher, wi not keeping *no* more Boxing Day dinner."

"Nope. Definitely not. Never again."

After a pregnant pause, we sighed simultaneously.

* * *

I was going to Sugah's wake alone. Annalise had refused to go although I had called her several times begging, so I was far from happy with her. I hated wakes. I had already instructed my kids that, when I died, they should chain up my gate and keep the lights off.

I had called Enzo to walk me to the wake. When he called to say he was going to be a little late because he was helping to cook, I did not mind at all. The rain had started spitting anyway, and if it continued, I would have a perfectly good excuse to call off. I used the opportunity to relentlessly pester Annalise into reconsidering, even shamelessly resorting to guilt tripping her, but I was the one who was left frustrated in the end.

Enzo came to escort me around nine-thirty. Truthfully, I could have walked myself there because the moon was brighter than stadium bulbs. However, I felt safer with company. When we started off, neither of us knew what to say, so to lessen the awkwardness, I began telling him about the dream I had had of Sugah.

He gasped and jerked to a stop, regarding me warily. "How yuh know Sugah smoke?"

I frowned. "What?"

"How yuh know Sugah smoke?" he asked again, his tone insistent.

I appreciated neither the look nor the tone. I shrugged. "I didn't until I saw him smoking in my dream."

The look of incredulity on his face told me he was not buying a word I was saying. "Yuh sure? Because yuh even know the kind of cigarette him smoke. Him nuh smoke regular cigarettes. Di ones him smoke expensive."

"I *honestly* had no idea he smoked until I saw him smoking in my dream," I said defensively. "And even then, I wasn't sure. You're the one confirming that for me now." My brows creased deeply. "How yuh acting like *nobody* knows that Sugah smokes?"

"That's because *nobody* nuh know seh him smoke." Enzo was not doing a good job of hiding how freaked out he was, but I could tell by the look in his eyes that there had been a shift in the way he saw me, and I did not like it one bit. "Not even him wife."

"What?" It was my turn to be creeped out. "That's crazy! I don't believe that."

"Well, believe it, teacher. Sugah hide his smoking from *everybody,* including him wife. I can't believe yuh find dat out in a dream."

"I know. Me neither . . . well, actually I can . . . story of my life."

"Really?"

I nodded and flashed my hand dramatically. "Long, long story."

A tiny smile touched the corner of his lips. "Dat kinda cool, still."

Relieved, but eager to change the subject, I asked, "Suh, you guys finish cooking?" We had reached the gate. I was so caught up in our conversation I had not even realized we had started walking again.

"No, but the mannish water's almost ready."

"Okay." I scanned the crowd. "Well, I'm not staying longer than an hour." I pointed to a spot on a wall, next to absolutely no one. "I'll be over there."

"Just let me know when you're ready to go home, teacher."

"Thanks, Enzo."

Wishing invisibility was a superpower I possessed, I reluctantly sat. I felt bad for having told Enzo my dream and perpetuating the belief that having someone 'dream you' was a good thing. I fidgeted and glanced around me nervously. It was going to be a brutal sixty minutes.

* * *

Holding out a tray of soup-filled-foam cups, Enzo interrupted my musing. "Would you like one, teacher?"

He was only the second person to talk to me in the thirty minutes I had been sitting there. The other was a guy, who must have had a few fingers of white rum in him, had asked if I lived nearby because he was cold and had forgotten to take a jacket. I had told him that it mattered not where I lived as I had no extra sweaters laying around to lend him. He had promptly proceeded to ask if he could get the one I was wearing—and had actually stood waiting for it.

I smiled and wrapped my hands around a cup, instantly warming my fingers. "Thanks, Enzo."

"You're welcome, teacher." He held up the tray to a few people who were reaching for soup as they walked by. "Remember, come get me when yuh ready. I'm busy, so I'm not watching di time."

"Okay," I called after him before turning my attention to the steam dancing out of the cup. Suddenly, the soup began to vibrate, as did the rest of my body. The DJ had arrived. Before my ears could start bleeding, I looked around for somewhere else to go. I spotted a couple, who lived one house up from me, standing under a tent towards the back of the yard. I waved at them, and when they acknowledged me, I immediately got up to join them.

We were there about fifteen minutes when I felt a sharp blow to the side of my head. A hot-white-numbing pain radiated from the area before I started seeing *mini-mini*. Tiny spots danced around, blurring my vision so much, I could see nothing else. Reflexively, I reached up to cradle my head, but had to drop my hand instantly as the spot was excruciatingly tender. People started gathering around, and someone led me to a chair.

"Yuh okay, teacher?" Enzo asked.

I was relieved to hear his voice. "No, not really." I gingerly peeled back layers of hair. "Can you check to see if it's bleeding?"

"It not bleeding, but it swelling up. I'm going to get some ice." There was something about his tone that was like salve.

"Oh, my God, how it just come loose suh?" one bystander asked.

"Shi lucky. It coulda kill her," another commented.

"Pfft. It nuh dat bad," a woman scoffed, apparently highly offended I had managed to make the night about me.

By this time, Enzo had returned with some ice cubes wrapped in paper towel. "Here, teacher." When the makeshift icepack was snug against my scalp, he handed me a bottle of orange soda. "Drink dis."

Giving someone something sweet to drink was a thing Jamaican people did whenever someone got a blow to the head. I never could quite figure if it served a medical purpose, but when I was little, I surely did enjoy being put into a sugar-coma.

"What hit me?" I asked Enzo between sips.

"A piece of bamboo dat was holding up di tent."

The wind had been blowing hard, and the tent had been wildly flapping about, but it never occurred to me that I would not be safe. With the force at which the wind had propelled the bamboo, I could have been killed. "Did anybody else get hit?"

"No. That's what everybody wondering. Dem wondering how you get hit and the other two people beside yuh nuh get a scratch, especially since you were standing in the middle."

I blanched. "I want to go home." I said softly, just for Enzo's ears. It was bad enough I had become the center of attention. The last thing I wanted was to further make a spectacle of myself by throwing up on Enzo's shoes.

"Okay, teacher," he said, helping me to my feet.

As he saw me home, the thought did occur to me that if I had any common sense at all, I would have taken myself off to a hospital.

* * *

The following morning, I dragged. I had not slept at all because sleeping after a big blow to the head was a no-no—knowledge I had picked up from watching a slew of medical dramas, and which I at least had had the good sense to utilize. I had promised Annalise I would come to the church early so that we could get a good seat for Sugah's service. At this rate, however, I probably would not make it there for the last amen.

My cell phone rang. I groaned as my head throbbed, and for a split second, I contemplated not answering, but I knew Annalise. She was relentless. "Hey," I said, my tone dry.

"Teacher, weh yuh deh? Sugah body reach."

Why was she being such a *Cheery Mary*? I did not want to go to the funeral, and worse yet, I did not want to view Sugah's body. "Really? Suh early? I'm still home."

"Seriously, teacher? Yuh said you were coming early," Annalise said incredulously.

"I know. I'm getting ready."

"*Cho*, teacher, hurry up and come. Yuh have to come look on Sugah."

"No, I don't," I groaned. "I told you already. I'm *not* looking at him."

"Teacher, you're going to want to look at Sugah."

"I doubt that."

"Teacher, just hurry and come," she said impatiently, ringing off.

I picked up speed a bit because, as horrible as I was feeling, I was feeling equally curious. I only hoped that when I got there, I could convince Annalise to tell, instead of show me, whatever she thought was so important.

As I pulled up to the church, Annalise rushed out to meet me. She opened my door. "Lawd, teacher. Yuh tek suh long to come. Come look at Sugah."

I shook my head. "Nah. Don't make me look at Sugah, Annalise. I *really* don't want to see him."

"Come. You need to see what he's wearing."

"What?" I perked up. "You're killing me to go look at him because of his outfit?" I shrugged. "Okay. But I'm not looking at his face."

She chuckled. "Yuh nuh have to look at his face, teacher."

I kept hanging back as we made our way inside and up to the front of the church. The closer we got to the casket, the more I felt like bolting. It helped when I fixed my eyes on one of the brass handles.

As Sugah's body came into proper focus, I gasped and turned to look at Annalise. She said nothing but gave me a what-did-I-tell-you look. He was wearing a wine-red-plain-long-sleeved shirt—the exact shade as my dress—and a purple tie, the exact shade as Annalise's hat, purse, belt, and shoes.

"Oh, my God. This is so insane," I leaned in and whispered to Annalise as we made our way to our seats. It was a good thing she had come early enough to put her stuff on a bench to save us seats because the church was already full.

"Yuh think that's crazy," she whispered back. "Look at what his family is wearing."

As I panned the hall, I stopped dead in my tracks.

All of Sugah's family members were wearing royal blue.

* * *

In the wee hours, one February morning, two angels came to me in a dream. I was standing in front of my garage, slightly off to one side. The Messenger, who was facing forward and standing at attention, did not acknowledge me at all, which gutted me although I knew this to be the protocol. I was looking for reassurance he was not mad at me, which was silly as he could not hold a grudge.

"Stay with her while I take a look around," The Protector said, walking off. After only a couple steps, he stopped abruptly and looked over his shoulder at The Messenger. "Do not take your eyes off her for a second." His tone made my insides slushy and my blood run cold. Without looking at him, The Messenger gave a slight nod, which I might have missed had I not been paying such keen attention.

I knew it was futile to question The Messenger with the Protector around, so I did not even try. However, as time passed, I began to grow uncomfortable in the stagnant silence, shifting from one foot to the other, willing The Protector to return. After a few more agonizing moments, I caught a movement out of the corner of my eye and turned, relieved to see him approaching. My hopes of being cued in were dashed, however, when he did not look at or address me.

"Check outside the gates," he called to The Messenger, who simply nodded and immediately moved to obey.

The Protector flanked me as the Messenger went up the street. As he passed by the gate, going in the opposite direction, The Protector turned to me and said softly, but firmly, "Go inside."

For some reason, the thought of going inside my house terrified me, but I did not argue. Instead, I stood board stiff and silent. I had a bad habit of arguing with him, but I was not going to make that mistake again, given the thin ice I was probably skating on with God where these angels were concerned.

"Go inside," he repeated a little louder and a bit firmer.

I started walking but not in the direction of my front door. As I hurried along the walkway at the side of the house, I called over my shoulder, "Do you drink smoothies? Because I could make you a smoothie. I have some bananas over here." Slowing only a little, I tore some ripe bananas off a bunch hanging low on a tree and kept walking. "I have some lemons over there." I pointed to the other side of the house.

Before I could round the corner, the angel blocked my way. "Go. In. Side," he ordered, the hard set of his jaw and his piercing eyes warning me he was not to be trifled with.

I immediately turned around. As I got to the garage, The Messenger was making his way back to the gate. Not at all happy, I placed my hand on the doorknob and opened my eyes.

* * *

Two weeks later, the United States, along with most of the rest of the world, was on lockdown. I was in Florida visiting my parents, and as the images of the dead came out of Europe, the bawling I had talked about only months before made sense; the incredible loss and grief I had felt also made sense. However, there had been no preparing for the magnitude of it all. Eventually, I had to stop watching the news to preserve my sanity.

By the time countries began opening their borders months later, I was ready to go home, but I had had to go to the emergency room and was in no condition to travel. Annalise, who was holding down the fort, called one Saturday to say that she could not reach Enzo, so she had asked someone else to cut the grass. I knew the landscaper, but not to talk to, so she wanted to know if I was okay with him. I told her I did not mind so long as the grass got cut.

About five minutes into our conversation Annalise said, "Teacher, I have to go. The man outside keeping church."

"What?"

"I'll call you back," she said, ringing off in a hurry.

I tried to distract myself by hanging out in the kitchen with my mom. However, after ten minutes, I had had it. I called Annalise. "Hey, what's going on?"

"The landscaper seh he's the one who had to come here today—*nobody* else—because you have to know that you are in danger. He says he's seeing everything that is going on here. He says he sees demons, one posted at each corner of the house."

My face blanched. "What?"

"And he's seeing who sent them. He says it's a woman."

My heart was in my mouth. "Oh, my God!"

"He keeps asking her what she's doing and telling her it's not right. He keeps telling her that she needs to stop what she's doing, repent, and seek God."

"Oh, my God!" was all I could manage to say.

"Not only that teacher. Mi si dem too, but he warned me to leave them alone."

"What? So, did *he* do anything about them?"

"No, him nuh trouble dem. He's only concerning himself with di woman."

"This is crazy," I began, but before I could add anything else, Annalise interrupted.

"Teacher, mi going back outside. I'll call yuh when I get home."

"Wait! What form did the demons take?"

"Frogs."

I frowned. "I've never heard of that. That's so weird."

"They can take any form, teacher. Anyway, mi going outside."

I had so many questions, but I backed off. "Okay. Fine."

I paced about a little after she hung up. "God, this is crazy. Somebody's trying to harm me? But who? Why would anybody do this? Who could be this wicked? I know what Annalise said she saw— but frogs, Jehovah? I'm finding that a bit hard to swallow."

Revelation 16, God said, instead of telling me to pick up and open my Bible, and I could understand why because I was nowhere near it.

I immediately searched for and found the passage on my tablet and began reading. When I got to verse 13, my mouth fell open. It read: "Then I saw three impure spirits that looked like frogs; they came out of the mouth of the dragon, out of the mouth of the beast and out of the mouth of the false prophet" (NIV).

"Okay, then," I said. "So, Jehovah . . . of all the questions I asked, *this* is the only one you're answering?

* * *

That night, demons haunted my sleep. *I was trapped inside my house when weird things began happening. Doors were opening and closing, seemingly on their own. Pieces of furniture were being moved around by no one I could see. I would go to pick up an object and it would slide or roll away from me. No matter what I said or how much I rebuked, they would not leave me alone.*

When I woke up, I was mortified. "God, what am I going to do? Nothing I said worked. They just kept coming, no matter what I said. Why does this always happen to me? Why do I always feel so powerless?"

I sat up so that I could breathe better, but it did not help. My skin felt like I was cooking from the inside out, and my heart was racing profusely. I rushed to the bathroom and splashed cold water on my face.

"God, I don't know what to do. What do I do? Please tell me what to do. I go home in a week."

His reply was succinct. *Fire.*

Immediately, I was shown an aerial view of my house and the four beasts, one at each corner.

"Okay." I timidly raised my right hand, and as I brought it down, I whispered, "Fire."

My mouth hit the floor when a ball of fire, the size of a boulder, fell from Heaven and consumed the first beast. With newfound confidence, I did the same with the second and third beasts, and by the time I got to the fourth, I had acquired a bit of flair.

I was super pumped, but before I could start rejoicing, God said, *Call a legion.*

"What? Why? There were only four," I began arguing before I caught myself and did as He asked. I watched for the legion of angels but could see nothing. My heart sank a little, but God reminded me of a conversation we had had about Elijah, and the fire he had called from Heaven. He reminded me of the promise He had made that I would be able to do the same.

I grinned from ear to ear and thought, *Oh, my God! I called down fire from Heaven? Just like You said I would? Me? A nobody? I've wanted to do that since I was little! Jehovah, what is my life? The craziest things happen to me.* I held up my hands. *I'm not complaining—I'm just saying.*

The Sum of Everything

Although I had had that amazing fire experience, I continued to be bothered by a lot. I did not like unanswered questions and found it difficult to move on from those. The two encounters that kept me awake at night, taxing my brain and troubling my spirit were the dream with the two demons I could not get rid of and the holiday encounter with the demon neither Annalise nor I could sense.

One day, when I absolutely felt I might lose my mind, I went to God. "I know it's everything in your time, but I'm going crazy. I can't stand it anymore. I *need* answers. Who can I call?"

Mark, He said.

I *so* was not expecting that. "What? Really? I can call Markie? Just like that? That was easy."

Mark Bartell was someone I knew for over twenty years, but we did not talk often, and although I was comfortable with him, I would not have called him about this on my own. Not sure why. Maybe it was the nature of the issue. He and Pastor James had two distinct counselling styles. Pastor James was who I went to for a firm kick in the behind, and Pastor Bartell was who I went to for a gentle shoulder. I was not surprised God was leading me to Markie because of where I was emotionally.

"Hi, my pastor and friend," I called out my usual greeting gleefully into the phone.

"Hi, my sister and friend," he replied, using his usual response.

We both chuckled.

We talked for a little while, touching on various issues before I got to the crux of my matter. "I needed to talk to someone, and when I asked God who, He sent me to you."

"Okay," he said in that calm baritone of his.

"So, I'm really calling about a dream that I had." I proceeded to tell him the dream and then added, "Nothing I said worked—no 'blood o' Jesus'—no 'in the name of Jesus'—nothing. Do you know like when you watch a vampire movie and people are holding up garlic, or a wooden cross, or splashing holy water, and the vampire is all like, 'where yuh going with dat?'"

He busted out laughing.

And I laughed right along with him, but then, got serious. "And yuh know the thing that has been bothering me the most about all of it? God said that my faith is not strong enough."

"So, let me ask you something." I pictured him sitting forward with both his hands cradled under his chin, one on top of the other. "Why do you say those particular words?"

"Umm . . . come to think of it, I don't know." I was stumped for a few solid moments. I had never thought about it before. "I guess I use them because it's what I've heard other people say." I scratched my head. "Come to think of it, I'm basically repeating what I've heard other people say." As the words tumbled from my lips, I felt rather silly.

"That's the thing enuh. We need to remember what the Word of God says—that the same Spirit, that raised Jesus from the dead, lives inside of us. Think about how *powerful* that Spirit is." He paused a little to allow me to do that. "That is the *same* Spirit we have inside of us.

Do you *know* what that means?" There was such passion and fire in his voice, it gave me the chills. "It means we can do *amazing* things through the power of that Spirit."

"Wow!" I said, my voice filled with awe. "I totally get it."

I could not believe the answer was so simple, and yet it had evaded me all this time. We chatted a little while longer, and by the time we hung up, I was grinning like a pleased puss.

* * *

Quite some time after that and while I was in Florida, *I dreamed I let myself into my sister's son's house. I had no idea where I was going because I had never been inside Dre's house before, so I walked around until I stumbled on him cleaning out a hallway closet. He was so focused on his task that he did not hear me come up behind him.*

"Hey," I called out.

He threw a quick glance over his shoulder and casually said, "Hey," before immediately returning to the task at hand. He was filling bag upon garbage bag with the contents of the hall closet.

I noticed a nursery straight ahead of me and walked past him to stand just outside the door. The room was empty, except for a rocking chair and a crib. The chair was at the foot of the crib, oddly facing the crib instead of facing outwards. The crib was stripped and bare—no toys, no bedding, no bumpers pads.

I shivered. There was an ominous force inside the room that I could feel but not see. "Dre," I said, turning around to face him, "something doesn't feel right. Do you feel it?" My tone was panicked—urgent.

"No." He was so hyper-focused on his task that he had not even looked up.

I frowned. How can he not feel that? I wondered. The energy was so overwhelming it was stifling. "You don't feel that?" I asked incredulously.

"No." Again, he did not bother to look at me.

Giving up, I turned back around to face the nursery. The hairs on the back of my neck prickled as the rocking chair started rocking. "Oh, my God! How is that?" I looked over my shoulder. "Dre, come look at this. The rocking chair is rocking by itself!"

He got up immediately, but by the time I faced forward, the chair had stopped moving. He came to stand silently beside me, but when nothing happened after a few seconds, he turned to move off.

"Wait!" I cried desperately. As soon as I said that, the chair started rocking again. "See that? I told you. Something is wrong."

Dre threw me a blank look—as though I were speaking a foreign tongue—and headed back to the closet to continue cleaning. Frustrated, I wanted to shake him and scream at him, but there was no point. Fear made me want to leave because this force was bigger than I was, but desperation made me stay. This was Dre's family.

I stepped into the nursery and held my hands out in front of me— right hand, palm up and left hand, palm down—like I was holding a ball. No sooner had I done that than a ball of pure white light—about the size of a coconut—with a bluish hue on the periphery, filled the space between my hands. The minute that happened the ominous force stepped up to me. I could feel it but still could not see it. The sheer power of it almost knocked me off my feet.

"I command you to leave!" I yelled.

The Force pushed hard against me, and I braced myself.

"I rebuke you in the name of Jesus Christ of Nazareth!" As I said that, I almost kicked myself. Those words didn't work, and I needed to remember that.

The Force pushed harder.

I stood my ground and pushed back. As I did that, the light in my hand grew bigger and glowed brighter. This goaded the Force into pushing back some more.

"Leave now!" I screamed frantically.

The Force pushed so hard I suddenly found myself back in my room (I could actually feel the sheets against my skin and hear myself screaming). I pushed back hard and found myself back inside the nursery.

"Leave!" I screamed.

The Force pushed hard, and once again, I found myself in my room. I pushed back harder until I was once again inside the nursery. I was getting increasingly mad as well as desperate because I was beginning to feel weak. My head felt light, my heartbeat was erratic, and my insides felt like scrambled eggs.

After being pushed out of the nursery several more times, I decided that instead of focusing on The Force, I would channel all my energy into the light between my hands. As I did that, the ball of light began to grow. As it grew bigger, The Force grew weaker, becoming unable to budge me.

When the light got big enough—about the size of a large beachball—I screamed, "You don't get to win. Leave! Now!"

I felt the moment the Force got sucked in by the light. I swung my hands hard to the left of my body and then swung hard to the right, releasing the ball of light as I did so. It flew out of the closed window, taking the dark force with it, and as it cleared the house, it grew until it exploded soundlessly, lighting up the entire sky.

The air in the nursery felt light. "Oh, my God! It's finally gone." I sagged, resting both palms on my knees. Looking up towards Heaven, I whispered, "Thank you," before calling out to my nephew, "Dre, feel that! It's gone!"

Without waiting for him to answer, I brushed by, anxious to check the rest of the house. When I was satisfied that all was well, I opened my eyes.

* * *

My entire body felt as though it had been tramped upon by a giant. Anxious to find out how Dre's wife and baby were doing, I tried to roll over to get my cell phone off the floor. However, I could not move. It took me all of fifteen minutes before I could scooch over on my back to the edge of the bed, but I still could not reach the phone. I could not turn onto my side either. I stretched with all my might, almost dislocating my shoulder, to pick up the phone. I messaged Dre, omitting the real reason I was asking after his family. When he said they were fine, I should have been relieved; however, I was not. I could not shake the niggling feeling in the pit of my stomach that all was not going to be well. They simply did not know it yet.

When I could finally move, I found my mom in the kitchen and told her the dream. "Are you going to call?" she asked, her face marred by worry.

I shook my head. "No, I messaged Dre already. I just have to hope and pray that everything will be okay."

"Maybe you should call and tell him to tell his wife to go to the doctor."

"No, I can't call."

"Not even to tell him to get the baby checked out?"

"No. What reason would I give her? And if I told her the truth, what would she tell the doctor—that she's calling because her husband's aunt had a dream? Besides, I really don't want to call and frighten anybody."

"I see. You're going to pray for them, though."

"Yes, but I get the feeling that whatever I was supposed to have done, I did it already in the dream."

"Okay. Well, we just have to wait and see—and hope for the best."

"Yup," I said, my heart heavy.

* * *

About a week later, Dre's baby was delivered seven-and-a-half weeks early, and his wife was in intensive care. Dre had not said what had gone wrong, and I had not pried. However, he assured me they would both be fine. Relieved, I asked him to keep me posted on their progress.

After we had said our goodbyes, I wondered if I would tell him about the dream someday. However, when it came to the things of God, I did not get to do simply because I could. I asked myself what purpose telling Dre would serve, and when I could not come up with one good reason, I decided to keep it.

A couple mornings after that, as I lay in bed waiting to thaw, I started up a conversation in hopes of getting answers because my mind was still blown.

"God, what was that spirit I was fighting at Dre's house?"

Death, He said.

I shot upright, my heart thumping wildly. "That's crazy! How is that possible?"

You have wrestled death before.

My blood ran cold. "What? When?"

God immediately brought up before me the dream in which an ominous entity was outside my mother's front door. As I had braced against the door, a white light had shone from beneath my palms, and I had been able to hold the door against the entity.

"Oh, my God! This is unbelievable!" I took a moment to let it all sink in. I thought about my faults—my stubbornness, my propensity to argue, my hot temper, my mouth, my tendency to question, my habit of procrastinating. "Holy Spirit, I don't understand. Why me? Why have you given me so many of your gifts? I am not worthy."

No, He said. *You are trustworthy.*

There has not been a word invented in any language that could describe how I felt in that moment, and I doubt there ever will be.

* * *

About a month later, *I dreamed that I was in a room full of people. Everybody was having a good time, but I was huddled in a corner.*

"Why are you in the corner?" God asked.

"Because I don't want to talk to anybody."

"You should be sharing the things I have told you."

I shook my head and pressed my back into the wall. "I am scared. I believe you for most things, and I'm willing to share those things. But I'm having a hard time believing you for Logan."

"Have I ever made a promise to you I have not kept?" God asked.

"No," I whispered, hanging my head low. It was then I noticed the white paper mat I was standing on. In the right-hand corner of the mat was a tiny-almost-microscopic-navy-blue dot. Heart fluttering, I bent down, focusing intently on the dot. It was actually a word: Quantum.

"Quantum?" I whispered, totally amazed I could see the word with the naked eye, excitement bubbling in me at the thought of a clandestine message meant for my eyes only. I looked around the room to see if anybody noticed, but they were all oblivious. It felt so spy movie, and I was loving every minute of it. "This is the third time you're showing me this word. What does it mean?"

I had seen it in two other dreams—once on a building, and once on a bus bench—and had not bothered to ask about it. However, this time, I felt it was important. When I got no answer, I impatiently forced myself awake.

"Okay, Jehovah, what are you trying to say to me? Please don't make me wait. What does *quantum* have to do with anything? What does it have to do with me?"

It is the smallest amount of faith it takes to effect change.

"What? The mustard seed? This is about the mustard seed? Why couldn't You just have said?" I squealed and burst out laughing. However, all too quickly, I sobered up. "Oh, my God! I'm so ashamed. I'm sorry my faith is so weak. With everything that has happened, I should be quickest to believe. The Holy Spirit said I was trustworthy, and I really want to be—but Jeshua—I don't want to look like a fool in front of the entire world. *Please*. I couldn't bear it."

I was a failure—a huge failure. I felt a warm wetness on my face and brought my fingers up to touch my cheeks.

* * *

The following afternoon, I was feeling dejected and super low as I went through the airport in Kingston. As I walked past a candy shop I had passed many times but had never been in, I got a strong urging to stop.

As I entered the shop, I heard someone say, "You don't need that."

I frowned and looked around at the man who had spoken. "What?"

He pointed at my face. "The mask. You don't need it."

I shook my head and said wryly, "Yuh notice I didn't say anything to you about the bling-bling you have around *your* neck?"

He laughed and said, "Point taken." He waited for me to stop chuckling. "Are you going to Fort Lauderdale?"

"Yes, I am."

"We are on the same flight," he said a little too cheerily. "I'll walk with you."

"Okay," I agreed a bit reluctantly.

We looked the odd couple—he like he belonged on a reality show about love and dancehall—and I like I belonged on a reality show about suburban housewives maneuvering midlife crises.

"I am Hebrew."

"Okaaay," I said skeptically because he was as Jamaican as I. Maybe he belonged to a weird religious group or something, but it was not up to me to judge. "That's interesting."

He frowned and studied my face before his lit up. "You're Hebrew too."

Seriously, Jehovah! Is this a joke? I thought. Immediately, a vision I had had years ago—of me kneeling at the cross—flashed before my eyes. *What is this?* I frowned at the stranger. "Who is Jesus to you?"

"He is my friend," the man said, quite easily and quite casually.

I shook my head vigorously. "No. Not the fluff stuff. Who is Jesus to you—really?

"Yeshua Hamashiach is The Word, who was made flesh and walked among us. He died on the cross for *my* sins." He touched his chest. "He is *my* Savior."

"Okay," I said, very relieved. "We can talk."

"I'm sorry about your marriage," he said. I gasped and gawked at him. "It's all spiritual. Everything that has happened in your marriage has been spiritual."

My heart pounded hard against my chest. I had so many questions, but I could not formulate the words.

"Your husband is out there wallowing in the pig pen. I see the woman he left you for. They didn't just meet yesterday. They've known each other for a while."

I frowned. "What? really?"

The man was not looking at me. He was staring off like he was elsewhere. "She looks like you—but your body type is different."

Goosebumps crawled all over my skin. I had a mask on, and he could not properly see my face. "That's not the one he left me for. The one who looks like me is the one he is with now—or so I've been told."

"Oh," he said contemplatively. "I see two of them, so the other one is the one he left you for. I get it."

As he started to describe her exactly—height, complexion, body type, hair—my mouth hit the floor. "Oh, my God! That's her."

"Yeah, well you need to know something about her. She is very wicked. She wanted to live your life. She wanted to be you. She wanted your house and everything you had, and she was willing to do *anything*. I could tell you what was planned for you, but I can see that you are already afraid—and I don't want to scare you further."

I blanched, bringing a hand up over my mouth, and took a step backwards. "Oh, God!"

"Your in-laws are always in church, yet they were behind this woman—backing her in everything she was doing against you. But you don't have to be afraid because you have some very powerful angels around you. One is standing here right now." He pointed to a spot slightly to the right of me.

I shivered and looked. Of course, I saw nothing. "Okay."

"Do not call your husband your ex. Do not change your name. The Most High says he's coming back."

Jehovah, what is this? I thought. *If things were up to me, then things would be fixed. But Logan doesn't listen to you at all. He lives to suit one person, and that's himself. He cares nothing of your will.*

This was the third person to tell me as much in the past three months. A stranger had approached me in Gainesville, a place I had never been. She had told me Logan was coming back, except her name for him was not *your husband* but the derogatory *that n*****, and she had been adamant I should not take him back because I deserved better. That was the first time I had seen my pain standing outside my body. She had held her stomach and said, "Oh, my God! You are in so much pain. You put on a brave face for your kids. You smile, and you make people laugh—but my God, so much pain!" The tears had run, unchecked, down her contorting face. It had been an unbelievable sight to behold, and it had brought me to tears.

I returned my attention to the stranger. "What do you mean he's coming back?"

"The Most High says it's all spiritual and that when you and your daughter are together again, you are both to pray for him for seven days."

I did not even bother to ask how he knew of my daughter. "I fasted for seven days already."

"It's not the same. This time you cannot pray alone. This time it has to be you *and* your daughter. The car accident"—he paused, a wistful look on his face—"The Most High says he's not going to die in it, but he's going to lose a lot. He won't lose everything. But he's going to lose a lot." He paused for a moment. "He has a business."

He looked at me for confirmation, and I hesitated because I was scared and unsure that I could trust him. But I found myself nodding. "Yes."

"He is a very ambitious man. He is all about status and achievement, and he is only interested in climbing." He stacked one hand on top of the other and then brought that hand on top the other until his hands were high in the air. "But he's going to be brought low."

He touched both his cuffs. "Long sleeve." He made a gesture like he was buttoning a shirt. "Button-down. White shirt." I frowned. "That's what your husband is wearing at the moment." Then he proceeded to tell me exactly where Logan was at the moment—not just the parish, but the town.

My eyes bugged. *Jehovah, what is this? This man must know us, somehow, because long-sleeved-buttoned-down-white shirts is all Logan wears. Plus, he gave Logan's exact location. Is this some kind of hoax?* "Where are you from?" I asked, my tone full of skepticism.

"I'm from Montego Bay."

Far enough, but no comfort. *Jehovah, I don't like this.*

"I see a tall, white man associated with your husband"—he held a hand way over his head to indicate someone taller than six-feet—"no, let me not say *white*—in case you find it offensive—*light-skinned*."

I gasped because I knew exactly to whom he was referring. "No. You can say white because that's exactly what he is." *How can this be Jehovah? This man is talking about Logan's grandfather, who has been dead for over forty years. I don't even know him. I've only heard Logan talk about him.*

Satisfied that I was no longer in doubt, the stranger continued. "When your husband comes back, he is going to ask for forgiveness, and you are to forgive him. Don't call him *dirty,* or talk about where he has been, or tell him that he has been with this one or that one—with Mary, Sue, or Jane. Don't do any of that."

"Why would you think I would do that?" I asked incredulously. God had brought up Hosea to me a few nights prior, but I was not going to tell him that.

He chuckled. "Who, you? You have an *aggressive* spirit."

I brought my hand up to my chest, feigning hurt. "Who me? I am here talking to you as sweet as can be."

He chuckled once again and gave me a do-you-know-who-you're-talking-to look. "You have a very *cross* spirit."

I laughed. "You've got me on that."

He got serious. "Your mother-in-law especially—she has been using her tongue as a weapon against you. The Most High says that the minute you say the words that you are supposed to, she is going to go dumb."

I pictured Constance on her bed, struggling to speak and shivered. "Oh, my God!"

"But first, she's going to turn around and curse your husband. She is going to ask him how he could do what he did after all she has done for him." I wanted to know what Logan could possibly do to upset Constance that badly, but before I could ask, the man's eyes widened, his face growing full of awe. "You can command the spirits, but you are afraid. Don't be afraid. They have to do whatever you tell them. You have the power to speak things into existence. Don't be afraid to do that either."

I brought a hand up to my chest. "Really?"

Instead of answering, his eyes widened further. "You're going to perform miracles." He walked away from me a little, and as he was coming back towards me, he raised his right hand toward Heaven and brought it down—just like I had when I was calling down fire. He stretched out the same hand. "You're going to tell the stone to move"— he swung his hand to the right of his body—"and the stone will have to move." He lowered his hand. "You're going to say to the dead, 'Get up!'"—he brought his hand up in a sweeping motion—"and the dead is going to get up."

I shrieked and covered my mouth. I caught movement out of the corner of my eye and looked off to the side. People were staring at us. I did not want anyone to think the stranger was harassing me, so I uncovered my mouth and forced a smile. "Oh, my God! This is crazy!"

The man smiled. "No, not crazy. True."

At that moment, our flight was called, and we boarded together. When we got to his seat, I said, "It was nice meeting you."

"Same." He smiled. "What's your name?"

"Jabez."

He raised his eyebrows. "Powerful name."

I smiled. "It's growing on me. What's yours?"

"Hezekiah."

"Cool. It was nice meeting you, Hezekiah."

"The Most High says we will meet again, and when we do, you will tell me that all is well."

"Really? That's good to know." I waved and walked off. As soon as I buckled my seatbelt, I googled the meaning of the stranger's name and grinned so wide my jaw hurt.

* * *

"Can I send something to your WhatsApp?" my mom called out to me, the following day, as I passed by the couch on my way to the kitchen to make some coffee.

I rolled my eyes. "Seriously, Mother? I told you about filling up my storage with stuff you get from people—like I need to be reminded what day of the week it is."

"That's why I haven't sent anything this long time. It's a song."

"Who is it?" I asked, approaching her. She held up her phone, and I did not need to see anything other than the 'd' in Donnie McClurkin's name to plaster a huge grin on my sulky face. "Okay, you can send it."

"Mm-hmm. Because it's Donnie McClurkin nuh?"

"Yup."

She shook her head. "If yuh don't hear me, I'm off to my doctor's appointment."

"Okay, Mother. See you later."

I put the pot on and went into my bedroom to listen to Donnie McClurkin and the Brooklyn Tabernacle Choir sing *The Song of Moses*. About a minute or two into the song, I was no longer sitting in my room but standing in a huge open space, and dead ahead of me was Jeshua. I gasped. He was clothed in a gown of purest white, so white it shimmered. He was facing forward, and I was to the right of him.

Although I was about twelve to fifteen feet away from him, it felt like I was right next to him, standing in the warmth of his glow.

As the line, "Nations shall come and worship thee," was being sung, I turned my head to the right and watched as, below me, a large group of Muslim men and women wearing traditional garb walked up to join the people already bowing. In a single, fluid movement, they all knelt—one knee to the ground—and bowed their heads. A group of Native Indian peoples in traditional garb came forward and knelt in like fashion. I looked towards the trees as a group of remote African Tribal peoples—some with face markings, loin cloths, piercings, lip plates and spears—emerged from a forest, stepped forward and knelt just like the groups before them. Far beyond that, a group of Aboriginal peoples—donned in loin cloths and carrying spears—also emerged from among the trees to come bow down. As I watched other tribes come forward, my heart welled with awe and wonder.

I caught a movement out of the corner of my eye and turned to see Jeshua walking in my direction. My heart skipped several beats before it broke into a full-on gallop when I realized He was looking at me. Coming to stand before me, his eyes met and held mine. Being so close to him was like standing next to the sun, yet my skin was not being burned nor my eyes blinded. As I basked in his glory, his eyes searched and touched the very core of my being, and warmth radiated off him to wrap around my heart. My eyes brimmed with tears.

Without saying a word, Jeshua raised his right hand and brought it up to gently touch my face—his touch featherlight, barely there. I gasped and brought both my hands up—one on top the other—to cup his as I closed my eyes and leaned my face into his palm, pressing my hands against his—greedy to feel more of His touch. The feeling was so overwhelming, it was almost too much to bear, yet I did not want it to end. Tears, like a river, flowed from my eyes.

As the vision began to fade, I called out, "Jeshua! Jeshua!" hoping He would let me stay a while longer. But just as suddenly as it had come, the vision was gone. When I came round, I was on my knees and my face was soaking wet. Wrapping my arms around my midriff, I hugged myself and wept.

* * *

Late in the day, I was pondering and wondering and second guessing everything. "Jehovah, I've been thinking . . . I can never tell anybody about what happened this morning. People are going to wonder how it is that I have the audacity to think that Jeshua would ever walk away from everybody else to come put his hand on *my* face. So, I'm asking you—*why* would He do that?

Instead of getting an answer, I got a strong urging to play a word game, which I tried to ignore. However, the urging would not go away, so I relented and began a game against the computer.

The first word the computer played was *OMEGA*. I smiled and thought, *Cool.*

It played *PE* next, and I thought, *Seriously? Physical education? Abbreviations aren't supposed to be a thing, but I guess, when it comes to the computer, the rules don't apply.*

When the computer played *ATONED*, I grinned and said, "Okay, Jehovah, what are you trying to tell me?"

He urged me to pay attention to the words in the order I had received them, and so I wrote what I found on a piece of paper:

OMEGA: 24th letter of the Greek alphabet.

PE: 17th letter of the Hebrew semitic abjad (also part of Psalm 119:129-136).

ATONED: sacrificed to amend for sins.

I scrunched my nose up. "Jehovah, I get what these words are by themselves, and the *PE* section of Psalm 119 sounds exactly like my heart . . . but I can't connect the dots."

I tossed the paper aside, only to pick it up again seconds later. I began writing, but with my brain having no knowledge of what my hand was doing. It was like there was a disconnect between my brain and my hand somehow, and I was watching someone else write.

I set the pencil down and frowned. I had written a three followed by a forward slash in front of the twenty-four; a two followed by a forward slash before the seventeen; and an eleven, forward slash seven beside the word *ATONED*.

I scowled. "Jehovah, this makes no sense to me. What are these numbers?"

As I got ready to toss the paper again, it clicked.

I slapped a hand over my lips.

"Oh, my God!" I whispered. "My kids?"

Acknowledgments

Thanks to G. H. Nolan, A. Heron, and Christine for their input and countless hours spent proofreading. Your help and support have been priceless.

Thanks to M. Green for his help with cover design and formatting. Your patience in working out the kinks did much to preserve my sanity. Of course, your skills come a distant second to your company.

Thanks to Nathan for a fantastic front cover. You took my concept and ran with it, and the result is better than I had imagined. Adversely, my IG photos have been trash. Hurry home. By the way, there isn't a word invented in any language that describes the way I feel about you.

Thanks to Christine for her artwork. I love, love, love your caricatures of me. The one on this book's back cover is my favorite. You see me like no one else does. You are very talented as well as beautiful inside and out, and I want you to know there isn't a word invented in any language that describes the way I feel about you.

Thanks to Michael for being brutally honest in his critique of my work. All those sevens out of tens motivated me to do better. Although you are growing faster than weed, you'll forever be my baby. Oh, and there isn't a word invented in any language that describes the way I feel about you. See what I did here?

To my parents: I've come to realize that everything that has happened to me happened to prepare me for what God has called me to do. I like the direction in which we're headed. I love you both.

Thanks to Annalise for countless hours spent around the kitchen counter. The day you walked in through my front door was a part of God's master plan, and I am extremely grateful. You are proof that there are no coincidences.

Thanks to my brother and friend, Pastor Bartell, for his encouragement and support. The nudge to inject a bit more of our culture into this book kept me up at night, but I think it turned out great.

Thanks to Dani for the emotional support, the three-hour conversations, and the messages and prophecies meant to encourage and sharpen me. Trust me, a blade of grass has nothing on me.

Thanks to my sisters Abigail, R. H. Curate, and M. Heron for their support. I'm looking forward to more good times because, not to sound cliché, life is short.

Thanks to my besties for their unwavering love and friendship. You are what was great about boarding school. Covid ruined our birthday plans, but I'm still looking forward to Greece.

Read to see how it all began

Before Journey's End

Available at Amazon.com
Available at Walmart.com
Available at Books-A-Million.com

The Three Rings

My dreams had been like common childhood dreams: falling, running but not actually going anywhere, peeing and then realizing that I was actually in my bed—that kind of stuff. However, at age eleven, shortly after I was baptized, that all changed.

I dreamed that I was walking alone along a rugged, desolate road when I happened upon an empty cave. As I entered, an image of a man was projected onto the wall in front of me. Although I had never met God, I knew Him immediately.

Dread gripped me, instinct prompting me to run. However, transmission glitches between my brain and my feet kept me planted firm.

In a fearsome voice, God said, "I'm giving you three rings to look after."

As He spoke, three intertwined rings of differing colors appeared in my right hand. I gasped, almost dropping them.

"Do not separate them, or I will be displeased," He warned.

I gripped them tightly.

"I will be giving you instructions regarding the rings. Instructions that you are to follow to the letter. Failure to do this will have dire consequences."

Almost immediately after He said this, a deafening boom resounded outside, shaking the ground beneath my feet and dislodging myriad rocks from the walls and ceiling. Dust fell, showering me and making it next to impossible to see. I brought my free arm up to my forehead, attempting to shield my eyes. The cave rumbled as if getting ready to jettison me from its bowels. I choked on the thick air, sputtering and coughing, glancing around frantically for the exit.

Clutching the rings to my chest, I bolted outside. I pulled up short at the scene of death and destruction. A multitude of dead people in white, tattered clothing were walking by me. But it was not like a scene from a phantasmagorical zombie movie. There were no gimmicks like partly rotted flesh, no incessant hunger for fresh flesh and no Frankenstenian stomp. The scene was no less terrifying, however. I watched, barely breathing, as they meandered by, unaware of my presence.

When I woke up, I was mortified. I was on God's radar. I honestly thought that when the big moment eventually came, it would feel a whole lot different than it did. I thought about the three rings for weeks, not saying anything to anyone.

Since I was five years old, I had been most drawn to the Bible stories in which God gave premonitions to His people. I never tired of shadowing Joseph on his journey to fulfilling his phenomenal purpose. No matter what happened to him, he had a single promise made to him in two premonitory dreams. Did the hope of that promise help him cope with the unfortunate circumstances of his life? That's where Joseph and I parted company. I had no dream. I had no promise.

My parents were ultra conservative. My father ruled with an iron fist, and my mother didn't do much without his say so. We occasionally had fun moments. However, the scale was unbalanced, the weights tipping heavily on the side of fear. I walked on eggshells because I never knew when the mood in the house would change, and it changed often, and in whatever direction my father's moods swung. My mother redirected her anger at my father towards my sisters and me. She was especially cruel to me, disparaging me at the slightest opportunity, her resentment palpable. Unlike the welts and bruises my father inflicted on my body with his belt and his fist, the scars left on my psyche by my mother's tongue were far more injurious. I was made to feel like No One. I worked up the courage to ask my mother one day if she was sure she had taken the right baby from the hospital when she brought me home. I didn't dare complain to anyone outside the house, but my face read like an open book, and the story remained the same—whatever page was turned. It didn't take a genius to read what was clearly written there. However, every time I was asked the reason for my angst, my reply was always, "Nothing." I knew that embarrassing my parents would be the worst possible offense, and I did not want to find out what the sentence for that would be.

When I was seven, I took matters into my own hands and devised a plan to run away from home. I packed the essentials, like a handful of Bustas (Jamaican hard candy made from brown sugar and grated coconut), a couple coconut drops (a confection made with brown sugar and diced coconut), a pack of Bubblicious bubble gum, two Hostess cakes, a bulla cake (kind of like a big, round gingerbread cakey cookie), a bar of Highgate chocolate with rum and raisins, two or three bags of Cheez Trix (Cheetos on steroids), my doll and way less clothing than was practical. I stuffed them into a pillowcase, which I tied to the end of an old, broken broomstick. Aside from the persistent problem with the darn pillowcase's refusal to stay in place (it had looked so easy on T.V.), my plan had a major flaw. When I was through packing, I realized I had not thought about where I was going to go. I ran down the list of all my relatives and my parents' friends, and I could think of one ideal place—my mother's sister's house. She had two sons but no daughters, and I knew my cousins would be happy for a little sister—at least I hoped they would be. However, I knew deep down there was no way my aunt would keep me. Dejected, I unpacked, but not everything made it back to the pantry. For months, I felt a strong sense of hopelessness and despair. However, it occurred to me, one day, that if God was the same as He ever was, then maybe I could have a different life. I just needed a dream. And so, for years, I waited most impatiently.

While Joseph's brothers and father immediately recognized the symbolism of his dreams, I wasn't quite sure what I was to be responsible for, but I did recognize that a ring wasn't just a ring. Worse than not understanding the dream was knowing that if I displeased God in the process, I would have to face His wrath. The dead walked by me every night I closed my eyes, and I found it harder and harder to sleep. The weight of the dream became so burdensome to bear that I finally told my mother about it. While she seemed amazed, the meaning of the dream eluded her. She reminded me that upon my birth she had given me back to God, so in essence, it was not surprising that I had had such a dream. She also said that my dream was a gift from God, and I should be thankful for it. Gift? It certainly didn't feel like it. Threat or frightmare would have been more apropos. Every day that something damning did not happen, the fear clawed and gnawed at me a little less until it eventually dissipated, taking with it any thoughts of the dream.

By the time I was to enter the ninth grade, my parents sent me to an all-girls boarding school two hours from home because it was reputed to be one of the best on the island at rearing up proper ladies. While I could care less about decorum and was more than happy to talk with my mouth full, chew gum noisily and rest my elbows on the table, I was relieved to finally be away from home. The rules were stringent, but I really didn't mind because funny enough, I felt like I could finally breathe. As the months passed, though, the novelty of my new digs gradually waned, and disillusionment set in. I felt out of place and alone. God was giving me dreams but remained distant. I had no one with whom I could discuss any of what I was experiencing. One of my housemates was Emma, my sister who follows me, but I had never told her any of my dreams, and I wasn't about to start. Although she was mature and very devout, our church belonged to a group of ultra-conservative Protestant churches, so I wasn't sure how she would react.

My other housemates were a bunch of eleven and twelve-year-olds with whom my most serious conversation was whether Michael Jackson was cuter than Prince.

I needed God to talk to me, but not as the God of wrath I had met in my dream. I was in desperate need of the God of everything else I believed Him to be. Each Sunday, I hopped from church to church in the town nearby, never feeling fulfilled. I looked for God, trying to find Him in everything: the smallest rustle of a leaf, the slightest brush of the wind, the softest patter of the rain, the faintest twinkle of a star, the mightiest roll of the thunder, the sweetest smile on a face. However, my favorite place to look for Him was in the vermilion of the sunset. Many evenings, I would drop what I was doing, hoping to meet Him there. I would sit on a metal rail outside my dorm and just gaze out at the vast expanse. No matter how often I did this, though, nothing changed because God was only what I imagined.

One moonlit Friday night, I sat alone on the stump of an old tree in a deeply wooded area below the quadrangle. I knew it wasn't wise, but I felt safe because the luminescence of the moon afforded me a modicum of visibility, and I could hear girls milling around in the distance. "God," I cried desperately, "I feel so all alone. I know you are everywhere, but it's like you are a gazillion miles away. Where are you?"

And, in the quiet of the woods, I heard God say, His voice soft and kind, "I am right here."

I slumped forward as I let out a huge sigh of relief. "What took you so long?" I whispered, tears slowly rolling down my cheeks. I really didn't care for an answer. I was just happy to finally meet Him in the physical realm. He was so much more than I had imagined, and I recognized exactly which God He was. I had met the God of love. And, for the first time in my life, my tears were of joy.

Made in the USA
Columbia, SC
12 March 2024

32537150R00164